2 - 16

Good Shepherd's Fold

By Anne Cawley Boardman

SUCH LOVE IS SELDOM
GOOD SHEPHERD'S FOLD

Good Shepherd's Fold

A Biography of
St. Mary Euphrasia Pelletier, R.G.S.

Foundress of the Congregation of Our Lady
of Charity of the Good Shepherd of Angers

by
ANNE CAWLEY BOARDMAN

Illustrated

HARPER & BROTHERS PUBLISHERS

NEW YORK

For
My Heavenly Mother
and the two men in my life—
my husband, Charles W. Boardman,
and my father, John S. Cawley

The illustrations appear following page 80

Preface

WOMAN was created to give life and she who gives it not, is a pervert, belying her destiny. The study of the great heroines of God through all ages shows them wondrously fecund, giving life with complete self-forgetfulness. That St. Mary Euphrasia fulfilled her destiny to a heroic degree is made eminently clear in the pages of this book. She gave life generously, burning up her own life in the process. Her desire to give the life of grace to souls to whom it had meant so little, left her no peace until she had daughters in every quarter of the globe, ready in their turn to give life. That life-giving work goes on and will go on as long as youth have need of the special help St. Mary Euphrasia's daughters have to offer them. She will always have daughters as long as generous, enthusiastic youth keep in touch with the vital fact so luminously understood by St. Mary Euphrasia. God so willed that the divine order be restored by man. And because He willed it should be restored in solidarity He teaches listening hearts that being members of each other, having been restored to Him, never each alone, they should take their share in lifting and restoring and reviving. I may add that she will have daughters as long as there are writers like Anne Cawley Boardman, ready to use their talents and their time to make her more widely known.

In the pages that follow the author shows one of God's great friends devoting a life to the building up of a highly specialized congregation dedicated to the service of restoring His Image where it has been defaced by ill-usage. She has shown much wisdom in the choice of her material, having selected the laudable plan of showing the greatness of her subject by the works of her hands, making no attempt to raise the veil hiding her deep, inner life, the mainspring of that extraordinary activity. Designedly I use the term praiseworthy, because too often lay writers mar their work by seeking to analyze the interior life of their subject. The depth of that interior life pulsates through each page of the book because it is so evident that her amazing activity flowed out of the superabundance of her charity.

The girl of nineteen who salted her evening meal with tears because of the flash of *His* understanding of obedience with which God pierced her intellect, never again lost that light. Her whole afterlife was proof. She who in the interest of souls was obliged to make weighty decisions, who had to tear herself away from loved tradition because her sure judgment showed her it was the only way to ensure the continuance of this work for souls, had an appreciation of obedience rarely equaled. How exquisitely painful it must then have been for her to have been so often taxed with lack of submission, a desire to shine alone, when in reality she was being most submissive to God and to Rome! The author unfolds this facet with an intuitive touch which does her credit.

St. Mary Euphrasia had a personal charm and attractiveness which drew to her side co-workers who stood stanchly by her when the whole world seemed tottering round them. She was so grateful to her daughters for their loyal love. She loved them as only the really holy can love. Her love cascaded down the pages of every letter she wrote to those of them she was obliged to send to the foundations. She had, in a very generous degree, the facility of showing her appreciation for their willing help in the building of the congregation. The author portrays this trait of articulate gratitude most clearly in dealing with the saint's relations with the two dear people we like to look upon as co-founders of our Mother House, Augustine, Count de Neuville and lovable Mme. d'Andigne.

In Chapter XVII * the reader will find an admirable range of case histories which show how dear the study became to the author and her psychological grasp of the significance of heredity and background in the building up of these cases. Her great faith is manifest in each page. Her book is a very substantial contribution to the understanding of the life and work of a very great servant of God.

(signed) SR. MARY OF ST. URSULA JUNG
Superior General

*Congregation of Our Lady of Charity
of the Good Shepherd of Angers*

---

* Chap. I as well.

Foreword

A FEW years ago I wrote the biography of an astoundingly simple and holy woman, Mother Mary Walsh, O.P., Foundress of the Dominican Sisters of the Sick Poor. Upon completion of her story I wondered if I would ever again be privileged to identify myself with anyone of her rare quality. For some time I sought such a person, using the ordinary techniques: the library, individual conferences, and an increased scrutiny of the various fields of social service. A number of organizations wrote me about their respective leaders. In each instance these leaders appealed to me—but not to my pen. Finally I turned to prayer, asking to be directed to one of God's servants who deserved a wider hearing. Someone, I said, who loved Him dearly and served Him devotedly through His children.

Months passed and my petitions appeared unanswered until a winter Sunday nearly three years ago when I was kneeling in thanksgiving in my parish church, having just returned to my place from the Communion rail. Suddenly a quiet voice spoke in my left ear: "Why don't you tell the story of St. Mary Euphrasia Pelletier? She founded the Sisters of the Good Shepherd. They do a wonderful work."

I was completely taken aback, for until that moment I had never once thought of St. Mary Euphrasia nor the Sisters of the Good Shepherd. I had never even met a Sister of the Good Shepherd nor been in any one of the Homes they operate for girls who have been denied a chance to lead socially useful lives.

Upon returning home I started to tell my husband of my experience, but I was afraid he might discount its credibility and so postponed mentioning it for several hours. Finally I told him—and waited for his reaction. If he had inquired solicitously about my health, I might have stopped my project right there; no one likes to be laughed at. However, what he said was, "That's interesting. Most interesting." Then his practical-headedness prompted him to add: "Have there been any other books about her?"

"None that I know of, but I'll find out."

Upon inquiry the following day, I learned that a juvenile called *The Little White Shepherdess* written by one of the Good Shepherd Sisters in San Francisco was the only book yet to be published in this country, although earlier biographies had been printed in France and England. When I reported my findings, my husband asked: "Where is the nearest Good Shepherd Home?"

"In St. Paul. It's a Provincial Convent."

"What does that mean?"

"A Provincial Convent is the Head Convent in a certain geographical area. The St. Paul area is comprised of eight separate Homes in a number of Mid- and Far-Western states. Each Home has its own administrative head, but all of them are responsible to the same Provincial Mother."

"How did you learn these things?"

"From an old reference book I have upstairs."

"Um-um," he spoke cryptically. Then he continued, "Let your idea simmer a few days. Either it will boil up or grow cold."

During the succeeding days it did not cool. I wrote to the Provincial Mother and an invitation for luncheon followed. Significantly my first visit to the St. Paul Provincial Convent occurred on the Feast of St. Francis de Sales—January 29, 1952—patron of Catholic writers and journalists. And, as I was later to learn, the legislator of the Congregation of the Good Shepherd.

Since that day the trail has been long and winding; yet it has been exciting and rewarding, bringing me into close association with one of God's saints and with the Good Shepherd Sisters, who devote their lives to re-forming the lives of the girls who come to them.

Naturally then I salute the "Sweet Voice" which directed me to the writing of this book, and the Good Shepherd Sisters everywhere, designating in particular Mother Mary of St. Ursula Jung, Superior-General, Angers, France; and Mother Mary of St. Paul Judge, Provincial, Mother Mary of St. Francis Hickey, Mother Mary of St. Jean Marie Schmidt, Mother Mary of St. Columba Gleeson, and Mother Mary of St. Germaine Loftus of the St. Paul (Minnesota) Province of Our Lady of Charity of the Good Shepherd of Angers.

ANNE CAWLEY BOARDMAN

Minneapolis, Minnesota
July 26, 1954

Acknowledgments

A WORK such as this is made up of the labors of many people. To all of them—judges, probation officers, case workers, librarians, ecclesiastics and religious as well—I wish to express thanks. To name them individually would be to offer an imposing list of persons. I am, of course, particularly indebted to my editors who early caught the scope and vision of this volume and became imbued, as was I, with Mother St. Euphrasia's magnanimity. From the beginning they have understood and appreciated my affection for her and my problems in encompassing it on the printed page.

Specifically I wish to thank Gabriel Francis Powers, earlier biographer of Mother St. Euphrasia, whose book *Redemption* I have found to be of invaluable help. Any quotations I have used from her work were made with her permission. I wish also to thank Burns, Oates & Washbourne, Ltd., London, England, for permitting me to quote from *Blessed Mary of St. Euphrasia* written by a Religious of the Congregation and published in 1933. Here with them, as with other publishers, in the case of books within and without the public domain, I have consistently given the volume, page and publisher. In addition, I desire to express my gratitude to anyone who at any time made any information about St. Mary Euphrasia Pelletier available. Who knows but what someday my efforts will help some future biographer? Foreseeing that possibility, I can sense the willingness with which Monseigneur Pasquier and others have aided me. A.C.B.

Good Shepherd's Fold

I

Let us by kindness endeavour to strengthen the "bruised reed" and prevent the "smoking flax" from being extinguished.

St. Mary of St. Euphrasia

CAROL looked directly at the big gray-haired man sitting across the table. "I won't go back to school. Talk as long as you want, you can't make me."

"But why do you object?" Someway he had to gain the girl's confidence. She was very large for her fourteen years and seemed almost frighteningly adult.

"I have my own reasons." And with these words she closed her mouth tightly.

He thought for a moment, recalling that her record stated she had already missed thirty-two days in the first three months of the semester. Then he tried again. "Carol, you must realize that you have nothing to gain by refusing to answer my questions. After all I am the judge of this Juvenile Court. We may be informal in discussing your problem, but I have the right to insist that young people answer my questions forthrightly and honestly. I have to know what is behind your chronic truancy. What is there about school that you don't like?"

The air grew tense with her continued silence. Finally, in a kind of desperation he asked, "Don't you like your classmates?"

"Like them? I hate them!" Caught off guard, she practically screamed the words. "They make fun of me because I'm bigger than they are. They call me 'Baby Elephant.' " Suddenly tears were streaming down her face. "I stood it until my Dad stabbed the tavern-keeper. After that they gave me the brushoff like I was poison, but still they watch me every minute and say things about me. It wasn't

1

my fault that he got written up in all the papers. If he hadn't been drunk, he wouldn't of gone to Jim's Place. I won't go back to school, your Honor, no matter what you say."

The judge pondered. He knew the girl's mother was an alcoholic. Now with her father in jail, she had no one to whom she could turn for counsel. No wonder she had built up an attitude that threatened to destroy her completely. Certainly he would be doing her a service to send her to the local Home of the Good Shepherd where the Sisters knew how to handle bewildered girls.

That same day in many corners of the land other young girls were sitting disconsolately, dazedly, belligerently, stubbornly, tearfully, pathetically in juvenile courtrooms, hearing similar words spoken with a legal but compassionate finality: "I am sending you to the Home of the Good Shepherd for an indeterminate stay." "For six months." "For a year or more." The men who pronounce the commitments are judges of the juvenile bench from various states. They issue their verdicts dispassionately and objectively according to the letter of the law, but their hearts are often moved by the tragic parade of errant girls who are the victims of unsavory social surroundings.

These girls range in age from twelve to twenty-one years. Among them are both first-time and practiced violators of the law. Most of them come from broken homes. Most are strangers to any kind of religious training; nonaffiliates of a church, as are their parents. Their mistakes follow a common pattern and yet each girl is unique as an individual.

Take Carrie Kate, just thirteen, who returned home from school one afternoon to find the door locked as usual, looked into the mailbox for the key as usual but found instead a hastily scribbled note from her mother. "Chin up, my big girl. I'm over the state line with Archie by now and I won't be back. Take care of yourself and forget me. You ought to be able to do that without half trying. I've never been much good to you. So long!" What Carrie Kate read was true; her mother had never been much good to her. She had never even allowed Carrie Kate to call her by any name but Evelyn. "My boy friends wouldn't like a big girl like you calling me Mother." Still she was her mother. As Carrie Kate took in the fact that she had been deserted she felt frightened. Where could she go now?

After curfew that night she was wandering about on the streets, uncertain and hungry, when a cruising policeman stopped his car to question her. Soon after, she was being received by a police matron who took care of her until morning when she was placed in the custody of a social worker. Temporary arrangements were then made for her lodging in a private home until her appearance in court as a dependency case. Finally the judge's words: "I am sending you to the Home of the Good Shepherd."

On this same day sixteen-year-old Jennie Kilbride tossed her saucy head and cried, "You may think you'll make me forget him. But I won't, I tell you. I won't. Sure, he has a wife and three kids, but he doesn't love them. He loves me. He's told me so. He's going to marry me someday. You just wait and see."

Then there was Diane George who had always wanted pretty clothes but had had few of them until she found how to shop without money. Easy pickings, she thought, until the store detective had stepped up to her quietly on the boulevard side of the city's largest department store.

One day some six months previous, Marcia, the best-dressed girl in her class at school, had said to her, "If you'd like a new cardigan like mine, I'll tell you how you can get its mate." Then she laughed. "People will think we're twins—both of us blonde with brown eyes— when they see us wearing the same kind of clothes."

Diane's mother, an overworked factory shirtmaker with a wracking cough, did not notice Diane's rapidly growing collection. Now Diane was in court. Much to her surprise her mother had actually seemed pleased because the judge was sending her to the Sisters of the Good Shepherd.

Economically speaking not all of the girls who come to the Home of the Good Shepherd are poor. Among them are always a few who have lived amid wealth. Such could be either Mary Beth Logan or Rosalie Owens, for theirs is almost an identical story.

Since her mother's death five years previous, thirteen-year-old Mary Beth had led an unhappy life filled only with the impersonal attentions of those employed to care for her. Had anyone questioned her father, an internationally distinguished research scientist at the state university, he would have said that of course he loved his only child. But his preoccupation with his investigations left no room for an excessively shy daughter. Mary Beth frequently wondered how her father could talk directly to her and yet give her the feeling that he did not know she was there.

One day she decided to leave home. She had accumulated enough allowance to last for quite a while; she would find someone who wanted a young girl around. She left the house for school at the usual time but she just kept walking, stopping now and then to buy a candy bar or some fruit. It was the fruit that brought "dear Mr. Smith" into her life. He was a kindly looking old gentleman with long white hair and a bow tie. The minute she saw him Mary Beth thought he looked like an artist. She was sitting on a park bench eating a Bartlett pear when he passed by, stopped, hesitated, and then asked politely, "Pardon me, but don't you need a napkin?"

At first Mary Beth did not understand that he was speaking to her. It had been a long, long time since anyone had purposely noticed her and longer than that since anyone except a servant had thought of her comfort. Later she could not tell exactly what happened next. All she could remember was the gracious manner in which Mr. Smith had offered her a clean white linen handkerchief to protect her dress. Soon they were sharing that substitute napkin as the gallant stranger also ate a pear. They laughed together and felt like old friends. After that it seemed only natural to tell Mr. Smith her troubles, explaining that she had plenty of money with her, but no place to go.

He listened attentively and then said generously, "I live alone in a very small house down by the river flats. I'd welcome you as my guest, if you'd care to share my poor quarters. They would cost you nothing."

Months later she explained to a psychiatrist how she had accompanied Mr. Smith home and how very good he was to her. "He was away a lot of the time on business, but whenever he was home he treated me like a queen."

Several weeks had passed, however, before Mary Beth's distraught father had located her. Then a difficult time followed for them both, for Mary Beth refused to return to her own home and her father hesitated to use physical or legal force. Finally she had agreed to come back after he had promised not to do anything to Mr. Smith. In desperation Dr. Logan then took his problem to one of the psychiatrists at the university. After due consideration, the psychiatrist advised, even urged the father to place his daughter immediately in the near-by Home of the Good Shepherd where the Sisters would endeavor to supply Mary Beth with the affection she so desperately needed.

No girl is ever denied admission to a Home of the Good Shepherd because of her race or color. For instance, there is Mabel.

Judge Jones studied the agenda of the day. His next case concerned an Indian girl charged with incorrigibility. Glancing up, he saw a tall slender young woman slowly entering his chambers, accompanied by the middle-aged social worker from the State Indian Agency. The girl appeared slightly older than most of the girls who came before him. She carried herself well and her clothes had an air. He motioned to the two chairs in front of him. "Please sit down while we talk this matter over together."

Then he addressed the girl. "I see that your name is Mabel Glory-of-the-Sunset. That's a truly beautiful name—yet you prefer to be called Mabel Adams." His eyes twinkled.

She nodded without smiling. "It saves me answering silly questions."

"With a name like Jones I don't have to answer questions either," he told her.

At this Mabel smiled wanly.

"What is your age?" he asked routinely.

"I'll be eighteen next month."

"And you are an orphan?"

"Yes, sir, I have been for nine years. That was when my mother died of tuberculosis and my father . . ." A tightening of her throat kept her from finishing.

The case history before him supplied the rest of the information. Mabel's father had been murdered the same year that her mother had died. Perhaps discouraged by his wife's lengthy illness, he had turned for solace to the wife of another Indian on the reservation. Jealousy on the part of her husband had resulted in a shooting fray and the death of Joe Glory-of-the-Sunset. The judge wondered what had been glorious about the sunset of Joe's life. He turned to the social worker. "Mrs. Lyons, will you please review this case for me?"

"Gladly, sir. Mabel has never really had a home since her parents died. For a time she lived with distant relatives on the reservation. Then she came to the city to stay with an aged aunt. Shortly after her arrival here the aunt died and Mabel, as a minor, was placed in a boarding school for dependents. She has been in several such schools maintained under civic or charitable auspices."

"What kind of a behavior record does Mabel have?"

The girl's face darkened slightly.

"I regret to say that her record has been consistently unsatisfactory. Each school has reported that Mabel has been unco-operative and generally difficult to work with. She is, and this she will admit, subject

to 'black moods' of depression. And she has an almost savage temper
that frequently causes her much trouble."

Mabel nodded in agreement.

Mrs. Lyons went on. "Not long ago we felt that it might be wise
to arrange a boarding-home situation for Mabel. After all, she'd spent
almost half of her life in institutions of one kind of another."

"Then you did find a boarding home for her?"

"Yes, sir, in a suburb to the west of the city. But the situation
proved intolerable."

At these words Judge Jones spoke directly to the girl. "Why was
that, Mabel?"

"The woman scowled at everything and she had no patience at all.
I got mad one day and turned on her. I didn't really mean to knock
her down, but I did. And afterward I wasn't sorry. I'm still not sorry.
She didn't trust me. Not even a little bit."

"Did you ever filch anything from her?"

"Once or twice."

The record indicated that Mabel had stolen several articles here
and elsewhere. But there seemed to be no definite pattern of stealing.
Perhaps the thefts had been her way of "getting back" at persons
placed in authority over her. On the preceding day, as a last resort,
Mrs. Lyons had taken Mabel to the Home of the Good Shepherd for
placement, but had been told that a court commitment was necessary before the girl could be accepted. So now she was requesting that
commitment.

"Do you want it too, Mabel?" Judge Jones inquired.

"Yes, sir." The answer was given firmly.

"What is your reason?"

"Well, I know I have to go somewhere, and I don't want to go to
the County Home School for Girls. I'd much rather go to the Home
of the Good Shepherd."

"Why?"

"On the reservation I knew two girls who'd been in homes. Mary
went to the County Home School and Genevieve went to the Home
of the Good Shepherd. I've been in lots of places like the one Mary
talked about, but I've never seen Genevieve's kind of place. Maybe
I'm just curious."

A few minutes later Mabel heard the words that committed her to
the Home of the Good Shepherd.

Generally speaking placements in a Home of the Good Shepherd are officially made by juvenile courts and established public and private social agencies such as the state or local Board of Social and Public Welfare and the Catholic Welfare Association, the Children's Service and the Children's and Family Service. Referrals also come through the psychiatric divisions of reputable educational institutions. Sometimes the Homes receive girls whose admission has been requested by parents or guardians. However, the Sisters discourage this practice, for experience has shown that family loyalties are often unpredictable, so that it is usually more satisfactory to work within the framework of the court and its allied agencies. Ordinarily, however, parents co-operate well when they understand that their assistance and interest are indispensable.

Certainly this was true of Dr. and Mrs. Scudder. Until their daughter Janet was fifteen she had never given them a moment's worry. Then she overheard a conversation between her mother and a house guest which made her aware that she was an adopted child. Beside herself with shock and insecurity as the days went by, Janet decided "to get even" by violating accepted standards of conduct. She became addicted to thievery, first stealing from her parents, then widening her scope. Whenever the Scudders tried to reason with her, she answered with scornful hostility. "You tricked me, didn't you?" she would say in effect. "Why shouldn't I double-cross you, too?"

Finally matters reached such a state that the harassed parents solicited Janet's admission to a Home of the Good Shepherd. Fortunately, a year or two later after the girl's confidence and equanimity had been restored, the family found happiness again.

It is only natural that a child should be fearful when entering an institution. No matter how unsatisfactory her home relationship and how unpleasant her surroundings, they have at least been familiar. When familiarity is taken away, she feels lost and helpless. Consequently she may close up like a clam or fight like a caged tiger.

Twelve-year-old Sandra Higgins was the quiet type. She had not committed any major acts of delinquency but recently had been spending most of her time at a public skating rink, going off after closing with strange boys and getting back to her grandmother's home at unreasonably late hours. Finally a social worker entered the picture and the child was soon taken to a Home of the Good Shepherd.

Upon her arrival Mother Josephine introduced herself to the tight-lipped little girl: "Welcome, Sandra, dear. God and I will be your friends and partners all the time you are with us. I think that we'll make a pretty satisfactory trio."

Sandra wasn't sure what those words meant. "Where's your stick?" she blurted out.

"We don't have sticks here," Mother Josephine answered.

"Aren't you really going to punish me?"

"Why, no, and neither will anyone else. Mother Euphrasia would never let us do that."

"Who's she?" Sandra queried.

"A kind and wonderful person for whom our school is named. You'll be hearing more about her."

As Mother Josephine and Sandra walked down a long hall and across a brightly lighted recreation room, girls called out spontaneously, "Hello, Mother!" and "Good afternoon, Mother!"

"Why do they call you Mother?"

"It's a Good Shepherd custom to call every Sister by the name of Mother." Seeing the distress in the child's eyes, she pressed Sandra's hand and said, "Already, I love you."

"Did you say 'love me'?" Sandra's tongue stumbled over the words.

"Yes, my dear. I love you and I want to teach you how much God loves you too."

Sandra looked up at Mother Josephine through tear-filled eyes. "No one ever before said she loved me."

Knowing that Sandra's mother, a widow of thirty-one, had resented being tied down by three children of whom Sandra was the oldest, Mother Josephine could well believe the truth of those words. Otherwise Mrs. Higgins would not have been at a tavern with her "boy friend" that night a year ago when fire broke out in the apartment in which she and her children lived. Sandra had done her best to save her baby sister's life but she had no chance against the flames that raced through the rickety halls. She had rescued her eight-year-old sister but she could not manage the baby too.

Now they had reached the reception parlor in the Juniors' Division. "Three other girls are living here," Mother Josephine said. "You'll meet them at suppertime. Till then I'd like you to take a hot bath and a nap. Miss Thomas, our school nurse, will take good care of you while I am away. She's a great favorite with our girls."

That night at Mother Josephine's suggestion the two knelt together in night prayers. Before a statue of a kindly figure holding a staff in one hand and with the other supporting a lamb on His shoulder, she heard Mother Josephine say: "Please take good care of Sandra, dear Lord. Like all our children, she is one of your own lambs. Give her a resting place where there is green pasture, lead her out by cool waters, and revive her drooping spirits. Lead her by sure paths and spare her from harm. In your Name. Amen."

Sandra's induction was well under way. In the days that followed she learned that particular emphasis was placed on the prevention of illness and the maintenance of good health among the girls. For almost a week she lived apart from the larger group, eating and playing with newcomers like herself. Their meals were served by one of the older girls who stayed to answer questions. "You'll find all sorts of recreation here," she said. "Movies, plays, concerts, television and practically every kind of sport—even swimming and skating."

"Skating! What kind of skating?"

"Ice skating in winter and roller skating the rest of the time. We have a big cement square that's perfect for skating."

"I love to skate," said Sandra.

And with that remark Sandra really entered the Home.

Day after day, the year around, the gates of Good Shepherd Homes are opening to girls who have been committed by judges, social agencies, parents, guardians, and in a real but unseen manner by the loving hand of God, to the care of the Sisters of the Good Shepherd. Some of the girls are orphans, some half-orphans, some are derelicts, some only mildly incorrigible but facing in the wrong direction. Sometimes two or even three sisters may come from the same family. Some are lost-looking children, some are ultrasophisticated adolescents. Some are frightened, some are bold. Some transplant easily and quickly sink thirsty roots into congenial soil; some withhold their rootage and refuse to flower until the steady sunshine of affection and even tears of longing have acclimated them to their new growing site.

How many Homes of the Good Shepherd are there in the United States? Do other countries have such Homes? How long have they been serving? Who started them? Why?

To answer these questions one must turn back to the early nineteenth century and cross over to a small town in La Vendée, France, when a little girl named Rose-Virginie Pelletier was hiding from soldiers and learning her catechism behind closed doors.

II

France, 1789-1810

A good name is better than great riches; and good favor is above silver and gold.

PROVERBS 22:1

THE fall of the Bastille in July, 1789, was the first serious act of violence in the course of the French Revolution. Louis XVI was then forced to approve the popular government, the National Assembly, and the new military force, the National Guard. A new way and a new day had arrived. In the beginning the new government's emphasis on the national unity of France and the popular sovereignty of Frenchmen elicited widespread fervor and enthusiastic support. Then came the inevitable reorganization of the state, which included extreme ecclesiastical reorganization by act of the National Assembly. Just before the first anniversary of Bastille Day the Civil Constitution of the Clergy was enacted, designating bishops and priests as a civil body, elected by the people, paid by the state, and only nominally associated with the Pope. In December a decree followed, compelling all the Catholic clergy in France to bind themselves by a solemn oath of allegiance to the Civil Constitution.

As might have been foreseen, this drastic action met with unrelenting opposition from both clergy and pious laity. Although many of the peasants had suffered hardship at the hands of the King's tax collectors and even at the hands of unscrupulous priests with an eye on political preferment, nevertheless they were faithful subjects and communicants. Immediately they banded together in protest. In the predominantly royalist and Catholic districts of western France they developed open hostility to the course of the Revolution. Throughout 1791 and 1792 uprisings increased steadily in La Vendée, until that province was in open rebellion against the new government. After the execution of the King on January 21, 1793, the Vendeans fought passionately and by spring had all but cut the national armies to pieces. In April, 1793, the National Convention entrusted the supreme executive authority of France to a special committee called the Committee on Public Safety, under whose direction the Reign of Terror was launched, primarily to bring the domestic foes of the new order into line. Although historians generally agree that its scope and magnitude have been exaggerated, they admit that in La Vendée its atrocities amounted to arbitrary slaughter of those who sought to disregard the mandates of the regime.

Like flash floods destroying everything in their path the government forces appeared for a time to have washed away forever the old order of life. But many of the clergy who refused to accept the Civil Constitution escaped butchery by going into voluntary exile, where they attempted to care for the spiritual needs of their people by moving secretly from one hiding place to another, administering the Sacraments and whenever possible saying Mass in cellars, caves, and all sorts of concealed and hastily appointed gathering places. The "underground" church functioned in homes, forests, and on farms. The tenacity of the clergy in carrying on God's work against tremendous odds sustained the faithful during those difficult years.

One night in the late summer of 1793 Dr. Julian Pelletier [1] and his wife, Anne Aimée,[2] admitted to each other that it was unsafe for them to remain any longer in their home town of Soullans.

"But where can we go?" Mme. Pelletier inquired anxiously. "It's hard to believe there is haven anywhere."

Her husband assured her. "I have been thinking of a quiet and isolated spot which stands a good chance of being overlooked by the Republican troops."

"Where? How far away?"

"Not far at all. It's the island of Noirmoutier."

She nodded slowly. She knew the island. It was in their own province of La Vendée. A small island some five or six miles wide. But few strangers would know about it, lying as it did off the west coast of the mainland and bulwarked by the sea. What was more, it was an unusually beautiful spot. But beauty and peace were no longer synonymous.

"Julian, can any place ever be peaceful again?"

Dr. Pelletier knew that she was thinking of Father Noeuf's death. A few mornings previous Father Noeuf—one of those who had refused to take the oath of allegiance to the new government—had been saying Mass at a temporary altar in a small cottage when a squad of soldiers had appeared and shot him and his server at the holy table. Mme. Pelletier had been shocked, of course, and deeply distraught. When such outrages could happen without warning, how were even the children to be safe? The doctor realized he must get the family away from Soullans; moreover, he must have some argument for persuading his wife to go ahead of him; to go immediately.

He spoke gravely, "My dear, a rumor is about that you have given shelter to a fugitive priest. That kind of rumor could lead to your arrest and imprisonment."

She looked shocked, as he had anticipated. He had hoped to spare her this knowledge but it was indeed better that she go. "I want you to take the children and leave at once for Noirmoutier. Do you agree?"

"What else can I do?" Then she realized that he meant for her to precede him, and a shade of terror came into her voice. "Won't you come with us?"

He shook his head. "I'll dispose of my practice and obligations here and join you in a few days. But one of our trusted tenants can accompany you."

So the Pelletiers were off for hiding, soon joined by several other families from Soullans. But none of them found the safety they sought. To be sure, the island was separated from the mainland, but with no means of exit other than the open sea that fact aided them scarcely at all.

The Pelletiers settled into "a spacious house on High Street," as some of the older records state. But it was in reality a modest, middle-class, two-story dwelling, except that it had a small spiral turret at one end, a perfect place for indoor games. The children insisted upon calling their tower a bell tower and punctuated their games with the ringing of an imaginary bell. They had no way of knowing that their tower would wait for more than a century to receive a real bell or that it would be hung in memory of their sister, Rose-Virginie.

During the next three years La Vendée became the tragic ground of attack, revolt, and counterrevolt. A directive from the new government ordering a province-wide conscription of all the young men capable of bearing arms went unheeded. Farmers and fishermen for the most part, the Vendeans knew little of politics and less of war. Theirs had always been a well-ordered life restricted by poverty but disciplined in joint service to their God and their King. The excesses of the new regime violated their sense of tradition and loyalty. They resented this arrogant order from the national capital to arm and join forces with the very people who were engaged in wiping out their preferred way of life and worship. They flaunted their refusal to bear arms by the unfurling of the only flag they knew—the standard of the Kings of France. In Paris this action was promptly declared treason and trained troops were immediately dispatched to Challans and Soullans to quell the revolt. As the bloody fighting approached Noirmoutier, the retreating Vendeans strove to defend their island fortress. Some twelve hundred Royalists who held the island were attacked by six thousand Revolutionists. Outnumbered five to one, the resisting forces went down like weeds before a scythe until they were powerless to offer any further organized opposition.

The victors then lost no time in establishing a military tribunal in order to try and punish the insurgents. Not content with the ordinary procedures of apprehension, a furious man hunt swept the place. Few people escaped the ire of the invaders. Finally in late February forty helpless women and children were deliberately drowned—Noirmoutier was a shambles of wrecked homes and hopes.

Across much of France open persecution, uncertainty, and gloom covered the land. In few places were priests permitted to come out of hiding to succor their people. This harsh state of affairs continued until the early spring of 1795 when suddenly the national government assumed a more lenient policy toward the unyielding Vendeans. A wise and kindly military administrator, General Hoche, was assigned to Noirmoutier, not in the role of an aggressor but as a trusted intermediary and peacemaker. Though he was not empowered to grant the residents freedom to practice their religion openly, he convinced them that that permission would come more quickly as a result of their passive co-operation. Under his direction peace and tranquillity were gradually re-established as prelude to the day when religion would be no longer proscribed.

It was inevitable that Dr. and Mme. Pelletier had witnessed many instances of savagery. Why and how they managed to escape with their lives will always be a topic of unresolved conjecture. Surely every member of the Military Tribunal sitting in judgment in the old

Abbey knew where their allegiance and loyalty stood. Why then did they spare the lives of the entire Pelletier household?

Later happenings support the idea that this devout couple must have been divinely protected for the purpose of bringing one of God's saints into the world. This child was born on July 31, 1796, on the Feast of St. Ignatius of Loyola.

"A good omen," her father said.

Mme. Pelletier smiled in happy agreement. For some years God had given them no children, but now after so much grief and sorrow He had sent them a harbinger of new life, surely a signet of blessing upon their home.

They regretted, of course, that the baby could not be carried to the village church for baptism. Since that was impossible the children together with Moise, their trusted nursemaid, formed a semicircle around the mother's bed while the doctor began the ceremony by making the Sign of the Cross over his infant daughter. With one exception all of them watched in quiet attention. Seven-year-old Julian was clearly confused. His parents had taught him about Baptism, but until now he had always associated this Sacrament with a priest and a church. He whispered a question to his twelve-year-old brother André-Constant.

"Sh-h-h-h!" André-Constant warned. "I'll tell you later. Listen to what Father's saying."

"I baptize thee, Rose-Virginie Pelletier, in the name of the Father, and of the Son, and of the Holy Ghost."

As he looked at his family Dr. Pelletier was moved by his twofold responsibility as father and husband, but even more by the fact that he was the human instrument by which his baby daughter had become a child of Grace. He bent down and kissed the child over the heart.

The succeeding months passed quickly until the late spring of 1797 when Rose-Virginie was carried by her parents to the home of their good friend, Mme. Frederic Richer. There behind closed doors a priest administered solemn Baptism to a number of infants and children, some as old as six years. The ceremonies denied those who had been privately baptized were now performed but the Sacrament itself was not readministered. The occasion was a happy and memorable one, though celebrated in guarded privacy. Father Gergand, formerly the parish priest of Beauvoir-sur-Mer, the nearest town upon the mainland, had survived the horrors of the last several years through the fidelity of the fisherfolk. There were countless tales of his tenacity and bravery. Everyone in Noirmoutier had known that some-day he would risk a visit to them to perform marriages and administer the other Sacraments. At last that day had come. In later years the account of this unforgettable event in Mme. Richer's drawing room became a family legend. Its beauty grew with its retelling. No further reference is made to Father Gergand, but his name and memory live on as a symbol of priestly courage.

Almost immediately after this event persecutions began anew. All over France hundreds of priests were exiled to Guiana in northeast South America and other distant lands. The murder of a Frenchman in Rome in 1798 gave the French an excuse for occupying the Eternal City and putting an end to the Papal temporal power. The Holy Father himself, the aged Pius VI, was taken as a prisoner to Valence, where he died of a broken heart. "The last Pope!" the maddened soldiers boasted to the sorrowing crowds assembled at the frontier. "The last Pope! There will never be another, we tell you!"

When Rose-Virginie was nearly three years old (some records say four) a son, Paul, was born to the Pelletiers. He was to be their last child. Thereafter he was his sister's pet and shadow in the same way that she was the shadow of another sister, Victoria-Emily, five years her senior. The three youngest Pelletier children had a happy child-hood together. Not even the struggle and uncertainty around them could rob them of this memory.

In 1799 Napoleon became First Consul of France, the same year that the Second Coalition of Allies waged war against the French. His army, though spectacularly successful, failed to defeat Great Britain, its major contestant. This fact infuriated the little General who was determined that France should emerge as the ruler of Europe. Naturally, then, the outcome of a sudden conflict between the English and the French in Noirmoutier had far-reaching effects. The English had long coveted this perfect naval base on the Bay of Biscay. On the first day of July in 1800 the English Fleet appeared unannounced on the horizon and twelve gunboats soon filled the arm of the sea between the mainland and the island, setting fire to vessels loaded with wheat which lay there at anchor. The natives of La Vendée gathered on the shore, watching in silent horror the complete destruction of their boats and priceless cargo. This kind of attack was quite unlike the earlier prolonged siege of the French Revolutionists. Against the mounting flames and the total consumption of the products of their toil they had no defense.

Then suddenly nature intervened as their ally. The English had overlooked one important fact—the tide. Drunk with success, they had delayed their departure. With the rapid lowering of the waters their vessels were grounded and a strip of land emerged to provide a quick and easy approach for a concerted attack by the Vendeans. They rushed forward like a human sea to envelop the English. Their arms were inadequate, but their fury was irresistible. When the struggle ended the Vendeans had captured the English gunboats and had taken two hundred of their men and officers as prisoners of war. In an incredibly short time the news of their success reached Paris. Honor had been satisfied. Napoleon summoned twelve of these heroic men, six from the coast and six from Noirmoutier, and acclaimed them as a "race of giants," receiving them in state and presenting them with gifts of money and personal arms in recognition of their gallantry. Not content with these usual tokens of appreciation he offered to reward them additionally.

"What more can I do for you brave gentlemen? Speak the word and I will act."

The men looked at one another with renewed hope. All had the same thought, but who among them was brave enough to utter it? Fighting was easy compared to speaking out unabashedly in the presence of this mighty man. Finally one of them stepped forward and spoke.

"Sir, you could give us back our parish priests. Without them we languish. Will you not restore them to us?"

This unexpected request undoubtedly surprised Napoleon. No mention can be found of his reply. Certainly no formal promise was given. But before the end of the year a few priests appeared from hiding to reopen their closed parish churches and resume their chosen work. The civic authorities did not protest. Presumably they had been officially advised that religion was no longer outlawed within their province.

The Pelletiers were heartened but not misled by this turn of events. They did not abandon their devotional practices which had provided their only sure means of worshiping together as a family. Mme. Pelletier stressed the importance of closing each day with a personal examination of conscience. Ordinarily she would have delayed this exercise until the children were older, but these had been no ordinary times. Even yet life remained insecure, so that she and her husband considered a daily examination of conscience an obligatory act, striving to emphasize love and not fear as its motive.

Mme. Pelletier had a happy way of explaining the matter of penance to her children. "When you ask God to overlook the mistakes you didn't plan or to forgive the ones you deliberately contrived, you should also offer Him a little gift. Then He will know you really mean what you say."

At that one of the youngest sometimes asked, "What kind of a gift, Mother?"

This question usually brought quick answers from all sides. Everyone had a specific idea, and each idea was satisfactory. "A prayer." "Several prayers." "A decade of the rosary." "A visit to a sick person." "Food for the poor." "A kind act." "Sharing your toys with a child who hasn't any."

Mme. Pelletier always nodded with pleasure at these spontaneous replies. Then she would add, "We call these gifts of prayer, or conduct, penances. They show God that you really want to be better boys and girls."

Next she would talk about the necessity of their joining in prayer for the Holy Father and the Church. "We should never let a day pass without praying for the Church. That doesn't just mean the Church in Noirmoutier; it means the Church everywhere. I sometimes wonder if you children understand what I mean?"

"Of course we do, Mother." This answer came from little Rose-Virginie. "You taught us all about that when we learned the Apostles' Creed. Don't you remember the part that says, 'I believe in the Holy Catholic Church'?"

Mme. Pelletier's eyes shone. "Yes, I remember. It makes me happy that you do."

There were other teachings that Rose-Virginie remembered equally well. One of these her nurse, Moise, reported years later to the Sisters of the Good Shepherd in Angers.

"Rather often after the child was undressed she would stand for some minutes in quiet reverence with bowed head. At first I thought this was some fancy that would soon pass, for, of course, the family said night prayers together as a group. I held my tongue until one winter night when I feared she'd catch cold standing there in her bare feet upon the floor. Then I ordered her to bed.

"She turned her big dark eyes on me and asked in open surprise,

'Why, didn't you know, Moise? I stand here in the cold whenever I haven't been a good girl. It's what Mother calls a penance. But I pray too.'

" 'Well, we've had enough of it. Now hop into bed.'

" 'But, Moise, I haven't yet finished my five Our Fathers and five Hail Marys for the Church. Please give me a few minutes more.' "

Rose-Virginie had her gay and mischievous side too. A healthy and a happy child, she spent long hours out of doors with Clementine Viaud-Grand-Marias and Sophie Duchemine, her best friends, and Paul, her little brother. This foursome was ingenious and congenial. They might decide to have a picnic on the seashore, take a climb over the rocks or make an excursion into one of the ancient caves along the shore. There were always wonderful things to do when one had a picturesque island as a playground. Together the children formed a plan for the day's games. When the sea was quiet, they could not retrieve the fascinating debris washed into the harbor but there were many times when the wind was brisk and the waves high. Then Rose-Virginie, more daring than her companions, would dart ahead with her brown hair flying to gather the flotsam drifting on the water's disturbed surface, calling back to the others, "Hurry, hurry, there's real treasure here." She loved running in between the waves. Whenever she got soaked by the spray she would hurry home to change into dry clothes and assure her mother she had not really gone out too far. Mme. Pelletier did not encourage this particular game, but she did not forbid it. She was certain that the children would observe her strict warning not to go into deep water.

Like a chameleon, Rose-Virginie responded to the moods of nature. She was quiet and thoughtful or frolicsome and exuberant according to the elements. She had no favorite season, for each brought its own kind of fun. In spite of unsettled political conditions, growing up in Noirmoutier meant both shrieks of joy and long silences. Together they provided the lights and shadows of a good childhood.

Midsummer when Rose-Virginie was eight years old, the heat was intense. One day the children were playing in the cool woods near their home, unknown to an elderly gentleman who was lowering himself to the ground in anticipation of a little rest in this secluded spot. First making sure that he was quite alone, he removed his heavy wig from his freely perspiring head. Then he stuck the point of his walking stick firmly into the ground, placed his wig aloft in safety on its knob, rubbed his moist brow with his handkerchief and settled himself for a comfortable nap.

A few minutes later the play of the children brought them over to the man. At first they did not recognize this stranger lying asleep against the oak tree as their neighbor and one of the town's most dignified citizens. When they did, they knew they ought to go away, leaving him to enjoy his nap in privacy, but instead they stood as though mesmerized. Never until now had they known that this man wore a wig, but here was a completely bald pate if ever they'd seen one, and a wig resting enticingly on the top of his cane. Just then a snore from the old gentleman almost convulsed his four young visitors. Monsieur with his head uncovered sprawling there in such an undignified posture!

Suddenly a daring thought flashed through Rose-Virginie's mind. Without a word she leaned over slightly, grabbed the wig from its perch, and flew ahead like a hare pursued by hounds with Clementine, Sophie, and Paul following close at her heels. She did not stop until she reached the home of the old gentleman. There she advanced demurely to the front door, lifted the knocker quietly and placed the wig securely under the handle. With that she hid behind a hedge where she was soon joined by her three companions. They found it hard to control their excitement.

After a long wait the old gentleman finally came in sight. The children had to hold their hands over their mouths to keep from laughing out loud. Certainly this angry man was anything but a picture of dignity. With his wig missing his tall stovepipe hat almost covered his eyes and rested loosely on his ears.

At the sight of his wig hanging from his door knocker he stopped short in wordless astonishment. Then he sputtered something about "rascally boys" and went into the house slamming the door hard behind him. Unfortunately the outcome of this episode is not recorded, but the fact that it has been preserved suggests that it was appreciated by the entire family.

Another happy year passed and then the Pelletier household was filled with grief. First came the grave illness of thirteen-year-old Victoria-Emily, who was Rose-Virginie's constant guardian, always welcomed by her young sister and brother and their companions, who found her good fun and a source of ingenious ideas for a new game. At their age the Revolution had denied her the freedom to roam at will, so she encouraged Rose-Virginie and Paul to take advantage of their opportunities to play out of doors. She aroused their interest in the possibility of hidden treasure on the island and shared her enthusiasm for nature lore and exploration. Before she became ill the children were well on the way to becoming juvenile naturalists and amateur archaeologists.

No wonder then that her death, on August 19, 1805, cast a heavy cloud over Rose-Virginie's life. For a while the younger child was inconsolable, crying incessantly. "Why did it happen? Why? Tell me why." Before long, however, she sensed the consolation of the faith that sustained her parents. Although they were heartbroken, they were resigned to God's will. Rose-Virginie tried her best to accept that Will and comprehend it. With less wise parents she might not have succeeded, but they had a special way of making the most profound truths clear to their children.

Without this shared understanding the dark days that followed would have been intolerable. For death returned to claim the lives of two other children, Nathalie and Sophie, both of whom were slightly older than Victoria-Emily. Unless one has experienced a similar loss he cannot appreciate the suffering that ensued, and unless he has experienced a similar trust he cannot hope to find a similar strength.

A few months later Mme. Pelletier was obliged to meet an even more severe crisis, and this time to meet it alone. Late in the fall of 1806 Dr. Pelletier became seriously ill. The nature of his seizure, heart most probably, held no hope for his recovery. The imminence of his death brought the priest hurrying to his bedside to administer the Last Sacraments of the Church. Fortified with confidence in the mercy of God, Dr. Pelletier died on the 27th of November and was buried a few days later in the little cemetery of Noirmoutier.

Now Mme. Pelletier's cup of sorrow was filled to the brim. The loss of her three children together with the sudden death of her husband threatened for a time to break down her spiritual defenses. She found it almost impossible to accept the fact that her husband had been taken from her. He had always been in good health; he was only fifty-four years of age. Yet he was gone, leaving to his widow, ten years his junior, a great emptiness of spirit and the awesome legacy of rearing and educating their six remaining children. Crushed and frightened by the mantle of responsibilities that had fallen so abruptly upon her shoulders, Mme. Pelletier wore it poorly in the beginning, but she never abandoned it because she could not ignore the needs of the children. If they needed her while their father was alive, they needed her more now that he had been taken from them.

She sought to ease her pain in various ways, attempting to offer her suffering to the Son of God in recognition of the greater suffering He had endured for her sake. But the humanity in her was weak and she grieved increasingly. Had it not been for a forthcoming event in Rose-Virginie's life, this depressing state might have been prolonged indefinitely. But her little daughter's approaching First Holy Communion aroused her to her obligation as a Catholic parent. Peace descended gradually upon her when she no longer resisted the dual role of father and mother that God had assigned to her.

Even before Dr. Pelletier died, arrangements were already under way for the ceremony of First Communion to be held the following spring in the ancient Abbey Church of St. Philbert. A knowledge of the catechism was a primary requisite. To Rose-Virginie, meeting such a requirement was as natural as playing on the seashore. Instructions at home by her parents and Moise, informal lessons at regular intervals by M. Moizeau, the assistant priest in the parish, and a concentrated series of quiz sessions given later at the rectory left no doubt that Rose-Virginie was thoroughly prepared to partake of the Sacred Banquet of the Eucharist.

Her interest in the truths of her religion increased during these months. She knew enough, the priest had said, but she was not content with that. Here she revealed a quality marked in her later as an adult and religious superior. "Good enough" never satisfied her; in her mind "status quo" signified retrogression. Consequently in the months preceding her First Communion she sought to be a better girl than she had been, extending additional courtesies to the aged and the ill, and helping with her mother's many charities. She tried to do her daily tasks "for God's sake" and not just because they had been assigned to her. Nevertheless, she was just as venturesome as ever, possessing a balance between the serious and the gay which she was never to lose.

Love of adventure brought her a rewarding experience when one day she accidentally discovered the deplorable condition of the lower church or crypt beneath the sanctuary. It, like the upper church, had earlier been desecrated by the irreligious, but unlike the upper church, it had not yet been repaired and restored. Immediately Rose-Virginie enlisted the aid of Clementine and Sophie—and Paul, no doubt, although the records speak only of the three girls or of "Rose-Virginie and her companions."

A little probing on their part revealed a stone altar covered with rubbish but still standing intact. The aisles were filled with accumulated trash, left no doubt by the Revolutionists who had hidden and plotted there. A careful search brought the girls to a square stone monument covered with a symbolic design.

"Clementine! Sophie! Do you think? Can it be?" called Rose-Virginie excitedly.

"You say it, Rose. You tell us."

"I think it must be the tomb of St. Philbert, the great Benedictine Abbot. Our church is named after him, you know."

"Is St. Philbert's body still here?" Clementine asked in uncertainty.

"No, not now. It hasn't been for centuries. But the tomb of a saint shouldn't look like this. It should be kept clean out of respect for his holy memory."

Then Rose-Virginie became very quiet. The girls knew that when she looked like that a new idea was brewing. Some minutes later Sophie said hesitatingly, "Time's up, Rose-Virginie. Tell us about it."

A smile lighted Rose's face. "I've thought of the most wonderful thing. Let's ask permission to clean up the shrine of our patron saint. Poor Father Bosseau is too old and sick, and Father Moizeau is too busy. Wouldn't you like to help make St. Philbert's shrine the kind of place he deserves?"

The girls caught her excitement. They dashed home to get their parents' permission to undertake this arduous job. Assured of that approval they had no trouble in persuading their pastor that they were really equal to the task which had long awaited such volunteers. Undoubtedly they enlisted others in this venture which, though hard work, was great fun too. They took turns at the various jobs so that their interest held.

"Sticks and stones! Rocks and bricks! Earth and rubbish!" made up a chant that the young toilers hummed or sang, indicating by their tempo and tone the progress they were making. Eventually the day arrived when they could call out, "It's finished! It's really clean at last! Hurray! Hurray!"

Then they brought linen cloths and candlesticks from their homes and secured candles from the priest after which they gathered armloads of flowers to decorate the scrubbed and shining altar. When everything was in place, people came to admire the renovated holy spot. In the beginning they may have been drawn by curiosity, but many of them remained to pray. Soon it became an accepted custom for pilgrims to visit the crypt regularly.

The re-establishment of this historic shrine was no passing fancy on the part of these three prospective first communicants. Years later Sophie Duchemin was to marry and remain on the island. As Mme. Lefebyre she cared for this little chapel as long as she lived and at her death left a sufficient sum of money for its continued upkeep.

Shortly after this, Rose-Virginie made her First Holy Communion. The recorded facts of that happy milestone are few; the later references many. It was a beautiful day in May preceding her eleventh birthday. A picture shows her in a thoughtful pose, her alert brown eyes expressing wonder and happiness. Her high-necked white dress and her coronet of spring flowers atop the fitted veil that covered her brown hair and fell in folds around her young face, make at first glance a typical First Communion picture. But on closer scrutiny it appears to be a prophetic picture of a dedicated child of Grace. Or is every First Communion picture a glimpse of the possibilities innate in a soul?

No one will presume to say that Rose-Virginie actually knew on this occasion that she was to become a nun, but later happenings make it appear that God may have chosen that particular moment to plant the seed of her future vocation in her heart. At this time she had never seen a sister—the Ursulines did not come to Noirmoutier until the following year—but she knew, as did her observant mother, that this day had touched her with spiritual wonder.

"I can't talk about it just yet," she said, "but this is like a day in Paradise."

Her wise mother pressed for no details, but she shared the inward experience.

A year passed before Rose-Virginie was confirmed by the Bishop of La Rochelle. Ordinarily the Bishop of Nantes would have administered the Sacrament of Confirmation, but that See was still vacant, following the widespread decimation of the French hierarchy during the Revolution. Everyone was delighted because the Bishop was coming to Noirmoutier. He had consented to go beyond his own diocese because of his close friendship with their pastor, Father Bousseau, a friendship which dated back to Seminary days when they had been classmates.

Eighteen years had elapsed since the last official visit of a bishop to the island. Nine of those years Father Bousseau had spent in exile in Germany. Now badly crippled with rheumatism and confined to his chair he rejoiced that his people were at last to receive the Sacrament of Confirmation.

Rose-Virginie rejoiced too. The catechism said that Confirmation made one a soldier of Christ, but the priest had explained that in their struggles against the enemies of the Faith, all of the residents of Noirmoutier had already shown that they were self-appointed soldiers of Christ. Now, through Confirmation, they would be declared official members of Christ's army.

The day of her Confirmation was enhanced by her first sight of a Bishop, and by the dramatic meeting between the aged priest and his ecclesiastical superior. Both wept unashamedly as they embraced each other on the porch of the rectory where Father Bousseau had been carried to await his honored guest.

The months that followed were filled with excitement. Throughout the summer the girls talked endlessly of something wonderful that was soon to happen to them.

"Just think, Clementine," Rose-Virginie would say, "in October you and Sophie and I will be starting to a real school. Can you imagine it?"

"No, but let's talk about it anyway."

After that their tongues would run on and on with a retelling of the great news.

"Father Baudoin from Chavagnes spoke to us at Mass, will you ever forget?" one recalled.

"Never," another added. "I thought I couldn't possibly keep still when he said he was going to bring the Ursuline Sisters to Noirmoutier this fall to open a school for boarders and day pupils."

"I wonder what Sisters are really like," Sophie inquired curiously.

"They are lovely ladies," Rose-Virginie answered. "They love God very much and work to make other people love Him. That means they love people too. If they didn't, they could never persuade anyone to listen to them."

"That sounds reasonable," Sophie commented. "But how will they dress? Do you think they will wear aprons and bonnets like our mothers?"

"They'll all dress alike, that I know," Rose-Virginie continued. "Their clothes will be a simple dark uniform—black I think Mother said—and they will wear veils over their heads instead of bonnets.

They'll wear aprons too, whenever they need them. But they won't wear them in church or on the street." With a smile she went on, "Seems to me it would be nice to have your clothes tell everyone that you were working for our Lord."

At last the day arrived when Father Baudoin, the Founder of this particular teaching Order of religious, brought five Ursulines to the island. A large crowd was at the boat to greet them with songs, flowers, and prayers, and to join in the procession that took them all directly to the church for the official welcoming. The coming of these teaching nuns marked the end of the long period of home instruction that until now had been the only means of educating the girls and younger boys. Meanwhile the older boys would continue to receive their instruction at the rectory.

When the Sisters came in view, Rose-Virginia shot ahead to inquire politely, "Please, may I carry your parcels? Oh, we are so glad that you are coming here to be our teachers."

With the opening of school, Rose-Virginie's life was completely changed. Before this she had had her lessons painlessly at home under the gentle direction of her governess, a former schoolteacher, whose knowledge had far exceeded her ability to hold the attention of active, growing children. Suddenly all was different. At the age of twelve Rose-Virginie found herself for the first time held to a strange and demanding schedule of arrival, recreation, and departure; study and recitation; homework and school marks. These marks were based not only on her own achievement but on competitive relationship to the class as a whole. Some of these things she found difficult; a few, irksome. She tried to adjust to the ordered program of school life and struggled to control her impatience when some classmate was groping for an answer to a question that to her seemed easy and obvious. But her endeavors sometimes miscarried and then she was soundly reprimanded for her impulsiveness.

One day she blurted out the spelling of a word that had been assigned to Clementine, and when the teacher scolded her she attempted to defend her action. This uncalled-for act caused the Sister to say vigorously, "Rose-Virginie, I am disturbed about you. You are too impetuous and outspoken. You must watch that tendency, for it could grow and cause you trouble. A quick disposition like yours will take you to heaven or to hell. Be careful, very careful. Which do you wish to be, a saint or a devil?"

"Oh, Sister, you don't understand," Rose-Virginie said. "I am going to be a nun."

The Sister was unprepared for this unexpected retort. She could only shake her head in utter disbelief.

Rose-Virginie said once more, "Yes, I am going to be a nun. I know I have lots to do before I am ready, but I'll learn not to speak out of turn. I'll keep working at it until I succeed. Won't you please believe me?"

By now the Sister had recovered sufficiently to reply, "I am most interested in what you say, and, of course, I'll help you in any way that I can."

Some weeks later Father Baudoin sent word that on his next visit to Noirmoutier he would examine the pupils from the Church History classes. He suggested certain topics for discussion, laying emphasis on the story of the Passion as told by one or other of the four Evangelists. He closed his letter by saying that he would award a prize to the one whose offerings he considered best. As is usually the case when a reward is in the offing, the pupils worked hard to merit it. Most of them wanted the prize for itself, and all of them desired Father Baudoin's approval. Rose-Virginie especially hoped to reinstate herself in Sister Marie's good graces.

At last the day of the contest arrived. Father Baudoin spoke of his pleasure at the size and appearance of the classes. He nodded his head in approval of the spelling and arithmetic charts shown him. Then he sat down in the big chair which the Sister Superior designated and listened attentively as one pupil after another demonstrated that she was well-acquainted with the New Testament account of the Passion. To be sure a few pupils had stage fright. But for the most part everything proceeded smoothly, and before long Father Baudoin realized that the contest was going to be very close. Several pupils were equally well-prepared. Surely such results were gratifying, but under the circumstances they were dismaying too. If this state of affairs remained unchanged, he decided he'd have to defer any awards until he could purchase additional prizes.

Then the final contestant, a dark-haired, bright-eyed, composed little girl took her place before him. Father Baudoin asked the expected opening question. "Which Evangelist have you chosen?"

"Do you have any preference, Reverend Father?"

"No, my child. None at all. I thought you understood that. Kindly proceed."

The little girl hesitated slightly and then continued, "I know the whole story from Matthew through John. I kept right on reading in order to see how the Evangelists differed in telling about our Lord's sufferings and death. Do you want it all, or just part of it?"

For a minute the priest thought the child was exaggerating, but he began his questioning and a careful examination showed that she knew the entire Passion almost word for word. Father Baudoin was truly amazed. He doubted that he could have done as well himself. The difference between finding an answer and giving it verbatim as she had done was the difference between competence and excellence. Moreover, this child knew far more than the words of the Passion. She identified herself with the various narratives.

When she had concluded, Father Baudoin complimented her highly. "A performance one seldom meets below the seminary level. Congratulations, my dear."

With that he presented Rose-Virginie with a beautifully bound copy of St. Alphonsus Liguori's *Visits to the Blessed Sacrament*, a book quite in keeping with the nature of the contest, but one rather far advanced for the average twelve-year-old. Rose-Virginie's genuine delight over her gift revealed far more than any comment on her acceleration in her studies, particularly in the fields of the New Testament and Church History.

Sister Marie whispered additional congratulations. "Your performance today has pleased me very much. I am sure it has pleased God too."

Always after that she treasured her prize book and kept it close to her, until many years later when she gave it to a lay Sister who longed for this particular book because she associated its owner so closely with it.

At this time the four oldest children lived away from home. Long before their father's death their schooling had become a grave matter to their parents, for the educational facilities in Noirmoutier were practically nonexistent. Several family conferences had failed to settle this vital problem. Finally Dr. Pelletier's sister, a wealthy widow with no children, opened a way. From her home in Bouin she wrote urging that her niece and three nephews come over to the mainland and attend school there. Anne-Josephine, she said, could live in her home and enroll as a day pupil and the boys could attend a boarding school near by. She would supervise them carefully and keep their parents informed about their progress. These plans were nearing completion when Dr. Pelletier's unexpected death occurred.

Naturally Mme. Pelletier's grief halted any further consideration of this proposal. Then one day it suddenly became clear to her that she could not put off this important matter of her children's neglected education. Belatedly she accepted her sister-in-law's invitation.

There were many tears on the day Anne-Josephine and her brothers left for Bouin. But each reminded the others that they were not going to a strange land and that when vacations came they would all be together again.

After their departure Mme. Pelletier, Rose-Virginie, Paul, and Moise felt quite alone. For some days it seemed as though they were in the wrong house. "It's so big and there are so few of us," Rose-Virginie said.

But all this had happened nearly four years ago. Now Anne-Josephine was about to be married to M. François Marsaud, a young man of means from an excellent local family. Mme. Pelletier thoroughly approved of her daughter's choice and was pleased that she was to have a home of her own. On the 10th of June the entire family assembled in Bouin for the wedding and everyone had a wonderful time. Rose-Virginie and Paul found it exciting to be related to the bride and enjoyed their roles immensely. Doubtless they would have been less carefree had they known that their mother had used this opportunity to inform the rest of her family of an impending domestic crisis.

Upon their return home Mme. Pelletier, encouraged by the approval of her older children, realized that she could no longer postpone telling Rose-Virginie and Paul that she had decided to sell their island home and go back to her native town of Soullans to live. She knew that Rose-Virginie especially loved every inch of Noirmoutier. Only a short time ago she had said, "Mother, isn't it really wonderful that we have our church and school and that everyone appreciates them as much as we do? It is hard to remember those ugly days when the soldiers were everywhere. The people are so kind and the ocean and the rocks and the woods so beautiful. Oh, I do hope I can live here for a long, long time."

It was no wonder then that her mother's announcement caught her by surprise.

"Leave Noirmoutier? Oh, Mother, why must we do that?"

"I have never gone back to Soullans since your father and I fled

it during the troubled days of the Revolution. We own property there
and it needs looking after. And I long to be near my girlhood friends
and relatives. Then, too, I'll be nearer Anne-Josephine. I feel so alone
here."

"You have Paul and me."

"But you will soon be ready to go off to school and Paul should be
entered in a regular school too. When that happens, I don't want to
stay on here. My heart has gone back to Soullans since your father's
death."

At first Rose-Virginie could not believe that her mother was in
earnest. In bewilderment she wondered how anyone could deliberately
decide to leave this lovely spot. Not until many years later did she
fully understand the claim that one's birthplace has on one's affection. In vain she remonstrated and coaxed her mother to change her
mind. But Mme. Pelletier was not to be diverted from the course she
had set.

Finally one late summer day in 1810, a weeping fourteen-year-old
Rose-Virginie waved a sad farewell to Clementine, Sophie, and her
other friends, and departed reluctantly from Noirmoutier, leaving her
childhood behind her. Throughout her entire life she was never to
relinquish her deep-seated affection for this wind-swept island off the
west coast of France.

III

1810-1814

I cannot forget them. I dream about them at night. Little black girls coming to me, putting their arms about my neck and saying: "Come to us, come and help us. Come and teach us how to know Jesus and to love Him."

ROSE-VIRGINIE PELLETIER

THE city of Tours, on the Loire River, has from the days of antiquity possessed a rich history. Today it is known primarily for its silk mills and for its picturesque old castles and bridges which draw throngs of tourists. But beyond the claims of industry, commerce, and travel it retains a recognized historical importance.

Evangelized about the middle of the third century by an Italian missionary named Gatianus, it has long been identified with one of his successors, the great St. Martin. For twenty-six years prior to his death in 397, Martin, the beloved patron of France, served as the Bishop of Tours. Four centuries later it was here that Charles Martel, grandfather of Charlemagne, led the Franks to victory over the Saracens, thus quelling the threat of a Mohammedan conquest of Europe. In 1170 the construction of its magnificent Gothic cathedral was begun, to be completed only shortly before the outbreak of the religious wars of the sixteenth century. Then Tours passed from Catholic hands to become a Protestant stronghold serving for a while as the capital of Henry IV. Following the revocation of the Edict of Nantes in 1685 its total population decreased markedly, although its Catholic population remained relatively constant. This state of affairs continued until the outrages of the Reign of Terror, at which time great numbers of its people died as martyrs in defense of their Faith.

During the Napoleonic era a renewed spiritual vitality permeated every aspect of the local and national life. Especially was this new spirit expressed in the long-neglected field of education, with the re-establishment of schools for the training of the young. The publication in 1687 of *Traite de l'Education des Filles* by Abbé Fénelon, then tutor to the Dauphin, had met a long-standing need in pedagogic literature, marking the beginning of all later developments in female education. In this treatise the author made it clear beyond any doubt that it was important that women should be educated, proceeding to a specific discussion of the ways and means by which their education should be provided. The overwhelming popularity of the Fénelon treatise gave an impetus to the growth of schools for young girls.

In Tours one of the best known of these schools was operated under the direction of Mlle. Pulcherie Chobelet, a member of a highly esteemed family, who had been among those imprisoned by the Revolutionists for her stanch fidelity to the old regime. This Academy, begun in 1804, had earned an excellent reputation, attracting pupils even from the distant provinces. Each term found it filled to its capacity of ninety girls. Included in the fall enrollment of 1810 was Rose-Virginie Pelletier, who came to Tours from Noirmoutier by way of Soullans. Her seemingly unimportant arrival was a prelude to the four years she was to spend in preparation for her work. None of her classmates would have surmised her destiny nor guessed that her achievements were to add another illustrious name to the list of the distinguished associated with this old city.

Upon her arrival in Soullans, Mme. Pelletier had investigated the local school situation. She had no trouble in deciding to enter Paul as a lay student in the Petit Seminairé of near-by La Garouche, but she learned to her dismay that the local girls' school offered no training beyond that which Rose-Virginie had already received. Consequently she had to look elsewhere.

As always, she prayed over this important matter. No doubt her decision was influenced by the knowledge that one of her lifelong friends, Mlle. Chobelet, headed a successful boarding school in Tours. To be sure, that center of culture and religion was 170 miles distant and travel by coach, slow and uncomfortable. One wonders why she did not favor the Ursulines at Chavanges, since she knew Rose-Virginie's desire to be a nun. The distance was considerably less and at Chavanges Rose-Virginie could easily have spent her holidays with her mother. But on all sides Mme. Pelletier heard enthusiastic reports about Mlle. Chobelet's flourishing school. She learned that the teachers were devout lay women banded together into a voluntary organization called L'Association Chrétienne, the Christian Association, the purpose of which was to provide a sound Christian education for young girls and women. These teachers wore secular dress and lived by a very simple Rule. An exchange of letters with her old friend convinced Mme. Pelletier that she should lose no time in enrolling Rose-Virginie.

Rose-Virginie heard the news in silence, and then exclaimed protestingly, "But Mother, Tours is terribly far away."

"Good things often are, my dear. I feel sure, though, that your experiences there will be ever so much more rewarding. You will have advantages that you couldn't possibly get here. I am confident that I am acting wisely."

She set about making the arrangements for their early departure, for they had to leave before the onset of bad weather. Once the roads became impassable there could be no traveling until spring. At best the trip would require three to four days, never an easy undertaking with roaming highwaymen abroad.

"Must we hurry so?" Rose-Virginie asked.

"The sooner we start, the better. I want to see you safely there and get back here within a reasonable time."

"How long will it be before I see you again, Mother?"

Mme. Pelletier had dreaded this question. "I can't really say, my dear. The school holidays are short, and the hazards of the journey many. You can't travel without an escort. It will be easier for us both not to dwell too much on the length of our separation."

"Do you mean that I won't be with you and Paul at Christmas?"

"I am sorry, my dear, but that will be quite impossible." Mme. Pelletier had to press her hand to her chin to steady its quivering. Then she drew her sobbing child to her and held her close.

There is no account of their journey to Tours other than the statement that "it took three days and three nights." [1] Just as is true all over the world today, the first few days following their arrival at the Christian Association Academy brought different reactions to the persons involved in the drama of new girl enters school. Mlle. Chobelet received her good friend, Mme. Pelletier, with courtesy and grace, and even affection, welcoming Rose-Virginie warmly for her mother's sake.

"You will like it here, I am sure. The girls are friendly and co-operative. All of them were newcomers once. One of them comes from Paimboeuf, which is quite near Noirmoutier. You will meet her shortly; her name is Marie-Angelique Dernée."

Rose-Virginie smiled politely but wanly at this bit of news. At that moment she was in no mood to exchange her mother for the possibility of gaining a new friend.

For her part, Mme. Pelletier was delighted at the size of the buildings and grounds. Situated at the corner of the Rue des Ursulines and the Rue du Petit Pré, near what is now the Parc Mirabeau, the Academy was housed in a former convent occupied by the Carmelites before their forced expulsion in 1790. Everything appeared in good order, for the school was then at its zenith. The Head Mistress, Mlle. Josephine Loisel, a young woman of twenty-five, and the Assistant Mistress, Mlle. Marie de Lignac, her junior by six years, gave every evidence of breeding, education, and a deep religious spirit. Together with Mlle. Chobelet, whom they addressed as "Madame" in deference to her position as Directress of the Academy, they assured Mme. Pelletier that they would leave nothing undone to promote her daughter's welfare.

"Have no fear, my good friend," Mme. Chobelet said. "This is the very place for a young woman like Rose-Virginie, who hopes to take her place later as a member of a religious community and a teacher of young girls. Here she will discover and enjoy the rewards of such a life."

Rose-Virginie found herself listening attentively. It was odd to be referred to as "a young woman" when she felt like a confused child. To be sure, part of what Mme. Chobelet said was true—she did want to become a religious [2]—but she had never even remotely considered the possibility of becoming a classroom teacher. Uncertainly she wondered now if all nuns were schoolteachers. Overwearied and unhappy though she was, her sudden anxiety about her future eased when she recalled the many stories she had heard about nuns who worked among the heathen, the sick, the poor, and the homeless; or of contemplatives who spent their days in prayer and sacrifice for the alleviation of the sins of mankind. Actually, in her day, there were few vocations other than teaching open to unmarried women except within the Church. Nursing, as a field of service, had not been commonly accepted, and the idea of a woman's entering the professions was unthought of. Social service was confined to the Church. Fortunately the services of the nuns were varied, for the nuns served all walks of life, in any capacity where they were needed, and in many parts of the world. Under these conditions Rose-Virginie would have a rather wide choice.

Before the week passed Mme. Pelletier was rested and ready to start back to Soullans. It was well that neither she nor Rose-Virginie knew that this was to be their last glimpse of each other, although undoubtedly the possibility was in the mind of both. Early on the morning set for her departure Mme. Pelletier looked out sadly at the bright autumn sunlight shining on the red and gold leaves of the ancient oaks and maples. She felt a similarity between the old trees and herself. Here they had decked themselves in their resplendent garments as a sort of recompense for the days ahead when they could no longer conceal their stark and forbidding destitution. And here she was, trying to appear lighthearted and matter-of-fact. Until now she and Rose-Virginie had never been separated, not even for one night.

She spoke to her unhappy daughter. "I love you very much, my dear. Always remember that, and remember too that God loves you even more. I have no doubt that He will take especial care of you and of me, giving both of us many tasks to perform for His sake. I, as a housekeeper, and you, as a schoolgirl, must always relate everything we do to Him. Remembering that will help you to overcome every kind of loneliness and discouragement. I know firsthand what I am talking about."

Rose-Virginie looked at her mother without smiling. "I'll try. But it won't be easy. Oh, mother, I'd much rather go home with you. Everything here is so very strange."

Mme. Pelletier was firm. "The new is usually strange, but it is also fascinating when we open our hearts to its message. Already I am looking forward to your letters and the reports from your teachers."

Sorrow gripped Rose-Virginie. She fumbled for the words, and blinked back her tears. "I'll do my best, my very best." More than that she could not promise.

With a flourish the stage, commonly called the diligence, hove noisily into sight to stop with a jerk. The luggage was strapped securely into place. Daughter and mother clung to each other. Then Mme. Pelletier was helped aboard, smiling. Soon she was off amid a waving of handkerchiefs and a chorus of good wishes and blessings. Once the coach had sunk from sight Rose-Virginie wept bitterly.

She found the days that followed hard ones indeed. Although she did her best to rise above her loneliness, she was thoroughly miserable, and no one seemed to care. Despite Mme. Chobelet's statement that all the girls had been newcomers not so long ago, the girls themselves had apparently forgotten that fact. To them there was nothing novel about a new girl. One came today, another tomorrow, and thus the school membership grew. Evidently it was each one's responsibility to adjust as best she could to the established routine. The school program was directed to the entire group and made slight provision for the orientation of one individual. Rose-Virginie longed for a friend with whom she could speak freely. Had Clementine or Sophie been here, things would have been much easier.

Mme. Chobelet appeared like an entirely different woman when seen in the role of school administrator rather than that of family friend. To be sure, she was polite, but she was usually in a state of deep preoccupation, forgetting Rose-Virginie for days at a time. Then for no apparent reason she would summon "Mlle. Pelletier" to her office. Rose-Virginie found this adult title an unscalable barrier between them. "Mlle. Pelletier" stood tonguetied in Madame's presence. Before her, she felt chilled and rebuffed and her tense manner invited no favorable reactions from the Head Mistress. Instead Mme. Chobelet became annoyed at the unresponsiveness of this student from Soullans. Always highly nervous and exacting under the most favorable circumstances, the Directress would lose patience with Rose-Virginie and dismiss her abruptly, pitying Mme. Pelletier for having reared such a taciturn child.

"And she promised she would be 'a second mother' to me!" Rose-Virginie sobbed aloud after one of these unhappy conferences. "I can't stay here any longer. I can't. I really think I'd rather die."

At such times she would transfer her troubles to paper, holding back nothing. Had she mailed any of these letters they might have brought her mother in haste. But she never sent them. She sensed her mother's predicament, as well as her own; an objectivity which served her well in later years.

In her loneliness she learned that homesickness is an illness of mind and body as virulent as any pox or infection. Gradually she realized that her condition was not uncommon. With that discovery was born a desire to help other homesick girls. Later as a Sister of the

Good Shepherd she always stressed the value of friendliness and warm personal interest as a means of aiding desolate and unhappy new-comers.

During the first winter Rose-Virginie made two new friends whom she was to cherish always. One was Marie-Angelique Dernée of whom Mme. Chobelet had spoken earlier, and the other was the Assistant Mistress of Studies, Mlle. Pauline de Lignac. As classmates and native Vendeans, Rose-Virginie and Marie-Angelique lost little time in becoming "best friends." It was exciting once more to have someone her own age with whom she could talk and plan. Within a short while each girl had confided in the other her desire someday to enter a convent.

"We'll pray and work and wait until we really know which Order we wish to join," Rose-Virginie said.

"But I know already," Marie-Angelique replied. "I'm going to be a Carmelite. Won't you?"

"It's too soon to make up my mind. I think I'd rather be a missionary Sister than live in strict enclosure. Time will tell. Right now it's telling me to study my New Testament lesson for Mlle. Pauline's class. She's given me a special assignment for tomorrow."

More than any other person Mlle. Pauline de Lignac was to influence Rose-Virginie during her life at the Academy. Consequently any account of Rose-Virginie Pelletier would be incomplete without a brief sketch of this extraordinary young woman.

Rose-Virginie's senior by only five years, she was quiet, personable, and intelligent, a young woman of genuine piety and varied talents. For over two years prior to the younger girl's enrollment at the school, Mlle. Lignac had worn the simple uniform of the Ladies of the Association, as the teachers at the Academy were called. Within that short period she had advanced to the post of Assistant Mistress, dividing her time between administrative and teaching duties. Her class in the study of the New Testament had won her a school-wide reputation for she had a special ability to make the greatest of all books live for others. Eventually their mutual love of the New Testament would prove a strong bond between teacher and pupil, but first came the bond of a real and lasting friendship.

One day shortly after Mme. Pelletier had returned to Soullans, when Rose-Virginie's spirits were at ebb tide and she felt completely lost in her new environment, Mlle. Lignac suggested their taking a short walk together around the school grounds. Later Rose-Virginie couldn't remember anything in particular that they had talked about, except Mademoiselle's saying she preferred a "brisk" walk to a leisurely stroll. That preference had rather surprised Rose-Virginie, for she would have thought a stroll much more in keeping with Mademoiselle's gentle manner.

Increasingly Mademoiselle's name appeared in Rose-Virginie's letters. To her mother she wrote that Mlle. Pauline de Lignac was an only child, the daughter of a widow of one of the victims of the Reign of Terror. Her father had been put to death by the Revolutionaries and she and her mother held prisoners for eighteen months in the former Convent of the Ursulines at Châteauroux. There they had sometimes attended Mass secretly as the Pelletiers had done under similar circumstances. Much later, after they had become confidantes, Rose-Virginie revealed that Mlle. Pauline had told her she had found it hard to leave her mother all alone in order to consecrate herself to God. She had purposely chosen to become one of the Ladies of the Association on account of their annual vows and simple Rule. Here she could follow a modified religious life and yet remain free to leave, should her mother's age or health make it necessary for her to return home. "But I am sure she never thinks of doing that. She is truly in love with Christ. You feel that all the time when you are with her, and you see it when she teaches about Him in our New Testament Class."

Rose-Virginie learned many practical truths from Mlle. Pauline de Lignac, some of which she would follow regularly in her later work of reclaiming wayward girls. One specific precept she was never to forget. Mademoiselle said, "Show the beauty of virtue rather than the deformity of vice, and you will so make the love of virtue to grow in the hearts of your hearers, that they will almost unconsciously forsake vice, without even dwelling upon it."

Now that she had friends, the school world seemed an entirely different place to Rose-Virginie. There were so many things happening, or about to happen, that time no longer dragged but flew ahead almost too rapidly. One custom in particular she found most appealing. This was the practice of what was at that time regarded as the frequent reception of the Sacraments. Most of the girls received Holy Communion fortnightly, but a few of the more devout ones, together with their teachers, approached the Holy Table every week. This privilege, so desired by Rose-Virginie, was withheld until she, as a newcomer, could prove herself worthy of it. In the beginning, she suffered keenly as the result of her confessor's inability to understand her. For reasons that are not clear the chaplain was overly severe and critical of this ardent, intelligent young girl, whose knowledge of things spiritual seemingly confounded him. His reproaches brought her prolonged grief. Finally she confided in Mlle. Lignac. One doubts that the teacher conferred with the priest, but she did succeed in comforting Rose-Virginie by reminding her that often the most faithful of God's servants are obliged to undergo trials far greater than those she was then undergoing.

On the surface everything in the Academy was proceeding happily. Never was there the slightest hint of any friction between Mme. Chobelet and the Ladies of the Association. Naturally then the announcement made early in March that Mlle. Josephine Loisel, the Mistress of Studies, was shortly to depart, came as a great shock. To the girls this news was entirely unexpected, but to Mlle. Loisel's colleagues it was no surprise at all. Some of the latter had wondered that it had not taken place earlier.

For a long time Mlle. Loisel had found things increasingly intolerable as they affected her life as a religious. Mme. Chobelet was a combination of irreconcilable qualities. As a perfectionist in spiritual matters and a born innovator she grew restless whenever things were progressing smoothly. To her, change meant improvement. Because of her unpredictable attitude the Ladies never knew when a directive from their Superior would require them to insert new practices into their religious pattern, discarding highly satisfactory ones. Even if Mme. Chobelet had only their best interests at heart, they found her proposals confusing and usually unnecessary. Their Rule, though simple, was sufficiently comprehensive and satisfying. Sometimes it seemed that Mme. Chobelet had only to read or hear of a new devotion, or an act of mortification, in order to adopt it straight off for the Christian Association. As a result their Rule had become almost unrecognizable.

The Bishop of Tours, Monseigneur [3] Barral, fully aware of Mme. Chobelet's mercurial temperament, admonished her to stop meddling in these matters of religious procedure. Later upon learning that his advice had not been followed, he refused to grant the Ladies of the Association permission to renew their simple vows. This denial, he asserted, would remain in force until matters improved. Because of this action Mlle. Loisel withdrew from the Christian Association and left her post, not without genuine regret, to join the Ursulines of Tours.

Surprisingly there were no other departures. Perhaps the calls to a religious vocation were not as immediate with the others, or they may have wanted to give Mme. Chobelet the opportunity to set things in order before they left. Perhaps she herself became less mercurial. Whatever the reason, the others remained. It was well that they did, for otherwise the Academy would surely have closed.

As it was, the upper school was in revolt. The older girls especially resented the appointment of Mlle. de Lignac as Mistress of Studies in Mlle. Loisel's stead. They felt insulted that a young woman only twenty years old was now placed over them, some of whom were already seventeen or eighteen. Deciding to make things thoroughly unpleasant for her, they ignored her presence, chatting audibly during her classroom instruction and appearing to be completely absorbed with their own affairs. One girl, more daring than the others, put her fingers into her ears to avoid hearing what Mlle. de Lignac was saying.

Mlle. Pauline was almost at her wit's end. She knew that she had to restore order, but she used one means after another only to see them all fail. Now she was overcome with her own inadequacies. Surely, she thought, there must be some way to win the co-operation of these upperclassmen. Late one afternoon after an especially difficult class period, she was walking down the corridor, tired in body and soul, when Rose-Virginie fell into step beside her. "You are in trouble, are you not, Mademoiselle?"

"What makes you ask?" Mademoiselle queried.

"I haven't seen you smile in ever so long. And you don't take 'brisk' walks any more. You stroll practically all the time."

That observation forced a weak smile from Mlle. Pauline. Reluctantly and yet with evident relief, she found herself talking over her troubles with Rose-Virginie. Immediately she felt better, although she clearly realized that many people would have thought her conduct unseemly. After all teachers were expected to give, and not to seek, solace from their pupils. However, Rose-Virginie's wisdom and maturity easily spanned the five-year difference in their ages. They were like two contemporaries intent on working out an amicable solution to a serious problem which, if not corrected, could weaken the morale of the entire school.

Rose-Virginie prayed to the Holy Spirit to show her a way to help

Mlle. Pauline. Suddenly she saw what she could do. Pentecost would soon be here. Why not try to interest the entire school in joining a novena in preparation for this great Feast? If she did her part, she had no doubt that the Holy Ghost would do the rest. Filled with confidence she hurriedly sought out Marie-Angelique.

"Oh, Rose-Virginie, you are clever! A crusade of prayer for nine unbroken days with everyone's going to Holy Communion on Whitsunday. That's a wonderful idea."

Rose-Virginie's plan was quite simple. They would ask another friend to help them spread the idea about. During recreation each girl would talk to one-third of the student body urging everyone to unite in making the school-wide novena. Its purpose was to prepare their hearts for the coming of the Holy Spirit. "We can't do that," Rose-Virginie said, "unless we shut out hate and replace it with love. We can't hold any bitter thoughts toward even one person. If we did, that would spoil everything."

At first the older girls were amused at the earnestness of the trio from the junior division, but they finally agreed to co-operate. One of them was overheard saying, "Those youngsters put me to shame with their zeal. Why, they actually act as though they were inspired."

And they were. Their fervor fired everyone to do her best to be charitable toward her schoolmates and teachers as well. Rose-Virginie did not hesitate to talk frankly to some of the older girls about the ways in which they might ease Mlle. Pauline's burdens. After that they worked hard to undo the harm they had already caused.

On the morning of Pentecost Sunday ninety young girls received Holy Communion together. It is easy to believe that each girl heard in her own heart "the sound from heaven as of a mighty wind coming where they were sitting, and they were all filled with the Holy Ghost, speaking the wonderful words of God." For the end of the novena saw the end of Mlle. Pauline's troubles.

Another year passed quickly and happily. In the autumn of 1812 Rose-Virginie received a letter which carried the news of the sudden death of her oldest brother, André-Constant. No one had thought his brief illness to be serious, and for that reason she had not known about it. Her mother's letter revealed that this sorrow had reopened the old grief caused by her husband's death six years before. At that time André, a strapping lad of eighteen, had supported her; now young, strong, and capable he had been taken from her.

Rose-Virginie saw the words of the letter but refused their meaning until her common sense forced her to accept the inevitable. Her impulse was to start for home at once, but her mother, anticipating such action, had advised against it. Instead she spoke of the solace of work and believed that it would be better for Rose-Virginie if she continued to apply herself to her studies. No doubt that was true, but Rose-Virginie's defenses crumbled before the thought of her mother's loneliness. She had already been away from home two years. Now the awful thought struck her that she might never see any of her family again.

Without Mlle. Pauline's understanding friendship she would have found her days far heavier. The young teacher succeeded in helping the grieving girl immeasurably until one day two months later when their roles were suddenly reversed. Then it was Mlle. Pauline who grieved and Rose-Virginie who comforted. Two letters came to Mademoiselle by the same post, one from her mother, and one from her mother's pastor. The first told her that her mother was gravely ill and wanted to see her daughter; the other, that Mme. de Lignac had already died. Immediately Rose-Virginie put aside her own grief and did her best to console her friend. In their shared sorrow, their friendship assumed a strength that was to hold for the rest of their lives.

Just six months later Mme. Pelletier died suddenly, on June 11, 1813, at her home in Vendée. The news brought Rose-Virginie near despair. The facts seemed incredibly cruel. Mme. Pelletier had been buried beside her husband in Noirmoutier before her daughter knew of her death. Reasons and excuses abounded, but they did not make clear the seemingly unpardonable oversight on the part of Rose-Virginie's sister and brothers. It was true that distance was great, communication slow, and Anne-Josephine not too well, with the birth of her second child expected almost momentarily. In their grief Julian and Paul presumedly had left everything in M. Marsaud's hands. As Anne-Josephine's husband, he was now the senior member of the family and could, they thought, be expected to act in their best interests. He did many commendable things, but he neglected to send for their absent sister at the time of their mother's last illness. Later Rose-Virginie learned that her mother had been in failing health over a period of months. The loss of André-Constant had taken away her prop.

Anne-Josephine wrote that Mme. Pelletier had asked them not to let Rose-Virginie know that her health was impaired after her son's death. Until very recently she had continued her letters filling them with comfort and reassurance, not meaning to be misleading, but centering on Rose-Virginie's needs and minimizing her own.

Now in retrospect Rose-Virginie could see that her mother had endured many sorrows during the fifty-two years she had lived. Suddenly Rose-Virginie gave way to remorse. She held no bitter thoughts toward her family for not having summoned her home, but she castigated herself for ever having consented to continue her studies at Tours. Why had she not realized that her mother had needed her more than she had needed an education? Better to have rebelled in the beginning than to suffer forever in mind and heart for the things she had failed to do.

Mlle. Pauline waited for Rose-Virginie's first grief to spend itself and then attempted to help her to rebuild her life. "To identify ourselves with another's sorrow is one thing, my dear friend, but to lose ourselves in our own sorrow is contrary to our Faith."

There were times when she was sure that Rose-Virginie had not heard one word that she had said. But she was not discouraged in her efforts to restore her friend to a sense of perspective from which she could view life as a corridor leading through death to eternal life. Had not Jesus said, "I go to prepare a place for you . . . that where I am, ye also may be."

One day to her consternation she found Rose-Virginie sitting in the middle of the floor packing her clothes and books.

"Whatever are you doing?" she cried.

"Getting ready to leave. I cannot stay here any longer. I am going back to Vendée."

"Does your family know?"

"I have written Anne-Josephine. I'll be ready to start as soon as I hear from her."

But Anne-Josephine and her husband responded unfavorably to Rose-Virginie's impassioned request. M. Marsaud, now Rose-Virginie's legal guardian, refused to grant the permission she needed to withdraw from the Academy. As he bluntly expressed it, he saw no sense in her leaving school before she had completed her course of study. That was his ultimatum.

Rose-Virginie accepted the decision. This harsh message served as a kind of catharsis. Face to face with the realities of life and death she acknowledged wholly, though somewhat tardily, the curative comfort supplied by complete trust in God. Always after that she wondered why she had wavered even for a little while.

In time she was given strength to carry the loss of her mother so quietly in her heart that few people were aware of it. But an incident that occurred thirty years later revealed the quality of her remembrance. On that occasion a friend from Noirmoutier recalled Mme. Pelletier's charity and kindness. Immediately Rose-Virginie burst into tears. Later when asked by one of the Sisters why it was she had never spoken to the Community about her mother, she answered, "Because never since I had the sorrow of losing her have I been able to utter her name without breaking down. I loved my mother so dearly that when I was told that she had died, I, too, nearly died." [4]

Rose-Virginie was always to remember that year for it brought, in addition to her mother's death, an awareness of the work of the Sisters of Our Lady of the Refuge and saw the departure of Marie-Angelique Dernée for the Tours Cloister of the Carmelites. Prior to her friend's leaving, Rose-Virginie had shown a deep interest in the recently opened Convent located opposite the Christian Association Academy. From the beginning she had listened avidly to Mlle. Pauline's account of the Refuge Sisters founded by the French missionary, Father John Eudes,[5] for the specific purpose of converting sinful girls and women and aiding them to achieve permanent rehabilitation. These Sisters, she quickly learned, had been in Tours for over fifty years at the time their Convent fell a casualty to the law of 1792 that wiped out all the convents and monasteries throughout the nation. Because each foundation was an autonomous unit, it had appeared unlikely that the Tours Community would ever have the means or the personnel to reassemble and resume its interrupted mission. But in 1804, after the storm had begun to subside, six of the older Sisters had emerged from hiding to reopen their school in a modest fashion. Gradually their work, so necessary in this industrial center, expanded, requiring them to seek more commodious quarters. At length under the direction of their Superior, Sister Mary of St. Joseph La Roux, they succeeded in locating an appropriate dwelling situated upon a small hill across from Mme. Chobelet's school.

Rose-Virginie's first visit to the Refuge probably came at the time of the official opening of the new Convent. Then the Ladies of the Association accompanied by a number of the older pupils attended some of the ceremonies held in the Convent chapel. The sight of those white-robed religious dedicated to the mission of snatching souls from Satan impressed Rose-Virginie unforgettably. After that she met every effort of Marie-Angelique to interest her in the Carmelites by saying, "I've always felt drawn to abandoned souls and sinners. I find this hard to explain, but I think perhaps it goes back to the stories I heard as a child from the deep-sea fishermen in Noir-moutier. They used to hold us spellbound as they pictured the plight of the African children who were sold on the market place and taken into custody as slaves. I cannot forget them. I dream about them at night. Little black girls coming to me, putting their arms about my neck and saying to me: 'Come to us, come and help us. Come and teach us how to know Jesus and to love Him.'"

About this time Mme. Chobelet reverted to the same unstable behavior that had brought about the departure of Mlle. Loisel. Unrest threatened to become open rebellion and many of the staff indicated their intention to resign their posts and go elsewhere. In desperation Mme. Chobelet acted on the advice of the Archbishop and in December, 1813, transferred the administration of her school to five Ursulines under the direction of a most able educator, the former Mme. Ronald de Bussy. She promised full co-operation to her successor, but as the weeks went by she failed to carry out her promise, remaining in the house and thwarting every change Mme. de Bussy initiated. At the end of two months Mme. de Bussy declared that she was unwilling to continue in such an anomalous position, and announced that she would withdraw to open an Ursuline Academy in another section of the city. Immediately five Ladies of the Christian Association, among whom was Mlle. Pauline de Lignac, asked to accompany her. In this state of uncertainty the school limped along for some time.

Mlle. Pauline had tried to prepare Rose-Virginie for their inevitable separation. Yet when it actually arrived, it saddened them both. For a long time each had known that the other wanted to become a nun and would someday leave the Academy to embark upon her religious life. Each had known too that after that they would no longer be together, for Rose-Virginie did not share Mademoiselle's desire to enter a teaching Order. Until recently, however, she had been content to bide her time, awaiting the day when God would show her how and when to act, but lately she had felt herself drawn almost irresistibly to the neighboring Convent of the Refuge. It was only natural for her to tell Mlle. Pauline about these stirrings in her heart. Mademoiselle counseled her to wait and pray, realizing the intense opposition that lay ahead should Rose-Virginie actually decide to affiliate herself with an Order whose emphasis and goal she felt sure would appear unorthodox to her conservative family.

Rose-Virginie was willing to wait and meanwhile made every effort to become better acquainted with the work of the Sisters of the Refuge. Once she went with several others from her class to a social function held at the Convent. On that occasion the students from the Academy provided the dessert for a party dinner for "those poor girls," as they called the Sisters' charges, serving the dinner themselves under adult supervision. Another time she visited the Mother Superior, presumedly in the company of Mlle. Pauline. For this visit she had not secured Mme. Chobelet's permission, preferring to act without it rather than in defiance of a permission denied, for she wanted to find out the requisites for admission into the Novitiate. To her great joy she learned that no impediments stood in her way, once her guardian gave his permission. Mother Mary of St. Joseph La Roux made it clear, however, that the consent of Rose-Virginie's guardian must first be secured. Rose-Virginie had no doubt that M. Marsaud would grant this necessary permission.

At that moment things were in a turmoil at the Academy because Rose-Virginie was not in her place when the students assembled for the evening meal. In her wrath Mme. Chobelet had failed altogether to notice the absence of Rose-Virginie's companion. Fuming and sputtering she watched the door as a hawk watches its prey. When Rose-Virginie came in alone, intending to apologize for her late entry, she was met by a barrage of questions screamed at her in the high and trembling voice of an infuriated woman.

"Where have you been? Do you not know that it is against school rules to be out after dark? What sinister things have you been doing?" Without stopping for breath, Mme. Chobelet continued to let fly a volley of ugly words and unfounded accusations. She refused Rose-Virginie her dinner saying that "even dry bread and water" were too good for such a disobedient and recalcitrant person.

Rose-Virginie's sensitive nature cringed under this attack, but she offered no defense. Later when the girls gathered around in sympathetic protest, pressing uneaten portions of their own dinner upon her, she held her silence. But she was unable to forget this unwarranted outburst on the part of the Directress.

It was shortly after this incident that Mme. de Bussy, Mlle.

Pauline, and their associates departed to form the nucleus of another Company of St. Ursula in Tours.

The ensuing months were not easy for Rose-Virginie. Sometimes she likened her last term at Madame's school to that first one nearly four years ago. Then she was a stranger in a strange land; now she was a stranger in a land that had grown strange. The school was in a state of obvious disintegration, with many pupils as well as staff leaving before the end of the academic year. Mme. Chobelet was petulant and unstable, and everyone seemed united in discouraging Rose-Virginie from carrying out her desire to become a Sister of the Refuge. Mme. Chobelet fought against the move both overtly and subtly, using every means to dissuade her from taking what she called a "rash step." She cajoled and threatened; she appealed to her mother's memory, saying that Mme. Pelletier would have disapproved, and that this headstrong determination on her daughter's part would have brought her both misery and unhappiness.

Failing to impress Rose-Virginie with such emotional reasoning, she then attempted to appeal to her social sense by praising the Society of the Sacred Heart and the Carmelites as religious Orders of distinction and respectability that "draw to them young French women of the better class." "Enter any one of these," she implored, "and I shall be satisfied. Persist in your senseless determination to go to an Order respectable young women ought to shun, and I shall write your guardian asking him to forbid such nonsense on your part."

As a result of Madame's inflexible attitude, Rose-Virginie engaged in an extended correspondence with M. Marsaud. He wrote that he was displeased at her request and supported Mme. Chobelet's position. Neither he, nor her brothers, would consider permitting her to enter the Sisters of the Refuge. Such work, they agreed, was entirely unbecoming to a young girl of her years and background. What did she know of the pitfalls of life? He was frank to add that he believed she was basing her reactions on impressions and not facts. Henceforth, he said, she was not to visit the Convent again. This was an expressed prohibition and, as his ward, she must respect it.

She obeyed him in deed, but not in spirit, for she had already left her heart at the Refuge where her lifework awaited her. During this period she prayed to be given the graces of Wisdom, Fortitude, and Perseverance that she must have in order to win over Monsieur. She longed for Mlle. Pauline's bodily presence, but she found comfort in the letters that came to her regularly from the Ursuline Academy.

Mademoiselle was happy and confident that Rose-Virginie would in time find similar happiness. She urged her friend to remain calm in the face of all this opposition, reminding her that human beings can delay the working out of God's plans only because He permits them to do so. In His appointed time God would reveal Himself as Rose-Virginie's active partner. During this present battle against the citadel of tradition and family solidarity, He had assigned her the task of defending their joint interests.

It was little wonder that Rose-Virginie's load always seemed lighter after these letters. Mlle. Pauline understood her almost as well as she knew herself.

The months dragged on slowly bringing her at last to her graduation day. That mirage had finally become a reality. Immediately after the exercises she left for Vendée, arriving there in time for her eighteenth birthday. M. Marsaud had invited her to visit Anne-Josephine and him at Nantes, where they were then living, but Rose-Virginie chose instead to go to her paternal aunt in Bouin. There she was assured of a welcome free from tension. Later she did visit in near-by Nantes, but she spent most of the next three months in the same home to which Anne-Josephine had gone shortly after their father's death.

Undoubtedly her visit to her sister brought delight as well as stress. Rose-Virginie had missed her family a great deal and reveled in being with them again. It made her happy to see her sister and her three little daughters, the youngest of whom was only two months old. It was obvious that Anne-Josephine enjoyed her role of wife and mother, which was reassuring, for Rose-Virginie's dealings with Anne-Josephine's husband had led her to believe that he must surely lack the understanding so necessary for a good marriage. Although Monsieur was unnecessarily strict and unreasonable toward her, he displayed none of these difficult characteristics in his own home.

In the beginning Rose-Virginie attempted to present her views serenely and objectively, but she quickly learned that the mere name of the Sisters of the Refuge was enough to arouse her guardian's ire. He remained adamant in his attitude; he would not, he said in agitation, permit his wife's only sister to engage upon a work that would take her among the outcasts of society.

But Rose-Virginie was adamant too. She stood her ground with the tenacity of those fighters from Noirmoutier whom Napoleon had once summoned to him. She knew that she was fighting for her life's happiness. Just when she was ready to admit that she had exhausted every resource at her command, she won her victory. Quite unexpectedly M. Marsaud agreed to permit her to enter the Convent, providing she would promise not to bind herself by formal religious vows until she had reached her twenty-first birthday. His animosity had dissolved before her persuasive arguments that there was no possible danger in her losing her purity by working among girls of doubtful reputation. She had quoted St. John Eudes to the effect that "Purity can no more be sullied when it goes hand in hand with Charity, than sunbeams which shine upon mire." Once he became convinced that further opposition on his part was unjustified, he no longer wanted the responsibility of keeping his sister-in-law from her holy vocation.

Once years later Rose-Virginie asked one of her nieces, most probably her godchild, Anne-Josephine's third daughter, to have a Mass said for her in Bouin "in atonement for all the sins I committed while I was there." She had won her cause righteously, but she had, she admitted, sometimes grown angry and impatient in the course of her struggle to bring about a change in her brother-in-law's attitude.

The day of farewell found Rose-Virginie turning tearfully yet happily toward Tours. This time the old city beckoned her enchantingly; her imagination outran the coach that carried her there.

Upon her arrival she returned briefly to the Academy. During those final days she was given an opportunity to catch glimpses of the Pulcherie Chobelet her mother had known before time, imprisonment, and ill health had turned her into a nervous and irascible woman. This well-meaning but pitiable figure strove valiantly to erase the memory of the stinging rebukes she had directed repeatedly to the young aspirant. She recalled her broken promise to Mme. Pelletier that she would be a second mother to her daughter and attempted to explain her harsh conduct by saying: "My child, you never understood me. I was severe with you, perhaps, but it was for your own good, for the formation of your character." [6]

Rose-Virginie accepted her apologies in a forgiving spirit. She was glad that Madame had offered them, but she held no animus toward her or anyone else. All her past disappointments vanished in the face of the fulfillment of her long cherished dream. She entered the Tours Novitiate of Our Lady of the Refuge on the solemn Feast of the

Sacred Heart of Jesus, which Feast St. John Eudes had established and for which he had composed the Mass and Office approved by the Holy See. Because she began her religious life on this Feast she was affectionately dubbed by the Sisters as "the postulant of the Sacred Heart."

That happy day was October 20, 1814.

IV

1815 - 1825

Remember, my daughters, that a soul is worth more than a world, and that consequently to lend one a hand to withdraw her from the abyss of sin, is a greater thing than to create an entire world and to draw it from nothingness into being.

ST. JOHN EUDES

"ROSE-VIRGINIE Pelletier, thou shalt not be known any more by the name that was thine in the world, but now henceforth in religion as Sister Mary of St. Euphrasia."

So spoke Father Danicourt, the Officiant in charge of the Clothing Ceremony on September 8, 1815, at the Convent of Our Lady of the Refuge. The candidate, clothed in the white habit and veil of this holy house, bowed her head in happy acceptance. On the inside of her habit at a point nearest her heart was stitched a small cross of blue to remind her forever of Christ's Passion suffered for her and the girls who were later to be entrusted to her care. It symbolized too the trials and crosses she would meet and accept willingly in a spirit of expiation for His sake. The color blue was symbolic of Heaven, her true home, just as the white of her outer garment was a mark of the purity of her own heart and the symbol of that virtue, the love of which she would ever strive to implant in the hearts of her young charges.

In her seat near by Mother Mary of St. Joseph La Roux thought quietly of the circumstances that had preceded the clothing of this novice. She reviewed the eleven months that had passed since Rose-

Virginie had come to them. Customarily the period of probation would have ended five months earlier, but it had been purposely extended so that her two years as a novice would not terminate until her guardian permitted her to speak her vows. From the moment she had crossed their threshold she had found her place in the routine of the religious life, accepting each responsibility graciously as a special privilege and showing a deep love for everything connected with their Rule. Her rare gifts of piety, simplicity, and sound common sense had made all of them realize that hers was no ordinary vocation.

Mother St. Joseph reflected further. "Rose-Virginie has never seemed lonely here, despite the fact that she and one other postulant [1] are the only two young people in the Community, and for a time the sole occupants of the Novitiate." It was obvious that she felt completely at home among the older Sisters whom she looked upon as Confessors of the Faith. She never grew weary of listening to their stories of the indignities and privations they had been forced to endure during the long years of their dispersal. They were much pleased one day when she remarked spontaneously that their lives gave her a firsthand model of dedicated service, adding that the Sisters seemed to her like God's angels and this hallowed convent, an adjunct to Heaven itself.

Undoubtedly Mother St. Joseph had these things in mind a few days earlier when she had asked Rose-Virginie, "Have you ever thought of the name you would like to bear in religion?"

"Yes, Reverend Mother. I would like very much to be called Sister St. Teresa of Avila," Rose-Virginie had answered quickly.

"What makes you desire that particular name?" came the surprised reply.

"I have loved it for a long time. I have read St. Teresa's life and many of her works. Then, too, my friend, Marie-Angelique Dernée, is now a Carmelite, Sister Mary of the Incarnation. In our letters we often share our love for St. Teresa. Most of all, I admire her great zeal for souls."

But Mother St. Joseph did not share Rose-Virginie's point of view. "I think you are rather presumptuous to aspire to this holy name. You must be humble in all things and especially in this one. I suggest you search in the *Lives of the Saints* for someone who is not so well known. Then come back and we will consider your second choice."

Rose-Virginie had not meant to presume, but she had hoped to have St. Teresa as her patroness. She left at once in quiet humility, an act that showed how far she had already advanced in grace. Not so long ago she would have found it difficult to acquiesce without protest.

Mother St. Joseph wondered if she had been too harsh. She was fully aware of this exceptional young postulant's many talents and had feigned disapproval only to emphasize the importance of true humility.

It took time for Rose-Virginie to find a Saint she considered obscure enough to satisfy the Mother Prioress and to chasten herself. Much later she returned, confident that her present selection would now be approved.

"Have you found another name?"

"Yes, Mother Prioress. It is that of a holy Virgin, a Greek girl, who lived as a cloistered nun and loved prayer and humiliation." She hesitated momentarily and then added quietly, "I guess I was drawn to her because I suffered humiliation without loving it."

Mother St. Joseph found it difficult to keep from smiling. "Who is this Saint?"

"St. Euphrasia. I had never even heard about her before. Do you know her?"

"Just slightly. Please tell me what you have learned."

"Her Feast is kept on the 13th of March. The Greek Church honors her for her gift of miracles and her victories over the devil. She should be a good protectress, for I'll surely be fighting the devil in my work."

The prioress agreed that the name was fitting. It was unpretentious and would emphasize the coveted quality of humility. "Now," she said, "many people will say that they are unacquainted with St. Euphrasia. Consequently, they will ask you endlessly about her."

To a certain extent Mother St. Joseph was correct, but she had no way of knowing that this postulant was destined to lift that euphonious name—which means "beautiful speech" or "one who speaks well"—from near obscurity to true fame in the conventual life.

The novitiate proper starts immediately after the candidate is clothed in her religious habit and white veil, and continues for two successive years. Throughout the first year the novice studies under the direction of her Novice Mistress the Rules and Customs of the Congregation, familiarizing herself with everything pertaining to the religious life such as the vows, the liturgy, and the history and spirit of the Order. Her daily routine is carefully planned and the development of her spiritual life emphasized almost to the exclusion of every other activity. During the second year, however, she spends a part of her time at certain tasks in the "Class," which is present-day nomenclature for the girls committed to the care of the Sisters, the earlier term "penitents" having long since been discarded. In the Good Shepherd system, the girls are divided into groups according to their needs. Each group is called a class and bears its own distinctive name. Each class is in immediate charge of a House Mother, or First Mistress as she is called in Good Shepherd parlance. Under her immediate direction the novices work with the girls, this work supplementing but in no way supplanting their spiritual training. It is easy to see how the uniform pattern of the first year of the novitiate limits the extraneous experiences of the individual during this important formative period. As it is today, so it was with Sister Mary [2] of St. Euphrasia, whose own personal experiences apart from those outlined by her Mistress of Novices were held to the usual minimum. Still she had some, and fortunately, an account of them has been preserved.

The first exterior duty she was assigned as a novice was the sweeping of the choir of the Sisters and the dusting of the thirteen stalls. This task she performed daily with care and love, but at best she could dispose of it quickly. No one, she said, not even a laggard, needed much time to do this job well. Before long her unfilled hours became a real trial. Always a vigorous, dynamic person, she needed some kind of an outlet for her pent-up energies. She knew that she had a capacity for much more work than she was being given. Finally after many sleepless nights she sought an additional assignment from her Mistress of Novices, explaining that this aspect of her present life was bringing her real unhappiness.

"You are asking to be given more work!" the Mistress of Novices said in a tone of surprise. "Why, my dear, the day will come and all too soon, when you will be crying for time to do all the things that will be your responsibility. We plan this period of preparation deliberately to be balanced in favor of study and repose, so that the induction into your active duties will be gradual and complete."

She had spoken with prophetic accuracy. Nevertheless as she listened to Sister Mary of St. Euphrasia, she learned that the young Sister had no liking at all for either knitting or embroidering at which arts the novices, as a rule, filled their leisure moments. After further thought and discussion she gave Sister Mary of St. Euphrasia permission to study and read extensively far beyond the demands of her regular classes, recommending in particular the Sacred Scriptures,

Annals of Carmel, the *Lives of the Saints,* and the *Origines,* or *Beginnings of the Order.*

This assignment served as a solace and a joy and proved a perfect preparation for her holy vocation. She immersed herself enthusiastically in these books and writings, learning many parts of them by heart. She was able to quote lengthy portions of the Holy Bible accurately and easily. Years later in her published conferences with her Community she referred to this experience.

"When I was a young novice," she wrote, "I was not skillful about manual tasks. I told our Mother that I regretted this awkwardness. She answered that, while I had leisure, I had better make use of it to read the Holy Scriptures and the *Lives of the Saints,* for that the time would come when I should be overwhelmed with work, and then I should reap the benefit; and indeed, the more I read of the Holy Scripture the more I loved its beauty." [3]

And again: "What I liked best after the Bible was the manuscript lives of our first Mothers, Father Eudes' letters, the abridgment of his life; [4] and when a Community letter arrived from one of the Houses of the Refuge, I was so delighted that I could not sleep at night for thinking about it." [5]

In addition Sister St. Euphrasia identified herself closely with the spiritual readings heard in common by the entire Community at their meals when each of the group in turn served as the reader in the refectory. One day at luncheon Sister St. Euphrasia found herself deeply affected by the reading which told the story of St. Dositheus,[6] a rich young man who became a Christian at Jerusalem and later, an Infirmarian monk at Gaza. In all respects but one, he was a paradox, for his chronic ill health made it impossible for him to observe the regular laws of fast and austerity prescribed by his Order. None the less he became a great Saint through his consistent and outstanding love for the virtue of obedience. Without reservation, he had completely given his will to God.

Perhaps the story was embellished by other details. In any case it stirred the young novice from Vendée deeply. On a much later occasion she explained her reaction in this manner: "One sentence stuck me with much force. It was this: "St. Dositheus quickly reached sanctity by perfect obedience.' I heard nothing else during the rest of the meal. Over and over again those words rang in my ears. 'St. Dositheus quickly reached sanctity by perfect obedience.' Light seemed to flood my soul. Obedience, then, must be the best means to become holy. If only I were allowed to make the Vow of Obedience, and at once!" [7]

Part of the account of Dositheus told of a questioning fellow monk who after Dositheus' death found it difficult to accept the vision he had beheld of his lately deceased brother until a voice from Heaven dispelled his doubt by these comforting words: "Dositheus attained this great degree of glory only through obedience. It is true he did not practice such austerities as some others, but, if he accepted certain modifications of the severity of the Rule, he did so with perfect purity of intention—to obey his superiors." [8]

At the first opportunity Sister St. Euphrasia asked her Mistress of Novices to permit her to make the vow of Obedience privately at the end of the first year of her novitiate. Despite its irregularity, this request to give up everything personal was granted and an impressive little ceremony took place informally in the Chapter Room before the assembled Sisters. Twelve months were to pass, however, before Sister St. Euphrasia would reaffirm this vow publicly before the altar of God in the presence of an authorized officiant.

In years to come Mother Mary of St. Euphrasia often drew upon her own experiences to illustrate the instructions she gave to the novices. Once when she was discussing the virtue of obedience she said, "At the end of a year of novitiate, our Mother allowed me to make the vow of Obedience, and she gave me the silver heart.[9] From that moment I felt more than ever drawn to this virtue. Oh, I really believe, my dear daughters, that perseverance in my vocation is due solely to the virtue of obedience. Attach yourselves, then, very much to this virtue, if you wish to persevere. Always obey whatever you may be told to do. Obey simply like children." [10]

Sister Mary of St. Stanislaus Bedouet, Rose-Virginie's first companion in the novitiate, has left this profile of her fellow novice. "That which struck one first in her was her ingenuousness, her delightful candour, and a great simplicity in her manners. She had such a humble way of accusing herself of her faults, and of joining her hands, that the Mistress of Novices called the attention of others (in the Community) to it. Never did she have an altercation with any one of her companions, nor indeed any difficulty with any other person. On the contrary she was always gentle, obliging, affectionate toward all; she was always ready to console those who were in trouble, and her unalterable gaiety entertained good humour among the persons who surrounded her." [11]

During the second year of her novitiate Sister Mary of St. Euphrasia was named the Second Mistress in the Class serving under Sister Mary of St. Victoire Houette. The Second Mistress as well as the other Sisters appointed to aid the First Mistress are her authorized lieutenants or auxiliaries, carrying out her instructions and implementing her program. Although lacking final authority, they are empowered by the First Mistress to act for her in given situations, serving as "angels of peace" between the children and the First Mistress. This premature appointment told its own story, for normally an inexperienced novice is seldom appointed to such a difficult and important post. However, her Superior had earlier sent Rose-Virginie, the postulant, into the Class to read to the "children" at their meals and to perform lesser duties in their behalf. In her mind there was no doubt that Sister Mary of St. Euphrasia was ready for this constant contact with the penitents, a number of whom were far older than she.

Soon the dignity, kindness—and no doubt the sense of humor— of the newly appointed Second Mistress won over her most obstinate charges; they sensed her honest desire to help them remake their lives. This re-forming, she told them, could not be done by a superficial glossing over of their faults. It must go far, far deeper than that. She had early realized that constructive ideals would lead to an entirely new life for the girls, only when these ideals were re-enforced by the warm personal touch of Christ and accompanied by interesting and worth-while projects of work, play, and prayer. One day she startled Sister St. Victoire by saying: "I think it is better not to preach too much; it only wearies them [the girls]. It is better to keep them interested and to try to be very just and always kind."

To her surprise she discovered that many of these girls had never been shown a real kindness by anyone. They scarcely knew the meaning of the word. Apropos of that discovery she said, "A cup of sweet milk given opportunely to one of our dear penitents will be more effectual in bringing her back to right sentiments than acts of severity." Another observation haunts one with its reasonableness. "If we had been plunged into misery, had we belonged to bad parents, perhaps we would have been wicked as many others." It was no wonder that Sister St. Victoire paused often in her daily tasks to utter a *Te Deum* for having been given such an able and understanding Second Mistress.

On July 31, 1817, Sister Mary of St. Euphrasia reached her twenty-first birthday. Immediately M. Marsaud as her guardian and the representative of her family asserted that his sister-in-law need no longer postpone taking her religious vows. Furthermore, he graciously added, he had been wrong ever to have doubted that she might not have been called to her particular vocation.

Thus on September 9, just two years after her clothing as a novice, Sister Mary of St. Euphrasia was received into the Tours House of Our Lady of the Refuge by Father Petit, the parish priest of the Church of St. Saturnin. In the presence of the Community and a number of her relatives and friends she pronounced the vows of Poverty, Chastity, and Obedience together with a fourth vow, to labor for the salvation of souls. This last vow had been prescribed by the Holy Founder, St. John Eudes, and is unique with the Congregations of the Refuge and of the Good Shepherd, the second evolving later as an expansion of the original Foundation.

It is the custom today for the Sisters of the Good Shepherd, upon the completion of their novitiate, to pronounce their simple vows annually for three successive years at the end of which time they pledge their final vows. But on the day of Sister Mary of St. Euphrasia's profession she spoke her vows once and forever and gave herself to Christ for all time as a co-worker in His task of redeeming souls.

To the four required vows Sister Mary of St. Euphrasia added one other voluntarily—the foregoing of her indulgences. After the established practice of the Church she believed that indulgences are a remission in whole or in part of the temporal punishment due to forgiven sin—certainly not the sin itself. These indulgences are granted by the Pope and the Bishops out of the Church's spiritual treasury, or fund of merits, produced by the sufferings and sacrifices of Christ, His Blessed Mother, the Saints and all the redeemed. Whatever the nature of the indulgence, it provides a proportionate cancellation of punishment for sin, which otherwise one would have to expiate by prolonged sufferings here and hereafter. All of this help, this succor, she gladly gave over. "I offer you, my dearest Mother of God," she whispered in fervent happiness, "all the indulgences I might gain throughout my life together with those others might gain for me after I die. This gift, my dearest Queen, is for you to apply to whatever suffering souls in Purgatory you may desire to aid, choosing them in your own manner and time." This act of renunciation tested her sorely when her only sister died unexpectedly, shortly after her profession. However, this sad event was only the first of many that would make this personally imposed vow a weighty but a willing sacrifice.

But at the time of her profession nothing marred the joyous day. Clothed in her white habit and black veil and wearing the silver heart and crucifix, all symbols of the professed religious, Sister Mary of St. Euphrasia, radiant with happiness, received the congratulations of her associates.

One of the older Sisters spoke in solemn prophecy: "The time will come, my dear, when you will be obliged to make a change in the formula of the vows you have taken today. You are destined to do great things for the Order."

The newly professed Sister smiled courteously, but she did not take these words seriously. Later, however, she recalled them when another elderly nun spoke to her in a tone of portentous revelation: "The day will arrive, Sister Mary of St. Euphrasia, when you will have great labors, very great labors." Even then she had no way of knowing how these predictions fitted her future role.

Following her profession Sister Mary of St. Euphrasia continued with her former work as Second Mistress of the Class. Hereafter she was to be under careful scrutiny, for her present accomplishments were already causing Mother St. Joseph and the Council to think that it would not be long before she would be ready to assume the responsibilities of the important post of First Mistress. Naturally then she underwent a strenuous apprenticeship. She knew that she was often observed by the Mother Prioress and the First Mistress, but she was unaware that their visits were prompted by any motives other than improvement of her work. Consequently she lost herself in the activities that made up the pattern of her day. Among her superiors she was spoken of as "a resourceful person"; "a real genius in handling the children"; and "one who is constantly vigilant with herself and others."

One experience of that period revealed her skill at transforming a potentially ugly situation into a happy one. It was a hot, sultry Sunday afternoon in late summer. No one had slept well the night before and the usual naps had been omitted on account of the stifling heat that hung over the dormitories. Outside the girls were sitting idly in small groups on the lawn, bored and resentful. Suddenly everyone gravitated toward one big tree. A side glance, a lifting of eyebrows, a shrug of shoulders—some small signal in pantomime—had brought the girls together into one compact group. Lowering skies seemed to intensify the fact that something much more than a natural storm was about to erupt. At that moment Sister Mary of St. Euphrasia appeared. Even before she spoke she knew that she must act quickly to divert the girls from whatever mischief they were contemplating. Her own account of this incident is dramatic in its simplicity.

"Remembering what I had heard an experienced Superior of a Community say about the danger of allowing ennui to take possession of the minds of her pupils, I took great care to prevent our poor children from becoming low-spirited. . . .

"I remember one Sunday many of them were in a dreadful humour. They paid no attention to the Mistress; on the contrary, they seemed to ridicule her. They were sitting together under a tree and appeared to be plotting mischief. I went up to them and tried to persuade them to walk, but they did not follow me as usual. I felt puzzled as how to act, and I prayed that God would inspire me.

"At last I saw a little grasshopper at my feet. I took it up and showed it to some of them saying: 'Is it not pretty?' One after another came to see what was going on. They laughed derisively, exclaiming: 'Oh! What a beauty! It is *really* well worth looking at, to be sure!'

"Pretending not to hear, I asked what name they would like to give the little creature, adding, 'We will keep it and build a little house for it right here beside us.' I continued to joke, and soon they began to be amused. Their bad humour changed, and in a few minutes it had vanished. They went gayly off to find a cage which they fashioned into a kind of castle. Thus the poor little grasshopper helped to amuse us for some time during recreation." [12]

Soon the skies opened and the rains fell, cooling the atmosphere sufficiently to permit the overtired girls to take siestas before supper.

"At the beginning of my religious life," she wrote many years later, "I was given the care of a class that was very difficult." She offered this as a simple statement of fact and let it tell its own story. When something went wrong, she admitted it calmly and did her best to prevent its recurrence. It was impossible for her to remain discouraged long— a trait that strengthened with the years—the ability to survive a disaster and forge steadily onward.

In the beginning she made the natural mistake of being a little too strict with the girls, but there was never a time when she used any kind of corporal punishment. Her instructions on this point have always been observed to the letter in every House of the Good Shepherd throughout the world. Her words bridge the years with a rare stability. "Never strike our poor children; never! however much they may provoke you. If you want to bring them back to God, you must, generally speaking, speak little and punish rarely. . . . You must make it a rule never to raise your voice when you are displeased.

"Sometimes their [the girls'] evil [13] dispositions lead them to court punishment—that is the time to look as if you had not noticed. . . . You must be careful also not to punish the entire class for the fault of a few; it would be most unfair. Poor children, who have done their best to work all day to satisfy their Mistress, should not be treated in the same way as those who have done wrong."

This injunction is never violated in the Order of the Good Shepherd. Anyone who knows the spiritual daughters of Mother Mary of St. Euphrasia knows that they never punish their charges corporally. They correct with kindness, example, and prayer. Not beaten bodies but happy holy souls are their goal.

But there were occasions when Sister Mary of St. Euphrasia found herself acutely tormented by some unresolved situation in the class. At times the girls would be restless and unco-operative, staring woodenly when directives were spoken or listening in a blandly deceptive manner only to miscarry with determined intent every instruction presented to them. One such day remained long in Sister's memory. The air was soft and the skies sunny, but the atmosphere was tense and the girls sulked forbiddingly. The curative of work had lost its effectiveness. Books remained unopen and an almost insolent nonchalance greeted Sister as she took her place at her desk. Her request for order went unheeded. The girls muttered among themselves or giggled in open disregard of her presence. She looked serene enough, but she was greatly agitated. What had she done wrong? What should she do to curb this defiance?

She proceeded with trepidation until the time came for her to be relieved temporarily by another Sister. Then without delay she hurried to the chapel prostrating herself before the Blessed Sacrament and begging Jesus to help her. She remained an hour, imploring earnestly all the while, "Show me what to do, dear Lord. Show me what to do."

Gradually a calmness entered her heart and she went back to the same group of girls confident that the earlier unpleasantness would now have spent itself. As she came in sight, the girls burst into tears and sobbed aloud, "We are sorry. We don't know why we acted the way we did. Please forgive us."

Soon after this episode Sister Mary of St. Euphrasia was named to

succeed Sister Mary of St. Victoire as the First Mistress, the latter
having been transferred to the position of Infirmarian. Both the young
and old Sisters realized that this was a most extraordinary appointment, for no one could recall when a young religious of twenty-two
years had been assigned to a post of such trust and authority. Sister
Mary of St. Euphrasia would have preferred to have continued as the
Second Mistress, but she accepted willingly the task that was now
hers. She would do her very best.

The office of the First Mistress (sometimes called the Directress)
is one of prime importance, requiring that its holder possess a variety
of qualifications. She must be a combination of seer and friend; leader
and associate; disciplinarian and counselor; administrator and supervisor. She must subordinate every personal taste and preference to the
reclamation of the group. Hereafter she is rarely separated from the
children even though she has a number of competent and devoted
assistants. Likewise she is the informed intermediary between the
girls and the Courts or Agencies that have assigned them to the Institute. Her responsibility calls for infinite tact, patience, and a con-
suming love of the girls. She must win and hold the affection and
loyalty of her charges, showing no favoritism to anyone. Perhaps more
than any other post in the entire Congregation, this one is the most
discouraging and the most rewarding. Within the class the office of
the First Mistress, or Directress, is analogous to that of the Superior
of the Community.

The next few months tested Sister's mettle. To her amazement she
saw how fickle human nature could be. At first the girls were overjoyed at her appointment; then suddenly even the most loyal among
them were swayed by the pressures of some of the more aggressive
older ones, who had made up their minds they would not accept such
a young First Mistress. They disregarded the fact that Sister Mary of
St. Euphrasia was their good friend, declaring that their objections
were based on principles and not on personalities. In this connection
Sister recalled the difficulties that Mlle. de Lignac once had had with
the upper classes at the Christian Association.

A deputation marched boldly to Sister's room to insist that they be
granted certain additional privileges. They should have known they
would find her firm and unyielding when a principle was in question.
In any case they soon discovered that young though she was, she was
far stronger than they. Her courteous refusal of their unmerited demands won their respect to such a degree that the account of their

unsuccessful efforts to intimidate her quickly became a school legend. Sister herself preserved this incident in writing.

"When I was obliged to thwart their [the girls'] wishes, they used every possible means to induce me to yield to them. One day I found five or six at the door of my room. I inquired what they wished, but no one dared answer. Knowing what they had in view, I said to them: 'What folly it is to suppose that a daughter of Our Lady of Charity would allow herself to be influenced by threats! Remember, she would die, were it necessary, in the discharge of her duty.'"

For eight years Sister Mary of St. Euphrasia served with success as the First Mistress. During that period her experiences fortified her earlier conviction that ignorance of religion and starvation for love were the chief causes of serious misbehavior. Lacking any knowledge of the restraints of God's Commandments and the comfort of His love, erring girls and young women saw little reason to obey man's laws. After the girls were well dressed and well fed, Sister made it her prime consideration to instruct them in the tenets of their neglected Faith. "Nothing else," she averred, "is as helpful or as lasting."

She felt keenly about this lack in their lives and devoted many of her future conferences to the ways by which it might be overcome. "The great means of labouring for the salvation of souls and the conversion of sinners is to instruct them in the truths of their faith. . . . Teach the catechism; explain the maxims of the Gospel to them, for these are the only roads to Christian sanctity. . . . I cannot recommend the study of the catechism too strongly. . . . Frequently read also Sacred History and Church History; such reading should form the foundation of many of your lessons. It may be said, that there is more danger for the salvation of an ignorant person, than for one who knows her religion. A person who is instructed may finally listen to the voice of conscience and yield to remorse. But what hope is there of converting a poor ignorant creature who has never heard of God, who does not know how to distinguish between vice and virtue? You know, my dear daughters, that there are seven Spiritual Works of Mercy, of which one of the most important is to instruct the ignorant. Therefore, instruct the young persons and children confided to your care thoroughly and solidly." [14]

But in this, as in other things, she knew when and how to act. She often said that "it requires a great deal of tact, a great deal of judgment, too, to speak of spiritual things opportunely. For instance," she asserted, "it would not be timely to speak to the girls of penance on a day when they had been given a dinner they did not like. On the contrary it would be better to say to them: 'Poor children, I am so sorry you had that dinner today. I was really vexed about it.' . . . On some other occasion tell them what a great evil sin is." [15]

Not all of these observations fell from her lips in her early years, but she practiced them consistently long before they were recorded for later generations.

One story that survives recalls an incident that began on a certain August 19, the Feast of St. John Eudes, some time during Sister's term as First Mistress of the Class at Tours. On this particular day she had gathered a basketful of the bright nasturtiums that bloomed in abundance on the Convent grounds, and draped them around the picture of St. John Eudes that hung on the wall of her classroom, transforming the dark and practical frame into one of living beauty. Upon entering the room the girls commented immediately on the gay decoration. On the following morning they noted with joy that flowers still garlanded the Father Founder's picture taking for granted that Sister Mary of St. Euphrasia had replaced yesterday's wreath with another freshly cut one. Their enthusiastic comment brought the surprising information that Sister had not touched the nasturtiums since she first put them there. She said she had been prevented from removing them at the end of the preceding day and had come early this morning with that in mind, but to her delight she had found the flowers as the girls now saw them and had assumed that someone else had been good enough to hang fresh flowers around the portrait. Once more the larger events of the day crowded out this minor one. On the next morning, though, to everyone's surprise the flowers were still fresh and erect, nodding a special welcome to each girl as she came into the room. Interest ran high. How could this be? Yesterday when Sister St. Euphrasia had surmised about the situation, she should have remembered that in a convent no one would ever take over another's work without invitation or directive, for each individual is expected to carry a task through to completion. Day after day passed and the flowers remained as fresh as ever. Each morning the excitement of the girls mounted and the young Mistress found herself marveling. Before long the entire Community had heard about the flower frame, and a number of the Sisters came to see the phenomenon for themselves. Careful inquiry ruled out every kind of natural explanation. For an entire month the nasturtiums lived; then one morning they were discovered limp and lifeless. The Sisters conferring among themselves spoke of "Sister St. Euphrasia's nasturtiums," not attempting to define their hidden message, but accepting the fact that the extended life span of those fragile flowers might in some way indicate the future vigor and longevity of the young Sister who had first arranged them.

It was a source of regret to Sister Mary of St. Euphrasia because the number of penitents did not increase. She noted with satisfaction the encouraging transformation that took place steadily in the lives of the girls who came to the Refuge and longed to make it available to all those outside who lacked an awareness of God's love for them and hence fell ever deeper into sin and sorrow. To be sure, the class at its current number of twenty to thirty girls kept her occupied and challenged, but she was not content to see the sun of faith light up only a small corner of the field when it could so easily shed its rays of warmth and healing over a larger area. She prayed that in some way her flock might soon increase. One day at recreation she startled her companions by exclaiming, "If we only had sixty penitents here! How wonderful that would be!"

The old Sisters threw up their hands in utter dismay at her naïve optimism. All looked askance, unable at first to give voice to their evident disapproval.

"You are not realistic, Sister Euphrasia," one admonished at last. "You would be inviting all kinds of trouble if you attempted to work with such a large group at one time. The newcomers would quickly band together to tear down what you had already rebuilt."

"Your imagination has run away with you!" another Sister added bluntly.

"Your hands are full now. What could you hope to do with twice as many girls?" a third inquired.

"You are young and enthusiastic, my dear," one of the oldest Sisters smiled in gentle understanding. "At your age it is quite natural that you should dream of the impossible." Then her face became grave. "Sister St. Euphrasia, I am sure you would not talk this way, if you had been with us during the Reign of Terror. It was dreadful to have to watch the dispersion of our classes. Those poor, unprotected girls! I hope you will never have to meet such a heartbreaking experience."

The young First Mistress was not a person to be daunted easily. She waited briefly and then spoke with confidence. "I would try to do

my best. Meanwhile I'll go on praying that some day I will see sixty
or more girls in the class."

Recognizing that with few exceptions the girls would have to earn
their livelihood by honest labor when they left the Refuge, she felt
they should be taught the specifics of work and the reasons for their
acquiring manual and vocational skills. She referred often to St. Francis de Sales' statement that the bees make honey from the flowers
near by, pointing out that the opportunities at hand were the means
by which the girls could sweeten their labors in the years ahead. She
recognized the merits of interesting work, and was consistently opposed to any kind of dead-end "busy work," insisting that whatever
the girls did should be related to their interests and abilities. Endless
mending, she observed, could quickly become a distasteful exercise,
but mending done as one small part of the art of needlework with
which one might later earn for herself a good livelihood assumed an
entirely different meaning.

Time brought a stream of changes, one of which was Mother Mary
of St. Joseph La Roux's retirement as Superior on May 27, 1819. She
was followed by Mother Mary of St. Hippolyta (Hippolytus) Bot-
milliau, a distinguished religious of considerable experience, who had
recently arrived from Vannes. Earlier she had gone out from Paris to
found the Convent of the Refuge in Versailles. She was a person of
strong character and a born leader, possessing the ability to inspire
confidence in everyone. Convinced that the Refuge could never expand adequately within its present cramped quarters she set about to
acquire the original Tours Convent which was situated in the parish
of Notre Dame de la Riche in the northwestern part of the city. With
the exception of one wing of the main edifice, which fortunately included most of the chapel, the surrounding buildings and grounds had
been laid waste, falling into the hands of several owners or proprietors.
In 1805, upon the emergence from hiding of the Carmelite Community, these Sisters had occupied the one habitable section of the un-
seized Refuge and there they remained. When they learned of
Mother Hippolyta's desire to secure and restore the original property,
they were glad to locate elsewhere.

Mother Hippolyta spent three years in effecting her goal, years of
intricate negotiations accompanied by interminable involvements and
exasperating delays. Even with tact and patience and the concerted
prayers of the Community there were many times when the outcome
appeared uncertain. However, none of them would admit the pos-

sibility of defeat and finally in August, 1822,[16] the last business detail was satisfactorily disposed of. Another fourteen months were required to finish the work of restoration. On the Feast of the Guardian Angels (October 2) the Archbishop of Tours, Monseigneur de Chilleau, came to bless their home and establish their cloister, using this occasion to pay tribute to the courage they had shown during their long exile, begun more than thirty years earlier. Understandingly enough his remarks caused the Sisters to weep with happiness at the fulfillment of their long-deferred dream.

Strangely though, their progress now stopped abruptly. For the next two years it was as though they had reached a plateau of achievement, and try as they might, they could not rise beyond it. They did their best to meet this situation philosophically, recalling that a halt in advancement is likely to be temporary unless through discouragement one permits oneself to lose the ground already gained. But they all agreed that it was indeed hard when no postulants came and only a few penitents were added to the Class. In addition the Sisters lost their beloved ecclesiastical Superior, the aged M. Danicourt, who was subsequently succeeded by M. Monnereau of the Cathedral staff. Somehow these combined trials served the purpose of sharpening their perspective and giving them a longer view of their work. Then suddenly the shadows lifted and a new breeze of hope floated throughout the entire Community.

In the spring of 1825 Mother Mary of St. Hippolyta found herself nearing the end of her second term as Superior or Prioress. Because the Rules of her Order forbade the same individual's remaining in office longer than six years, it would soon be necessary for the Community to choose her successor. Who would this person be? No one was able to answer that question satisfactorily. Speculation usually brought the name of the young Mistress of the Class into the realm of the discussion only to see it quickly dismissed on account of her youth. Everyone knew that the Constitutions required that a Superior be forty years of age and eight years professed, and that the Council of Trent had set thirty years of age and five years of profession as the minimum requisites for this important post.

Prior to the approaching election Mother St. Hippolyta shared her concern as to her successor with her good friend, the widowed Mme. d'Andigne, a wealthy and generous noblewoman then in her early sixties. Mme. d'Andigne divided her time equally between her estates in Angers and Paris, stopping frequently in Tours, which lay directly in her path of travel. Her regular visits to the Refuge enabled her to identify herself closely with many of the problems of the Mother Superior and her associates. That particular day Mother St. Hippolyta remained lost in her own thoughts, as the Countess talked to her. Knowing that only a serious matter could have brought about this distraction, Mme. d'Andigne inquired, "Pray tell me, my friend, are you ill or worried? You appear quite unlike yourself."

At this query Mother St. Hippolyta looked up. Immediately she collected her wits and expressed her anxiety over the coming election. "The new Superior will have many heavy problems related to the further growth of our Community. Now that we have started again to expand, we must not retrogress. Who among our Sisters is the best qualified to direct us?"

"Why not Sister Mary of St. Euphrasia? I have long been impressed by her alert and efficient manner. She possesses the desired qualities of social and spiritual leadership. She is a devout religious and an able organizer and administrator—what more could you ask for?"

Mother St. Hippolyta gazed at the Countess in undisguised astonishment. She knew, of course, that Sister St. Euphrasia was the logical candidate possessing all the necessary qualifications but one.

"She is not yet twenty-nine years old, a far distance from our minimum requirement of forty."

"Don't you think the age barrier might be set aside under the circumstances?"

"To date it has always been observed."

"But has the question ever come up before?"

When the conversation ended Mother St. Hippolyta had agreed to discuss the matter with Canon Monnereau, the Vicar General of the Archdiocese as well as the present Ecclesiastical Superior of the House. He gave his close attention as she outlined her hopes for the future of the Community and nodded his head in vigorous agreement when she suggested rather hesitantly the name of Sister Mary of St. Euphrasia.

"I do not believe that her age is an unsurmountable obstacle," he assured her. "I shall be happy to apply to Rome for a dispensation, reinforcing my request by a statement of my convictions that this particular Sister, more than any other member of the Community, is the one most capable of filling this important office."

The dispensation was granted expeditiously and the date for the election set. On May 26, 1825, with Canon Monnereau presiding, the Tours Community of Our Lady of Charity of the Refuge chose Sister Mary of St. Euphrasia by unanimous vote to be their new Mother Superior. She was only twenty-eight years and ten months of age when the staff of leadership was first placed in her hands; from that day until her death four decades later she was never to be without it in one form or another. It was to serve alternately, sometimes simultaneously, as her ladder and her cross. In the beginning she found it difficult to realize that the mantle of authority had fallen upon her. Then in humility and obedience she accepted this honor as a deep obligation, never forgetting that "to govern and lead a soul in the spiritual ways of grace is a more excellent thing than to rule a world with regard to temporal things." [17]

V

1825-1828

ST. MARY MAGDALEN

You claimed the false
Until you found the true:
Your beauty wounded
Until beauty wounded you:
And plunged your soul
Into so clear a spring
Your tears fell as chaste pearls
At Mercy's Feet.

A. PAGE, C.S.C.[1]

ONE day some of the older girls came to Mother St. Euphrasia with a pressing request for a private interview to discuss "something very special." She named a time, and as they came into her office their serious faces indicated that whatever was on their minds was important to them. Even their voices were subdued and they had that look of ardent, even holy, intent which marks the young when they throw the weight of their longing behind some high endeavor. Mother knew all of them well for until her election as Mother Superior of the Tours Refuge less than six months previous, she had been with them steadily as the Mistress of their Class.

"Now what may I do for you?" she asked, as eager to hear as they to speak.

The girl appointed as spokesman for the little group stepped out, but if she had a rehearsed speech she forgot it and instead stated their request in a few quick words spoken with a kind of passion. "Reverend Mother, we want to be Sisters. Not Sisters of the Good Shepherd, but Sisters just the same. There must be some way we can spend our lives in service as a return"—she hesitated—"a return for the graces God has given us."

For a moment Mother St. Euphrasia did not speak. Were these girls mind readers? Finally she said, "Give me a little time to think over this request." She paused again. "Actually God has already heard your prayer for He has already given me a concern for the same matter. Soon I can give you an answer. And in the meantime, let us all pray for wisdom, shall we?"

The rest of the day she turned their request and her own plan over and over in her mind, recalling that in the founding of the Congregation of the Refuge it had been deemed wise to restrict admission for membership to individuals of unimpeachable conduct and reputation. Obviously, such a restriction automatically excluded any former member of the class from affiliation. These limitations were believed necessary because society expected the Sisters who looked after young charges to come from families not given to irregularities, and the children themselves looked to the Sisters for example as well as for teaching. But much more important was Mother St. Euphrasia's conviction that there was no substitute for a life of untarnished purity, for purity carried its own radiance and was bound to influence the children whom it touched. She sighed as she considered the obstacles for admission to her beloved Order. No one knew better than she that there were many grievous sins not easily discerned or regulated. She knew young women in the class of great strength and purity. Indeed, it sometimes seemed that human beings who had sinned or been sinned against became the stanchest servants of their Lord, once they found themselves and received His pardon. Some of the most sensitive girls she had ever known were among those who had come under her care in the class. She felt humble before them; she loved them; they deserved the best which in her eyes meant a chance for a Sister's selfless service. It was because she knew these things and was moved by pride in these charges of hers that she had already been considering some kind of a new order which would offer a special place for them.

That evening she assembled the Council to conference. She stood before them with expectancy on her face, an inner eagerness to which they responded in mood.

"Last May you chose me as your Mother Superior," she said to them. "But when it comes to making a significant innovation or embarking on a new venture, we all come together seeking guidance and mutual agreement. For some time I have been considering a new undertaking, a desire near to my heart. And today I was given evidence that already this desire is shared by others. Tonight I wish to propose to you that we devise a way for those girls in the class who have a sense of vocation to enter the religious life. There are among our older girls real Magdalens, repentant souls already on their way toward the same goal we ourselves are striving to reach."

Her words fell into a pool of silence. This was an entirely new idea, an innovation indeed. Finally one of the older Sisters said, "But, Mother, the Rules and Constitutions of the Refuge as formulated by St. John Eudes make no provision for the reception of penitents into our Congregation."

"I am aware of that," Mother St. Euphrasia said, thoughtfully. Then she smiled. "Still, you must admit that our Founder did not rule out such an arrangement as I am presenting."

Once more the room grew still. Mother St. Euphrasia waited again until another Sister spoke. "What would the clergy say to this idea?"

"Father Alleron, my confessor, approves wholeheartedly. Canon Monnereau, speaking for the Archbishop, has encouraged the enterprise." Then she continued eagerly, "Not long ago I wrote to the Paris Refuge seeking information about a group of penitents who live there in retirement. You see this concern has been with me for some time—years in fact—and today a handful of our girls approached me with much the same request." She told them about the interview.

Following her description of the girls' call, the Sisters relaxed and questioned more freely.

"What is the name of the Paris group?"

"Les Madelonettes," Mother St. Euphrasia told them.

"Is theirs a successful undertaking?"

"Apparently not." Then Mother St. Euphrasia went on candidly, gravely. "The Sister in charge sent me a discouraging letter. She went to much trouble to explain her problems, assuming that ours would be identical."

"Don't you think they would be?" asked a skeptical Sister.

"Quite the contrary." Hope and determination again lit Mother St. Euphrasia's face, a characteristic expression. Then she outlined her plan to form a separate Community for eligible aspirants attracted to the religious life, following their conversion from a life touched by sin. Certain rights must be a vital part of such an Institute of Penance, chief among them its complete and valid religious status. She felt that its members should be permitted to bind themselves to God's work by holy vows according to established Constitutions, thus ensuring the stability of a recognized sisterhood. In the story of St. Mary Magdalen herself she had found the inspiration for such a Community. It must be a Community open to all persons regardless of their past, "provided they give proof of a spirit of penance and a true religious vocation and are not bound by lawful impediments and are capable of the burden of the religious life." [2]

As the evening wore on the other Sisters caught her spirit along with her vision. They made suggestions. The meeting adjourned in considerable excitement. During the ensuing weeks Mother St. Euphrasia was in touch with the cloistered Carmelites of Tours. She believed that the Carmelite Rule, written by St. Teresa of Avila, would form a feasible basis for the Rule she needed for this inner community. She sought permission from the Carmelite Council to alter their Rule for her purposes. Through her good friend, Sister Mary of the Incarnation, nee Angélique Dernée, and through their joint ecclesiastical superior, Father Monnereau, full co-operation was forthcoming. The Carmelites assured her they would also be happy to have the Sister Magdalens wear the brown habit of Carmel. Mother St. Euphrasia then made certain distinctive adaptations, including the substitution of a black mantle for the white mantle of Carmel. The Carmelites also loaned their books and study outlines and asked for the privilege of making the habits for the first four Magdalen novices, themselves supplying the brown serge. Nothing short of such generous co-operation would have satisfied the zeal of St. Teresa's spiritual daughters. They understood well the life the Sister Magdalens would follow, knowing firsthand the struggles toward attainment that await every true contemplative in her search for detachment from the world and attachment to the life of intercessory prayer and hidden service.

On November 9, 1825, the Rule and Ceremonial of the new order received episcopal approbation and a fortnight later the first clothing occurred. Four Sister Magdalens embarked with joy and courage on a life of expiation in behalf of all those needful ones who might yet be so far from God as not even to know their need of Him. The Magdalens would themselves become channels, empty of self, through which His grace might effect the conversion of souls.

Tears of happiness welled in Mother St. Euphrasia's eyes as each aspirant received her new name, prefaced by the Community's patron, St. Mary Magdalen. She was confident that these candidates would persevere and yet she was aware of the trials that lay ahead before their spiritual triumphs would be manifest. She rested her faith on the spirit of the Magdalen Rule which would surely help them to overcome their frailties. Six years later on August 28, 1831, this new establishment was confirmed by the Council of the Angers Community of the Good Shepherd. From that time on the history of the Community is one of steady growth in numbers, service, and silent power.

Among the Sister Magdalens is a community of spirit but a wide diversity of backgrounds. There are some whose earlier misdeeds were forced upon them by circumstances beyond their control, some whose errors were unintentional and unpremeditated, some whose misconduct was willful and deliberate. Some have always come from the top social brackets, leaving a family name of distinction for the name of a saintly patron. Some have always come from broken homes or from no home at all. Some have excellent formal education and some but scant schooling. Some bring artistic excellence; others only the desire to serve with their hands. In any Convent of the Sister Magdalens the story of one may be the story of a score, for after all life's tragedies and misdeeds are largely unique in their similarity, in the fact that all human hearts tend to stray but also turn at last toward God.

From experience Sister Mary Cuthbert knew that no one shortcoming is responsible for more disaster than the capital sin of pride. Her life attested this fact frankly, bringing her both desolation and reconciliation. She came from a cultured and wealthy family of jurists and legislators; her education included extensive study abroad which brought her advanced degrees in the fields of social studies and administration. When she first made known her desire to enter the convent, her family received the news in amused tolerance. "Imagine Mary Jo's ever being a religious. Why, she wouldn't take direction from anyone." Had she not always refused to listen to their advice? However, the family soon realized that Mary Jo was in dead earnest. Almost before they could adjust themselves to her decision she had entered the novitiate of a well-known teaching order, giving herself wholeheartedly to her new life. Then came the happy day when she took the vows, along with the name Sister Mary Cuthbert. Two years later she became a teacher and after three terms of teaching was made principal of Resurrection Academy. In her eyes, as indeed in the eyes of the community, the school was unprogressive. She soon took care of that defect. She revolutionized the curriculum and the regulations. She left nothing undone to make the school an elite and exclusive one, developing this concept so effectively that her religious superiors were obliged to reprimand her for her excessive pride amounting to the misdirection of the girls who came to the Academy in their formative years.

Sister Mary Cuthbert continued to disregard the admonitions of her superiors, evidently reasoning that because her education and knowledge exceeded theirs, she was freed from the necessity of obedience in regard to her determination to strengthen her school. She thought of it as her school. Finally pride and recalcitrance resulted in her demotion, later followed by dismissal from the Order itself.

Several months later a thoroughly chastened young woman sought entrance into the Reparatrix Community of the Sister Magdalens, which occasionally accepted former religious from other Communities. She told her story frankly and asked for the privilege of serving God as a cloistered religious in expiation for her sins of pride and self-will. Her motives stood the test of careful scrutiny but she was advised to wait a year and reminded that the life of renunciation, prayer, and penance she asked to embrace would offer no opportunities for her specialized training. Had she thought about these things? Her answer was affirmative. She had indeed thought about these things.

Twelve months later the former Sister Mary Cuthbert entered the novitiate of the Sister Magdalens. In due time she became Sister Mary Magdalen of the Resurrection, a name she begged to be given as a reminder of her former pride and as an impetus to an unselfish life. For forty years she lived a life of reparation and devoted service. Her patience with the older Sisters seemed endless; during recreation she listened to their stories as attentively as if she had never heard them before. She loved the Sisters whose formal education was limited because they seemed to hold up the chalice of their service for God's blessing the more modestly. She fostered the gaiety of the younger Sisters even when she grew old and ill and weary. Let no one think that her good mind and training were "wasted" in the cloister

for quality of perception and mental discipline will express themselves in a thousand ways and add dimension to life within the
cloister as much as to life within the college. The other Sisters said
of her that she was not known to complain, to presume, nor to speak
unkindly. Few in or out of a convent could lay so sweet a garland of
unostentatious virtues on the altar, and their fragrance permeated the
community life. Who shall say how far such fragrance carries? At
last an inoperable brain tumor blocked consciousness for considerable
periods of time. One day during a period of lucidity she turned to the
Mistress with that look of appraisal which reflects a keen mind,
"Without this gradual impairment of my intellect I would never have
known how I would have reacted to such an affliction." Soon she
added, "Christ emptied Himself of all honor in order to become the
means of my salvation. I hope I have renounced my self-will in complete surrender."

Then there was Sally Taylor. As a child Sally was known as a dare-
devil. She took delight in defying the laws of chance, probability, and
gravity. She could scarcely be said to have defied the laws of God because to Sally those laws were nonexistent, there being no God. She
was casually matter-of-fact in her dismissal of a deity. "That kind of
stuff makes no appeal to me. Let's forget it, pal, and the sooner, the
better." On one occasion when she was in juvenile court on a charge
of speeding, she pitied the earnest julge in his attempt to get her to
recognize a power beyond herself, a higher power he called God.
People always seemed to get around to God when they tried to reason
with Sally but no one made a dent in her self-sufficient philosophy.
"Maybe I am a pagan or a heathen, but I'm my own boss, and no one
—and I mean no one—can change that. Get me?"

Most of Sally's companions were not interested in spiritual things
and consequently had no qualms about leading Sally astray. "Astray
from what?" she would ask in a pixielike manner. As a result she
tasted all of the thrills and dangers that come so easily to one without
inhibitions. At nineteen Sally was an undisciplined young woman
whose actions exemplified her personal credo: "Live dangerously; it's
much more fun."

And it was fun of a sort until one February night when the car in
which Sally and her current boy friend were racing skidded on the
slippery pavement, somersaulted, and rammed into a tree. Dick
never knew what happened for he died instantly. Sally didn't know
either for she was unconscious when the rescue crew arrived. Several

hours later, when she came to consciousness, she realized she was swathed in bandages like a mummy. But before she could inquire, she lapsed again into forgetfulness. For some days her hold on life was precarious; the cuts on her face and body were numerous; her skull was fractured; both legs broken.

The Sisters of Charity ran the hospital in which Sally lay. Its accessibility had saved her life for she could never have survived without the medical care given her within minutes. During her long months of suffering Sally found herself obliged to accept the ministrations of others. The idea of insisting upon being her own boss seemed silly under the circumstances. She could not eat or sleep without help; she could not take a bath or comb her hair. She could not even shift herself in bed, locked in traction as she was with heavy weights and casings all about her.

At first she merely lay still and moaned fretfully, later becoming impatient and restless. "A dirty trick," she'd say over and over. "This shouldn't happen to a dog." After a time she realized that her complaints made no impression on the Sister nurses who tended her gently. She was always their "dear child," no matter how ugly she acted toward them. One day she rang her bell insistently. When the Sister appeared, Sally demanded, "Take that awful looking thing down. I don't want it in here." She pointed to the crucifix high on the wall facing her.

"Oh, my dear, I couldn't do that. Let it remind you that you're never alone."

"But I hate it. I've looked at that ugly figure long enough. Take it away."

"He was not ugly until we drove the nails into His body."

"Are you crazy, Sister? I never drove a nail in my life."

One night when Sally could not sleep, Sister Margaret sat beside her bed and in a low voice read the sixth chapter of the Gospel of St. Matthew. She was not at all sure that Sally was listening. Slowly she closed the book. The unbroken silence was baffling. It could mean that Sally was marshaling her forces in order to renew her attack and yet it might possibly mean that Sally had been touched by some word of eternal promise. Sister formed a silent petition.

Sally's next words told her that her petition had been granted. "Those are really beautiful words, Sister Margaret. I mean those last ones. Will you please read them again to me?"

Sister spoke them aloud without opening the treasury that held them. "But seek ye first the kingdom of God and His righteousness; and all these things shall be added unto you."

"The kingdom of God sounds like a beautiful place."

Sally's heart, the nun realized, was no different from the heart of every wanderer far from home; it, too, longed for surety that it would eventually reach home.

Sally's transformation was not a rapid metamorphosis. Much of the time she suffered great pain. Often she was bitter and resentful. But her interest grew and her spirit gentled. When the hospital chaplain began to visit her informally she was full of questions. A day came when she asked for baptism, a day when she sat in a wheelchair, a day when she could be pushed into the chapel for services. Then finally the day when she was dismissed from the hospital. But on that day she asked if she might come back for further instruction. She wanted to hold onto the hands which were holding the Hand of God. Then finally there was the day when she herself reached for the Hand of God and sought admission into the Community of the Sister Magdalens. And after that a long succession of days—half a century of them—distinguished by her relish for life proclaiming itself in zestful service, varied, determined, triumphant. She was a very happy person.

An outsider might think the lives of these cloistered Sisters is monotonous, but how could they be when there is such diversity of personality and talent among them? Take Mademoiselle the actress who became Sister Magdalen of Mercy. In 1904 the French theatrical world was startled when it learned that one of its favorites was withdrawing from the stage to enter a cloistered community. Was this a whim or a bid for even wider acclaim? Mademoiselle was at the peak of her career. Those who knew her best insisted that Mademoiselle's personal life was regular enough. Widowed and the mother of two children in their teens, she had left no stone unturned to provide for their well-being. On the stage, however, she played the most daring and unconventional of roles. Art was art for her, and an actress with a voice and a figure like hers could not be expected to hide them in a nunnery. But that was exactly what she was going to do.

Her fellow artists had seen a change coming on. Finally her manager had protested to her. "Whatever's happened to you? Are you turning pious on us?"

"I hadn't thought of it exactly that way, but I guess I am. What's more, I don't care who knows it. Just as soon as I have finished my current contracts, I plan to spend the rest of my life in reparation for the harm I may have done. Monsieur, I assure you that this is no temperamental gesture. I was never more serious in my life."

On Holy Saturday the convent bells had just rung out the Paschal Alleluia when this beautiful young woman sought admittance to the Angers Community of the Sister Magdalens. Naturally the Mistress of Magdalens, a Good Shepherd Sister charged with their spiritual direction, questioned the validity of Mademoiselle's motives. However, she found her doubts dispelled as she listened to Mademoiselle's story.

"It happened in Paris near the end of a particularly successful season. That night the applause was at its height when suddenly an inner voice intruded, 'How would you feel now, if you knew that your own daughter was out there in the audience watching you?' Overcome with guilt I headed toward my dressing room when a most extraordinary thing happened. Before me hung the Crucified Christ, His poor beaten body one open mass of wounds. Then I heard Him say, 'See how you are treating me.' I fell to my knees and wept for forgiveness. The vision disappeared, but the words remained. How could I hope to atone for the harm I'd done to other women's daughters, glorifying the false and the untrue? The rest was inevitable, dear Mother. Everything was completely changed. Earlier commitments prevented my leaving the stage immediately, but now that I have fulfilled my contracts, I beg leave to join the Magdalen Community. Both of my children are nearly grown and well provided for."

Her request was granted and from the day of her admission until her death on May 6, 1933, Sister Magdalen of Mercy loved much and suffered much. She knew that "to suffer was to love and to love was to repair." Her memory still lives in her influence in the religious vocations of her grandchildren who are fulfilling her hope for them as expressed in one of her most fervent ejaculations: "Would that I were that last drop of water causing the cup of Mercy to overflow."

The appeal of the Sister Magdalens is wider and more varied than is generally recognized. For example, many Sister Magdalens are converts to Catholicism, their numbers sometimes exceeding those who were born into the faith. Then, too, there are to be found among them individuals who were eligible to enter a different type of religious Community, but chose instead this cloistered penitential one wherein to expiate the sins of others. Such persons are far too humble to appraise their actions by any man-made rule. In every sense they are their brother's keeper.

Donna Walsh was one whose record was impeccable. An honor graduate of Cathedral High School, she had been awarded a scholarship to a Dominican college in a near-by state. With the exception of her spiritual adviser and one of her teachers no one knew that she planned to renounce an academic future for a penitential one.

Until Donna's father had died at the beginning of her sophomore year, her mother had always been a good woman. "The very best, Mother St. Joseph," Donna said, "kindly and charitable and above all devout in her spiritual life." It was common knowledge, however, that following Mr. Walsh's death his wife had changed, flaunting openly the laws of society. "I can't remember exactly when mama first started breaking the sixth Commandment. Sometimes she drinks too, but she's seldom intoxicated. Once in a long while when we are alone, she smiles blandly and says in a defeated tone of voice, "God has already punished me by taking your father away. Nothing He does to me here or hereafter will ever be as hard as that. That's why I'm going to take my fun where I can find it."

Donna had sought this interview with her pastor's blessing. Still the Mother Superior demurred. "Do you feel reasonably sure that you have a vocation to the religious life?"

"Yes, Mother, I do."

"But why are you drawn to the Community of the Sister Magdalens?"

"I'd like to have the opportunity to give my service in expiation for my mother. I tell you, she is a good woman in spite of her conduct. I'm ready to accept whatever hardships Christ may send me. But perhaps mama's return to the Faith will be among His gifts."

"And if it isn't, my child?"

Donna's expression remained unchanged. "Why, then I'd know that it was not His will. I'd never let myself forget that there is always such a possibility."

Mother St. Joseph continued. "Are you familiar with our usual custom of asking one who wishes to become a Sister Magdalen to spend a specified period of time in the class?"

"You mean in the delinquent department?"

"Call it that, if you wish. We prefer to speak of it as the class; its members are our girls."

"I'd heard that this was the procedure, but I'd forgotten about it.

Just why is membership there a prelude to entrance into the Sister Magdalens' Community?"

"Primarily because the Sister Magdalens take a fourth vow—to pray for the salvation of souls, particularly for all the works of the Good Shepherd.[4] Because of that we think it wise for all candidates to this auxiliary institute of Penance to know our work firsthand. Above everything else we strive to teach our girls to establish the right relationship between themselves and their Creator. Living and working with the girls is enlightening and rewarding but it calls for perseverance and genuine humility."

For several minutes Donna remained quiet. Then she asked, "Mother, how soon may I become a member of the class?"

Mother St. Joseph had nothing more to say, for she knew that Donna Walsh was the material of which religious are made.

Economically the Sister Magdalens are a self-sustaining unit, earning their livelihood through various kinds of service performed with their hands. Some do fine needlework, particularly children's clothes, liturgical vestments, and altar linens. Some make baptismal dresses, confirmation and wedding dresses for a very special clientele. Others are enthusiastic apiarists, preparing a first-quality honey for domestic sale. Many make altar breads for churches, near and far. Whatever they do comes under the heading of "employments" on their daily schedule, employments accepted as the will of God. Approximately five hours of the day go into these practical services.

Many people have seen the exquisite and delicate products of the Sisters' needles, but few have seen them sewing. Even fewer have seen them make the altar breads. In the Altar Bread Room, the wafers are baked and cut into two sizes, the smaller ones to become the individual communicant's Bread of Life, and the larger ones to be raised aloft at the Consecration of the Mass or at Benediction, as well as during other periods of public exposition.

The Altar Bread Room is God's laboratory staffed by His dedicated handmaidens who perform their tasks amid immaculate surroundings in prayerful silence under the direction of a Sister of the Good Shepherd. Mechanical appliances, including refrigerators, ovens, storing cabinets, and electric cutters, recede into the background alongside the cheerful industry of those entrusted with this work. The altar breads are made from an unleavened paste for which the grain has been especially grown and milled. Usually the breads are baked in the morning and sorted, packaged, and wrapped for mailing in the

St. John Eudes (1601-1680)
Founder of the Order of Our Lady of
Charity with its two observances of the
Refuge and the Good Shepherd

Rose-Virginie Pelletier at eighteen, shortly before she entered the Convent of the Refuge, Tours, France

Sister Mary of St. Euphrasia Pelletier as a novice, September 8, 1815

St. Mary of St. Euphrasia Pelletier, Foundress of the Congregation of Our Lady of
Charity of the Good Shepherd of Angers
(1796-1868)

Mother Mary of St. Francis Xavier
Hickey, St. Paul, Minnesota

Mother Mary of St. Ursula Jung, present
Superior-General of the Good Shepherd

Philadelphia, Pennsylvania

Los Angeles, California

St. Paul, Minnesota

Peekskill, New York

Cincinnati, Ohio

Photograph by R. J. Westrich

St. Louis, Missouri

Baltimore, Maryland

THE MOTHER HOUSE AT ANGERS

THE GOOD SHEPHERD GIRLS IN THE UNITED STATES AND ELSEWHERE

AT WORSHIP

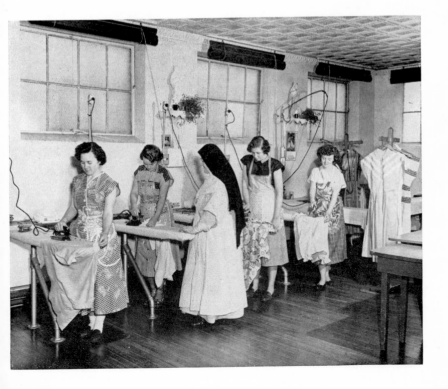

Canonization of St. Mary Euphrasia Pelletier by Pope Pius XII
in St. Peter's, Rome, on May 2, 1940

afternoon. The electric cutters assure uniformity of size and design, but manual checking and packing provide a personalized and accurate service that the workers prefer. The Sisters who pack the altar breads identify themselves with those persons for whom they are destined, saying a short prayer for their welfare. The words of the prayer are not always the same, but its meaning is unvarying. "May the one who receives this wafer sacramentally find himself strengthened through its power." This thought is further emphasized by a copy of a hymn which hangs on the wall. The hymns differ, but this one is representative.

SONG OF THE HOST MAKER

Jesus comes to feed His people,
Yet He bideth in retreat
While we fashion fitting garments
Spun of flour, water, heat.

Meekly Jesus waits our pleasure
While His raiment we prepare:
Spotless wafers, great and little,
Are the clothes He fain would wear.

Shepherd Jesus stayeth hidden
Till His sheep their wool supply,
Then He cometh forth to feed them,
Lest they, hungering, faint and die.

Sing, my heart, amid the labor,
For thy King His garments spread;
Only through our joint providing
Can the multitudes be fed.

Little hosts, O how I love you!
Mine to make, but Christ's to be:
Soon are you to change, O marvel,
Into His Divinity!

—ANONYMOUS [3]

In most Communities the Sisters rise at a quarter past five in the morning and retire at half-past eight at night. Their employments are not continuous, but are interspersed by spiritual exercises, averaging about four and a half hours, and by two and a half hours of recreation, including singing. Naturally age and health help to determine the sort of recreation engaged in. Young postulants and novices usually prefer active games such as volley ball and badminton. Hop-scotch and jumping rope redden the cheeks. During this transitional period from the worldly to the religious life roller skating, too, is a favorite diversion. Gardening appeals to many, the care of birds or bees to others, and strolls about the grounds to almost everyone. The high walls which surround the enclosure insure privacy. Indoors the Sisters play quiet games, prepare informal programs, act out charades or pantomimes, rehearse choral and orchestral numbers to be used at some Feast Day celebration, or assemble in little groups to knit, mend hosiery, chat, plan, enjoy the changing days and seasons.

The noon recreation lasts for an hour, the evening recreation for an hour and a half. On each occasion one of the Sisters designated for a week as "the Angel of the Recreation" signals three different times for momentary silence, reminding her companions that here as else-where they are in the presence of God and adding a reference at midday to "this morning's Holy Communion" and in the evening to "our Holy Communion tomorrow morning." During inclement weather, or when the Sisters prefer, the Mother who is presiding reads aloud from an approved book of general interest.

Thirteen years must elapse before a Sister Magdalen can be admitted to perpetual vows. During her first year as a postulant and her second and third as a novice she is always free to leave on her own volition. However, at the end of the third year when she receives the silver cross to be worn about her neck and pronounces the religious vows for the year ahead, she waives the opportunity to return to the secular life until the expiration of her vows a year hence. Thereafter she renews her vows annually for nine additional years, after which she pledges herself "wholeheartedly and without con-straint," confirming forever her vows of Poverty, Chastity, and Obedience together with her undiminishing prayers for the souls and the works of the Good Shepherd. Should anyone ever desire to leave the Community after she has taken perpetual vows, an "indult of secularization" from the Holy See would be required to dispense her honorably. Very rarely, however, does one ask to be released, the long period preceding her admission to perpetual vows having fully acquainted her with every aspect of the life to which she gives herself.

The reason that so high a percentage of the girls who come as postulants remain permanently is a very simple one; they are happy as Sisters. To be sure, there are times when a nun's heart, being human, must turn with longing toward her family; perhaps times—

at least at first—when she wonders why she ever left. There are times of difficulty when spiritual progress seems slow. There are times when the work is hard. There are days of illness. There are griefs, not less heavy because they are inflicted by someone the Sister has never seen but who she knows continues to shun God and His mercy. Yet the roll of any monastery of the Sister Magdalens is a roster of happy lives. The Sisters do not have to fill out a questionnaire to prove that their vocation was well chosen. Their faces are their spiritual biography. Oddly, with many the skin is unusually clear, almost transparent. Not the transparency of undernourishment or lack of sunlight but the transparency which comes to those anywhere whose inner minds know no lag, who have come to terms with their reluctances. The Sister Magdalens laugh easily, the way children laugh, and the greatly good. Their voices are soft, because they have caught the rhythm in life and have nothing to be strident about. Their hands are useful hands and there is dignity in their bearing.

A nun's vows are not negations. She does not so much give up riches as choose poverty. She chooses poverty as one long earthbound might choose wings. She lays aside impediments, the easier to be conscious of another element she may enter at will. She gives up the possibility of a married life, seldom because she does not care for children or wants to sidestep family obligations, but because she knows that the life of prayer demands a peculiar and persistent energy. She lays aside self-will and espouses obedience not because she is irked with the day-by-day demand for choices but because in the larger matter of ordering her life she feels that her spiritual director will chart a wiser course in the light of wider perspective. Like a corpuscle in the bloodstream, she puts the good of the organ and the welfare of the whole body ahead of her own predilections.

But perhaps it is the fourth vow,[4] the last one to be granted as a special privilege of the Sister Magdalens, which is the most demanding and the most rewarding. Through it each Sister binds herself to pray for the conversion of sinners everywhere, and especially for the conversion of persons living in the Houses of the Good Shepherd. Since this duty is the particular end of her Institute she enters fully into the spirit of reparation by praying for all the needs of the Congregation. She allows this purpose to inspire all her actions, offering her work and all her daily exercises in order to repair the indifference and forgetfulness shown God by so many of His careless children. Whether she uses the transforming prayer of adoration or the unceasing prayer of intercession, she knows that she is approaching the throne of God Almighty. With that knowledge she proceeds, "Thy will be done," ever guarding her deepest thought.

True prayer is energy-consuming beyond all other mental effort. It requires a disciplined mind but it also requires a physical discipline. The body cannot be ignored, for it is the instrument of prayer. It is actually the temple of God and unless it remains in balance it cannot stand the stress of the charge it may receive. This fact accounts in part for the insistence upon physical exercise and well-being. These Sister Magdalens are the dynamo behind the work of the Good Shepherd Sisters. They know that they do not need to beg God for His mercy in behalf of any needy child, for His love is always available —"Closer is He than breathing, and nearer than hands and feet"— but they know, too, that in some manner not well understood the one who prays actually makes it possible for His power to reach the recipient who needs Him. Does the groundwire understand the intricacies of a radio's mechanism? Or itself call, or even hear the melody? But would it therefore, because of itself it is so little, withhold its services? So also do these praying Sisters help to accomplish true miracles of salvation.

The groundwork for the growth and strength of the Sister Magdalens was laid well by the first four penitents. Fearful lest they should ever again offend God, they prayed that they might be spared such a defection even at the cost of their lives. Within a few years all of these young Sisters were called to Him in the exact order in which they were professed.

Meanwhile, in May, 1828, Mother St. Euphrasia had been unanimously re-elected Mother Superior of the Tours Convent. As she entered upon the second term of her superiorate, she wrestled increasingly with one problem: should she not set plans in motion to establish another House of the Refuge so that the expanding Novitiate could serve others beyond this immediate area? The increase of novices both heartened and dismayed her. She rejoiced to see the growth of religious vocations, yet she knew that their numbers would soon exceed the size and needs of this particular Convent.

Remembering that every Refuge with the exception of the original one at Caen founded on February 8, 1651, by St. John Eudes had been started from some other House, she reasoned that the time was near when the extension of their field of labor should be revived.

What ought she to do? To act precipitously would be unwise, but it would be equally unwise to blind herself to the imminent expansion of the work for which she was responsible. With that in mind she put everything in the hands of God, deferring any action until she had received some token of assurance from Him. In the interim she regularly visited the only living member of the original Sister Magdalens, who lay gravely ill of an incurable malady. Prior to the young Sister's death she opened her heart to Mother St. Euphrasia. "You have always been so good to me. In the class when I was a trial, you gave me your patience and love unstintingly. I owe you my conversion and vocation. Without the one I could not have found the other, and without you, I would have been denied both."

"My dear, dear child, you have surely merited God's love. Soon you will be seeing Him in His full radiance. That we both truly believe."

The young Sister smiled. "And when I see our Lord, I shall thank Him for your many kindnesses to me."

Touched by her childlike confidence, Mother St. Euphrasia said, "Will you then ask Him to let me know in some way, if He wants me to found other Houses?"

"Oh, Mother, how can you doubt that He does? However, I'll gladly deliver your message."

The Sister's obsequies had scarcely been completed when Mother St. Euphrasia received an urgent invitation from the Bishop of Angers to establish a Convent of the Refuge within his diocese. Some may see this timing as a coincidence, but Mother St. Euphrasia saw it as God's direct answer to her query. The Sister Magdalen had talked with Him and He had replied. Everything was as simple and as profound as that.

VI

Angers and Tours, 1829

*Reject not the petition of the afflicted,
and turn not away thy face from the needy.*

ECCLESIASTICUS 4:4

ONE morning in late May Father Breton jogged along contentedly in the diligence headed for Tours. Several of his fellow passengers recognized this stocky, middle-aged cleric as the genial and outspoken rector of the ancient Cathedral of St. Maurice in Angers. Although they knew nothing of his present mission their silent consensus ran like this: "Something worth while, or he wouldn't be doing it."

And they were right, for Father Breton was being sent by Monseigneur Charles Montault des Isles, the Bishop of Angers, to urge the Mother Superior of the Tours Refuge to establish a similar Convent in his episcopal city. Hopes for success were high because Monseigneur Montblanc, the Archbishop of Tours, had promised his full co-operation, assuring his suffragan diocese that he was heartily in accord with this idea, provided the Sisters could be persuaded to extend the field of their service to Angers.

Father Breton had asked that the Sisters not be told of his impending visit. Always an individualist, he liked to do things his own way. This time he preferred to make an unannounced call on the Refuge so that he might observe their work under normal and ordinary conditions.

There is no doubt that Mother St. Euphrasia was surprised by the

unexpected arrival of this ebullient stranger and more surprised when
he announced bluntly that he wanted to enter the enclosure, or
private residing place of the religious, as well as visit all the different
departments of the House.

"Only recently," he informed her, "I've learned that you have four
departments: the classes for the Penitents, the Monastery of the
Magdalens, an orphanage, and a boarding school."

Before Mother Euphrasia could catch her breath Father Breton
produced a letter from her Archbishop supporting his rather startling
request with the necessary seal of approval and permission. Then he
asked, "How does it happen that you also have orphans and boarders
here?"

Mother St. Euphrasia explained that she had established the
orphanage, called the Preservation Class, in order to afford protection for the appalling number of homeless and abandoned children.
"In most instances, these waifs would have no nursery but the
streets," she said. "I'll admit that it is a big job to feed, clothe, and
educate the eighty or more children we now have because of course
they bring in no income. But their expense is partially offset by the
fees from our boarding school. It was the Archbishop who asked us
to undertake the boarding school because there was no similar institution in this vicinity for Catholic children of the better class. Here we
are able to provide for their spiritual and educational training in their
own separate quarters." Then she added earnestly, "But, Father
Breton, our chief concern is for the wayward girls and the Sister
Magdalens. With us they will always come first."

Mother St. Euphrasia's direct manner and gracious courtesy appealed tremendously to her energetic and impetuous visitor. His
bluff and hearty way of doing things was novel to her; yet she
indicated no surprise, listening absorbed to what he had to say. True
she had never met a priest like him. As they traveled through the
corridors, workshops, and classrooms his booming voice often broke
the silence and serenity of the house. At first it was a discordant note
in a muted symphony; yet later it sang its solo well and in key.

When the tour of the Refuge had ended, Father Breton knew
without any doubt that Mother St. Euphrasia was just the person
needed at Angers, and he told her so. "And Countess de Neuville
would have agreed with me, that I know," he added with conviction.

"The Countess de Neuville?" Mother St. Euphrasia looked
bewildered.

So Father Breton told her about the late Countess, a wealthy and gracious gentlewoman, who had returned from exile to spend her widowhood in extensive works of mercy among God's less fortunate children. She had long been interested in aiding girls and young women who were the victims of false companions or tragic home circumstances. Convinced that a haven for such girls was greatly needed she had contemplated reopening a former local hospice, Le Bon Pasteur, of the Good Shepherd, which had remained closed after the holocaust of the Revolution as had so many other social institutions. However, upon investigation the Countess had concluded that this kind of project would thrive best in the hands of a qualified religious group.

"Sadly enough, she died before such a group could be located," Father Breton continued. "But first she authorized her only son, Count Augustine de Neuville, to give the Bishop of Angers 30,000 francs from her estate for this purpose so dear to her heart." Then he said feelingly, "If she were alive she would warmly approve of my visit here."

In a moment he went on. "Other factors have fostered this idea. The priests of the city augmented the Countess' gift by special collections in their parishes. But the spark that really ignited us all came from a penitent—a young girl—who died not long ago at the Caen Refuge. She was a former member of an Angers parish, by the way. Before her death she talked at length with an older woman from Angers who was then spending some time as a paying guest in another section of the Refuge, begging her to implore our Bishop to establish a Refuge in Angers for girls who otherwise would have no chance to remake their lives. Oddly enough the letter written at the dying girl's insistence reached Bishop Montault almost simultaneously with the Countess' legacy. Naturally he was deeply impressed by this coincidence."

Mother Euphrasia's interest ran high. "But how did the Refuge of Tours come into the picture?" she inquired.

"By the Providence of God, I truly believe. Only lately the Bishop and I decided that our funds justified going ahead with the purchase of a property. But what good would a property be without the right religious community to operate it? I consulted one of my own parishioners, the Countess d'Andigne, presently in Paris, asking her to suggest a community qualified and available for the project. Do you know what she replied?"

"No," Mother responded. "But we are good friends. Perhaps she told you that?"

"Indeed she did, and far more." He took a letter from his pocket. " 'There is at Tours the very thing you are seeking. I know the Reverend Mother of the Refuge well. She is full of zeal for souls and longs to launch out in fresh directions.' Mother, you must come to Angers. I will not take a refusal. Bishop Montault won't take a refusal. I bring you the prayers and the welcome of all the clergy of our city. Will you accept them?" [1]

Her first impulse was to answer in the affirmative but she knew that without the endorsement of her advisory Council she was not free to act. Nevertheless, as she later reported, her "joy was so great when Monseigneur Montault sent a messenger to Tours to propose the Foundation I almost thought I was in Heaven." [2] However, it was a fleeting joy, for when the Community Council heard the purpose of Father Breton's visit, they flatly rejected his invitation. They could not understand why he had brought his problem to them. Had he forgotten that they were an autonomous and cloistered group? Busy with their own affairs, they had little time and less desire to expand beyond their present confines. Politely but steadfastly they counseled this zealous priest to contact another community. Quite as steadfastly he refused their advice, insisting that only Mother St. Euphrasia and her associates could help him. Meanwhile she added her voice to his eloquently pleading that they accept this call "unsought but surely divinely inspired." The Sisters loved their Superior, but the older ones could never forget the fearful experiences they had encountered during their years of dispersion. They were unwilling to court disaster and they feared that this venture came under that category, believing with many others that a second period of terror was imminent and recalling that as late as June of the preceding year oppressive measures had been taken against the Seminarists and the Jesuits. Who knew when the Sisters of the Refuge might also be singled out for further persecution? They remained unmoved until Mother St. Euphrasia cried, "Are souls in Tours more important than souls in Angers? How can we possibly justify our fourth vow, if we turn a deaf ear to this appeal from God sent us through His chosen courier? How do you think our holy Father St. John Eudes would have acted in this matter?"

Many weary hours later the Council consented reluctantly to their Superior's returning with Father Breton in order to see the foundation she had been asked to direct and make any necessary preliminary arrangements. They then appointed Sister Mary of St. Victoire, the former Mistress of Penitents, as Mother Euphrasia's traveling companion. "This visit must be brief, very brief," they insisted. "We shall look for your return shortly."

Mother St. Euphrasia wished her victory might have been more wholehearted but she knew that it was at least a step in the right direction.

The trip to Angers was made by private coach with Father Breton taking care of all of the arrangements. Because several calls on his relatives and friends were made en route the three travelers did not reach their destination until midmorning of the third day. The sun was hot and the Sisters jolted and wearied by the discomforts of their journey. Nevertheless Mother St. Euphrasia felt only an inexpressible happiness when she saw the city which had summoned her. Often called "The Black City" because of its many slate-roofed buildings and the numerous stone quarries that pinpointed the landscape, it appeared to her a shining abode of hope and promise.

Father Breton's capacity for doing the unexpected now asserted itself. He deliberately chose the meanest and least attractive approach to the city. Apparently he wanted Mother St. Euphrasia to view the vast field that awaited her; at the same time he wanted the working people to be the first to gaze upon the Sisters.

At the crest of the hill he suddenly halted their carriage, opened the door, and cried aloud: "The Holy Apostles went on foot among men. You like them are God's disciples. Descend, descend, and imitate them. They did not ride through the towns and villages— they walked. So shall you. Follow me."

The sun beat down, but the curious stares of the townfolk burned the Sisters even more. To two women come directly from the cloister this public exposition was hard to endure. Not so with Father Breton. Walking ahead with his large umbrella held aloft he was completely unaware of either the sunrays or the Sisters' confusion. With assurance he led his two companions by grimy and circuitous routes to the episcopal residence of Bishop Montault.

The cordial welcome extended them made Mother St. Euphrasia quickly forget her dusty habit and aching feet. After a time the Bishop sent for Count de Neuville who lived near on the Rue de la Touissant. "He will be your benefactor, that I know," Monseigneur Montault said. "It was his mother, you know, who first called my attention to the need for a protective Home for the wayward children of my flock. Her son is a noble Christian gentleman, and deeply interested in furthering his late mother's wishes."

These words were a cautious understatement, for thereafter Count de Neuville and Mother St. Euphrasia proved to be in complete accord on everything that pertained to the Angers Foundation. The rest of his life the Count was to assume the lion's share of the responsibility for its material growth and expansion, winning for himself the title "Father Founder of the Angers House." In the years ahead he often spoke of this "work of my heart," manifesting the truth: "For where your treasure is, there will your heart be also." But on that day no one could have foreseen the role that this ascetic and kindly philanthropist was destined to play.

In the late afternoon the Bishop suggested that Father Breton take the Sisters out to view the property that had been selected for their possible use. Count de Neuville quickly placed his carriage at their disposal, adding that he would like to accompany them. Thus escorted the Sisters approached the site of what was destined to become the Angers Convent and much later, the Mother House of Our Lady of Charity of the Good Shepherd of Angers.

Father Breton explained that the buildings had formerly been used for the manufacture of fabrics printed with gayly colored designs and known in the trade as "*indiennes*" or Indian prints. "In addition to the main factory," he said, "there are several small dyeing and drying sheds that could, we think, be used to advantage."

Located across the Maine in the extreme southwestern section of the city this area was almost entirely removed from traffic. Although the buildings were woefully run down, Mother St. Euphrasia knew that they were not beyond repair. She feasted her eyes on the winding river near by, the wide expanse of land in all directions, and the abundant groves of beautiful fruit and shade trees, envisioning the buildings and grounds extended and occupied by happy and dedicated religious and by busy and contented girls working together. Her feet were on the ground, but her eyes were on the stars as she mentally transformed this neglected and isolated spot into an oasis of natural and spiritual beauty.

Father Breton's crisp comment that the transaction had been held open until she had seen and approved the property brought her attention sharply into focus. If she sanctioned its purchase, he said, they would proceed immediately to close the deal. By now Mother

St. Euphrasia was convinced that there was only one course of action before her. In a vibrant voice and with a happy heart she accepted officially the gift of the Diocese of Angers in the name of the Sisters of Tours whom she represented. In the light of future events it was especially fitting that the chief witness to the little ceremony on that early Saturday evening in late May, 1829, should have been Count Augustine de Neuville.

On Sunday morning Mother St. Euphrasia and Sister Victoire attended Mass at the ancient Cathedral of St. Maurice where Father Breton was the pastor. Before his sermon he introduced the Sisters to his parishioners, adding his own original touch. "These saintly women will cure Angers of its ills and disorders. . . . Bring your sick to them. All will be healed."

Many interpreted these words literally, later flocking in droves to the sacristy where the Sisters had gone at the end of Mass. The aged and the infirm, the poor and the desolate came in good faith expecting to be cured. When Mother St. Euphrasia tried to explain the real nature of her work, they cried aloud in vexation, "But Father Breton said you would cure the sick."

It required tact and empathy to make them understand that their pastor had not meant to mislead them. With a smile Mother said gently, "My friends, we work with spiritual diseases rather than with physical ailments. When spiritual maladies cause physical illness, then we do indeed cure the sick. You will agree, I am sure, that bodily ills are slight in comparison to these more serious ones. Won't you please believe and trust me?"

Some were reassured and went away satisfied. Some still shook their heads in disbelief. This incident though embarrassing to the Sisters, resulted in their being talked about from one end of the parish to the other. Off to such a start Mother St. Euphrasia was never again to be a stranger in Angers.

Early the next day the Sisters left for Tours. Almost immediately upon their arrival a meeting of the Refuge Council was convened at which the chapter eventually agreed unanimously to accept the offer of the clergy of Angers for "a large house and spacious grounds, the necessary furniture, and funds for the maintenance of persons to the number of six, who are required for the foundation of this establishment." [3]

Bishop Montblanc and his Vicar General, M. Dufêtre, were then in Rome, but in anticipation of the establishing of this convent M.

Fustier and M. Dugied had been empowered to act for them. The latter approved wholeheartedly of the matter, supported by other members of the clergy including M. Alleron, Mother St. Euphrasia's long-time spiritual adviser, and M. Suchet, who did his best to convince the hesitant and timorous members of the Council that this proposal was undoubtedly the Will of God and should not in his opinion be thwarted with a selfish veto. Consequently on May 29, 1829, the following resolution became effective. ". . . the foundation of an establishment of her [Mother St. Euphrasia's] congregation in the said city [Angers], for the same ends and to fulfill the same functions conformably to the object of the institution, which is to bring back to religion and good conduct such girls and women as shall voluntarily put themselves under their guidance; to instruct them, according to their talents and capacity, in all sorts of work, and to admit also, into another separate class, young persons whose unfortunate characters or moral tendency give rise to well founded anxiety. . . ." [4]

Three days later the Council named the religious for "our Sister-House" as Mother Euphrasia affectionately called the infant Angers Foundation. They designated Sister Mary of St. Paul Bodin as the Superior, her appointment to become effective when Mother St. Euphrasia had finished the job with which she was already identified in the minds of Bishop Montault and his associates. As soon as things were running smoothly there she was to install Sister Mary of St. Paul in office and return directly to her post as the administrative and spiritual head of the Tours Refuge. Meanwhile Sister St. Paul was to remain in Tours.

This document or "obedience" signed in the name of the Archbishop of Tours by his duly appointed representatives read in part:

"We authorize Mme. Pelletier, in religion called Sister Mary of St. Euphrasia, Superioress of the said Community of Tours, to go to Angers together with five religious of her Order and house, chosen by herself and her Council, to carry into effect the beginning of the proposed establishment, in all things conforming to the statutes and rules by which their Institute in its various monasteries is governed.

". . . We also enjoin upon Mme. Pelletier, present Superioress of Our Lady of Charity, that, when she shall have sufficiently organized the establishment at Angers, and shall have installed the Superioress who shall be sent from here to govern it, she shall herself return to the house at Tours, which consents to be deprived of her presence

only for this short time. We recommend, moreover, to the said Sister
Mary of St. Euphrasia to curtail the time of her absence as much as
shall be reasonably possible." [5]

The 3rd of June saw the departure of the party which Mother St.
Euphrasia headed—six religious including herself, a young girl from
the Tours class who had been selected for her industry and dependa-
bility, and most fittingly, the Countess d'Andigne. Henceforth the
Countess, or Mme. d'Andigne as she preferred to be called, was to
be closely associated with all of Mother St. Euphrasia's undertakings,
using her talents, time, and means in promoting or defending them.
Despite the disparity of their ages—the Countess was then sixty-eight
and Mother St. Euphrasia not quite thirty-three—the two women
were much alike in disposition and outlook. Both thought in terms of
the future while doing well the task at hand.

This ability to spread her attention without diffusing it was one
of Mother St. Euphrasia's most helpful endowments. It gave her the
authority of perspective. Physically she was not a large or mighty
woman. Of medium height, firmly but slenderly built, quick in movement, always alert, she gave an impression of attention to the matter
at hand. Her eyes spoke more quickly than her tongue. She had big
brown eyes, serious in her moments of earnest inquiry or appraisal,
sometimes large with grief, but more often sparkling with anticipation or sheer joy. She got her relaxation in seeing to it that others
got their relaxation. She was a great believer in recreation as the
renewer of mind and body. Sisters dealing every waking minute with
tense unhappy children who must be led to lay aside their belliger-
ence in favor of friendliness and co-operation must themselves maintain verve for living. The best proof of Mother's resilient nature and
flexible mind is the quality of the group which developed about her.
She seemed able to hold the loyalty and promote the spiritual growth
of all sorts of temperaments. Because she loved deeply, she understood broadly. And where work was concerned she gave herself no
quarter; not as a slave to duty but as an emissary of compelling good
will.

The Countess and Mother St. Euphrasia were always amazing each
other by the matter-of-factness of their service. When Mother St.
Euphrasia was about to leave Tours, the Countess arrived posthaste
from Paris. When the nun expressed her surprise, the Countess
expressed surprise at her surprise. "Why, of course I'm making this
trip to Angers too. After all I am your sponsor. Does the godparent

stand by idly when her godchild embarks on a strange and perilous mission?"

"Perilous? That dark pronouncement is not like you," Mother replied.

"Well, it won't be easy."

"Nothing worth doing ever is."

"You should know that," the older woman commented meaningfully.

From the start the trip was a kind of nightmare. The sultry weather and the constant lurching and jolting of the carriage made Mother St. Euphrasia carsick, her illness becoming more aggravated with each turn of the wheel. No doubt she was over fatigued as a result of her recent trip to Angers and the heavy responsibilities she had taken upon herself.

"Our driver quenched his thirst too often," she later recalled, "and once he was so intoxicated he didn't know what he was doing. It was then that he drove us dangerously near the embankment of the Loire. Our carriage actually stood in a vertical position with the frightened horses hanging over the water's edge. I am convinced that only a miracle kept us from plunging to our deaths. How else could we explain our being saved from that near tragedy? Somehow we managed to get out of our coach unharmed and wait alongside the road until succor came. That in itself was providential, for we were powerless to help ourselves and our driver was in no condition to aid anyone. It was a long time after that before he was sober enough to resume the journey. All of us would have felt better with another driver, but there was nothing we could do but go along with the one we had."

At midnight three days later they reached the outskirts of Angers, the darkness of the night increasing the proverbial "blackness" of the city. Mme. d'Andigne solved the problem of their lodging by taking them to her old friend, Mlle. Blouin, the Directress of the Hospice for Deaf Mutes on the Saumur Road. Here they were greeted as though their coming had been momentarily awaited. Few hostesses could hope to match the spontaneity or quality of Mademoiselle's reception to her unexpected guests.

On the following morning they arose refreshed and ready for the strenuous day ahead, but they delayed their starting until Mother St. Euphrasia and Mlle. Blouin could talk over the common elements of their respective tasks. On many future occasions Mother St.

Euphrasia was to say: "I could never forget the warmth of Mlle. Blouin's hospitality. My coming to Angers was made brighter by it."

Mother's second arrival in the city was quiet and inconspicuous. With Mme. d'Andigne and the others she went directly to the Bishop's home where their coming was expected. First Monseigneur Montault received them officially in the Hall of the Synod after which he welcomed them informally and pledged anew his support. He was visibly touched by their willingness to take immediate possession of their new quarters despite the fact that that place had not yet been made habitable and closed the interview by conferring his blessing on these pioneers whose later achievements would cause him to exclaim: "They are one of the glories of my episcopate."

At this point Father Breton took charge, Mme. d'Andigne leaving the party temporarily. Had she remained she might possibly have dissuaded him from his next course of action. Instead of starting at once toward the former cotton factory he deliberately set off in the opposite direction choosing as their paths of travel unsavory lanes and streets of ill repute. In a penetrating voice he repetitiously called: "Let all bad girls come out and go with these good ladies to be converted."

It was natural that this group fresh from the cloister found such an experience a trying ordeal. Mother St. Euphrasia had told her companions not to be surprised at anything Father Breton might do, but she later admitted that his behavior far exceeded anything she had anticipated. Whenever his enthusiasm asserted itself in queer ways his friends and fellow parishioners always smiled tolerantly. "After all, if Father Breton acted like us, he wouldn't be himself. Don't fear, his heart is in the right place."

When the uncomfortable little band arrived at their destination, the priest quickly dropped his eccentric role for one the Sisters found less dismaying. After a short speech of welcome he presented the key of the old factory building to Mother St. Euphrasia with these words, "Now this is really yours, Mother. I am sure you will do great things here." In that mood he left the newcomers to their own devices.

Under such unauspicious circumstances the Sisters of the Refuge came to Angers on June 6, 1829. All of them knew that this particular Pentecost Eve would live forever in their memory.

In the next few hours Mother St. Euphrasia's ingenuity was sorely tested. Clearly nothing at all had been done since her visit a week previous. Of course, she had known that the repairs were not yet under way, but she had taken for granted that at least adequate food and bedding would be on hand. A thorough search revealed neither. "How can we ever spend the night here?" she wondered. She was careful to keep her thoughts to herself knowing that the Sisters trusted in her ability to see them through any distressing situation.

By agreement the committee in charge of arrangements had promised "to furnish the house with the most indispensable articles" and "to give the Community a small pension to care for their living expenses," the latter sum having been set at 1500 francs monthly.

With that promise in mind Mother St. Euphrasia asserted that their present inconveniences were "awkward but necessary." Consequently they slept without mattresses, retiring by the light of a tallow candle stuck in a broken bottle. The next morning, Whitsunday, a very weary group attended Mass at the near-by Church of St. Jacques. When no provisions had been delivered by midday, Mother St. Euphrasia was forced to send word of their hunger to Father Vincent, the pastor of St. Jacques. In turn he sent them the dinner from his own table expostulating, "If I'd only known earlier!"

Thus their first day passed amid the lowliest kind of poverty while succeeding days were filled with continued hardships and deprivations. It was evident that something serious had gone awry. Even the workmen needed so urgently failed to appear. "The whole place was in such a tumble down condition . . . that a drunken man who had found his way in through a hole in the wall was discovered sleeping in one of the haylofts." [6]

The records shed no light on the reason for the delay of the necessary furniture and the nonpayment of the promised pension. The unsupported assumption is that no particular individual had been given the responsibility of caring for the Sisters' needs, each potential benefactor remaining unacquainted with the true state of affairs.

Saddened but unafraid Mother St. Euphrasia appealed to her associates: "Before long this unfortunate mistake will be discovered and corrected. Until then we'll do the best we can with the little we have. It would be foolish to spend our time in futile regrets. Whenever we are tempted to look back, we should try to remember the fate of Lot's wife."

The Sisters smiled wanly, for they were hungry. Then they smiled broadly when Mother suggested that they have boiled nettles without salt for supper. "Our crop of nettles is heavy; we'll gather all we can eat." In the days that followed the Sisters grew to know the taste of nettles well.

Necessity steadily challenged Mother St. Euphrasia's inventiveness. For instance, there was the time she came by accident upon a fairly large carrot patch hidden away in the garden. Finding the carrots fresh and tender she called Marie, the young girl she had brought along from Tours, and together they picked and tied them into bunches, Marie selling them at the market in town. With the money she earned they were then able to purchase a few staples such as yeast, flour, and tallow dips.

Meanwhile the Sisters went to work to prepare living quarters for themselves and separate accommodations for the girls who would eventually be sent to them. Five weeks would pass before the old cotton factory could be transformed into a semblance of a clean and ordered refuge. In view of the problems that beset Mother St. Euphrasia one wonders at the speed with which this change came about.

Present and ensuing obligations were taken care of by the Sisters or by volunteer workers, the inference being that in spite of its sanguine expectations the committee in charge did not find it possible to pay the cost of repairs and contribute additionally to the upkeep of the buildings. Corporate responsibility had evidently ceased with acquisition of the property. In any case, Mother St. Euphrasia was forced to live with the idea that from now on she and her associates might have to make their way alone. She was not without heartaches, but these were eased considerably by the loyalty of the Sisters. Especially was she comforted by her assistant and long-time friend, Sister Mary of St. Stanislaus Bedouet, who would say cheerfully, "Things aren't too bad for us, dear Mother. We know your disappointment is much greater than ours."

It was not a part of Mother's nature to harbor animosity or resentment toward anyone. "The poor priests have done their best," she said in their ready defense. "We should be glad that they were inspired to set this project in motion. Certainly we must not criticize them for the problems they cannot solve." For such expressions some people praised her for her wisdom while others denounced her for her foolhardiness. To some she was "a remarkable woman"; to others "an impractical and dangerous innovator." By such diverse pronouncements the profile of her future was taking shape.

During all this time Count de Neuville and Mme. d'Andigne

called regularly as did Father Breton and other members of the clergy.
But in the beginning even these close friends were misled by surface
impressions for the Sisters had managed to clean and make livable a
reception room beyond which their guests did not go. It may have
been the Sisters' close application to their needlework with an
unusually keen interest in its sale which first focused attention on
their needs. In any case when their friends discovered how things
really stood, they lost no time in rallying to Mother St. Euphrasia's
support, berating themselves for their naïveté and selfish neglect of
the little Community. She must believe they were not fair-weather
friends! No matter how the wind blew they stood ready to act in her
behalf.

Mother was encouraged by their renewed interest. Also she never
forgot that in order to purchase the property Count de Augustine de
Neuville had personally added 38,000 francs to his mother's legacy.
It was because of this generous contribution that she had very carefully refrained from imposing further upon his good graces. Otherwise she would have consulted him directly when she decided to
provide the Sisters with some sort of chapel before she returned to
Tours.

Instead, she and the Sisters went ahead on their own initiative,
choosing one of the less run-down and lighter rooms for this special
purpose. With an abundance of love they made it ready to house the
Blessed Sacrament. The place was scrubbed bright and clean and a
few humble effects gathered together. Naturally their industry could
not long be overlooked. Once discovered, the friends of the House
vied with one another in helping to furnish the chapel. Mme.
d'Andigne gave a monstrance to hold the consecrated host, and a
censer for the incense; Monseigneur Montault, silver cruets for the
altar wine; M. Breton and M. de Neuville everything else that was
required for the altar and sacristy.

The first Mass in their own Convent was said on the Feast of
Corpus Christi, less than a month after their arrival in Angers. M. de
Neuville was among those present. Hereafter the Sisters could attend
daily Mass on their own premises without going back and forth to
the Church of St. Jacques, although they had to depend upon an
aged volunteer chaplain whose time of arrival was usually determined
by his convenience rather than the Sisters' schedule. On mornings when he was very late the Sisters would have to eat something
and were thus denied the privilege of receiving Holy Communion.

Incredible though it seems "erring sheep had begun to find their way to the fold." [7] At first they came singly, but before long they were arriving in twos and threes. Just how many made up the first class is a matter of conjecture, but it was sizable as to numbers and obstreperous and unruly as to conduct. Many of the girls were the illegitimate offspring of the Revolutionists. Seemingly they had inherited the rapaciousness of their forbears, acting more often like untamed young beasts than human beings. Many of them had worked in a large match factory amid intolerable conditions. Their chronic dissatisfaction with life sometimes asserted itself in bodily attacks upon one another, accompanied by screams of thwarted rage. Until now they had never heard such words as "discipline" and "co-operation."

"Savages, little savages, that's what they seem to be," the frightened Sisters whispered. "How can we ever hope to appeal to their better selves?"

Without Mother St. Euphrasia they might not have succeeded. In open admiration the Sisters watched her as she circulated freely among the rebellious girls treating them with firmness based on kindness and love. Before too long the girls were her slaves saying, "I'll do it, if the Mother says so . . . I'd do a lot for her." [8] It was a tedious and discouraging process to teach them to do a "lot" for the other Sisters as well, but happily for all that day did come.

Mother's next act was to give their new home the beautiful and comforting name of the Monastery of Our Lady of Charity of the Good Shepherd of Angers. She chose this name in deference to the late Countess de Neuville and out of consideration for the townspeople who had regarded highly the earlier local foundation of that name. In addition she wished the new Convent to stand before all men as a living witness of the Good Shepherd's willingness to make all wayfarers at home in His fold and to lay down His life for His sheep.

At the end of two months the Council recalled Mother St. Euphrasia to her post as the Mother Superior of the Tours Refuge. In their letters Mother sensed their mounting impatience and implied criticism of her delay. She knew that the members of the Council were acting within their rights, but she also knew they were too far away to appreciate the tremendous difficulties that lay ahead for Angers. She wondered how she could even leave this poor struggling Community. Her dilemma was a matter of duty versus duty. Common sense told her she should not leave Angers, yet obedience dictated her return to Tours.

A deputation of the clergy led by Father Vincent of St. Jacques personally interceded with the ecclesiastical authorities in Tours, asking that Mother St. Euphrasia be left indefinitely as the Superior of the newly founded Convent. However, they quickly learned that Monseigneur Fustier, the Vicar General, and the Refuge Council were unwilling to modify their stand that Mother St. Euphrasia's place was in Tours, not Angers. In this decision they were supported by the cradle of their Institute, the Refuge of Caen. Though holding no jurisdiction over the other Houses of the Order, Caen's decisions were usually sustained. Consequently Mother's immediate return to Tours could no longer be postponed.

Following that decision Mother Mary of St. Paul Bodin arrived in Angers, accompanied by a Sister *tourière*, or extern, who would serve as a liaison between the Convent and the public. The following day Mother St. Paul was installed as the new Superior, after which the enclosure was formally established, the impressive ceremony presided over by Monseigneur Prieur, acting in Bishop Montault's place. Among his assistants were Monseigneur Maupoint, later the Bishop of Bourbon, who could never forget the poverty and difficulties that attended the opening of the Convent at Angers.

On this occasion the little chapel was filled to overflowing with the clergy and invited guests, the small crowd spilling over into the hallway and garden. "That happy day," Mother often recalled, "some of us knelt in the rain and mud, but we didn't find it too hard. Instead we rejoiced because at long last we were a cloistered house of religion."

Her statement meant that according to Canon Law no one was henceforth to be permitted to enter the section of the Convent assigned to the Sisters, and the religious themselves were not to go abroad. The exceptions to this rule would be rare occasions when serious illness or a similar emergency arose. Most interestingly the Angers enclosure was effected on Mother St. Euphrasia's thirty-third birthday which fell on the Feast of St. Ignatius, who had himself once founded a refuge for penitent women.

Early the next morning Mother St. Euphrasia set out for Tours. Tears blinded her eyes as she bade farewell to the Good Shepherd Convent. When and how she might see it again were matters in God's hand, not hers. Yet she did not doubt that someday she would come back to Angers. Until then her work lay far beyond this place. To have minimized its importance would have gone contrary to her philosophy that the immediate task should never be slighted for one that might never arise. So fortified, she adjusted her sight and let her thoughts run ahead of the coach. After all it would be good to be home again.

VII

Tours and Angers, 1829-1831

Without a spirit of sacrifice and self-denial, you can effect no good, but with zeal and devotedness, you will succeed in accomplishing the most difficult works.

ST. MARY OF ST. EUPHRASIA

IT WAS not easy for Mother St. Euphrasia to resume her position as Head of the Tours Refuge when a number of the Sisters continued to criticize her for ever having gone away. Being fiercely loyal to their own Convent, they resented the growing claims of the Angers House as an unjustified intrusion. Fortunately these critics were in the minority, but they made themselves felt in the same way that a thorn in the flesh pains and festers, remaining a constant threat to Mother's peace of mind and the morale of the Community. A house divided against itself is never a relaxed nor happy place. Try as she would Mother St. Euphrasia failed to persuade the dissidents that she had not changed during her short absence from them.

There was no open rebellion, but the situation was strained and difficult. When it persisted, Mother suggested to her spiritual adviser that perhaps it might be better for all concerned if she would resign her office as Superior. Father Alleron discouraged this drastic act saying, "The Rule that limits an incumbent's service to six successive years will free you of these burdens at the end of your present term. Until then have patience and do the best that you can."

In the meantime the affairs at Angers were also in a bad way. Mother St. Paul, though an excellent religious, was a poor administrator. She was timid and lacking in confidence, discounting her own ability to meet the extraordinary demands of her new assignment. Aware of her own limitations she did not trust herself to make decisions. As a result she grew tense and unco-operative, rebuffing curtly those who wanted to help her. Soon she lost her sense of objectivity, magnifying each problem out of all proportion to its true value. Not infrequently she found herself overwhelmed by the day's events. It was unfortunate that this good woman should have been subjected to such acute unhappiness, but it was even more unfortunate for the good of the institution entrusted to her.

Before long Mother St. Paul's overcautious manner lost her the services of their chief benefactor. Distressed because the convent chapel was too small and inadequate Count de Neuville had made up his mind to erect a larger and more commodious one, presenting it to the Community as a memorial to his late father. When the tentative specifications were drawn, he took them to Mother St. Paul for study and evaluation, urging her to suggest whatever revisions she desired.

He was completely unprepared for Mother's rather casual dismissal of his proposal. "You are very kind, but for the present we can make our chapel do," she said with quiet finality. "I believe it would be unwise to enter upon a building project until our nation's economy grows more stable. Hard times lie ahead for us all."

Here she spoke truthfully, for as soon as the Count understood that his gift had been rejected he withheld his purse and his presence. Several months were to intervene before he visited the convent again.

In succession others followed his example, all of them nursing a deep regret over the steady decline of Mother St. Euphrasia's groundwork. With the coming of winter even the clergy came less frequently, using as a double excuse the pressing urgencies of their parochial obligations and the bitterly cold weather that held them in its grip.

The winter of 1829–1830 remains on record as one of the worst Angers has ever known. How the Sisters and their charges managed to live through it without outside help cannot be explained. They were both cold and hungry with too few blankets and too little fuel. Their clothing was inadequate, their diet insufficient and of poor quality. The Sisters voluntarily placed themselves on short rations so that the girls could have more to eat but even then everyone went hungry most of the time. Strangely enough the girls made no attempt to run away, undoubtedly realizing that their lot would be as bad and perhaps worse were they to desert the Sisters. Being human they grumbled and complained, but they were much too busy trying to keep warm to plan any concerted mischief. Among themselves the Sisters called the girls "docile and industrious" and "heroic and helpful."

Mother St. Paul's letters to Mother St. Euphrasia were sad. Once she wrote: "This House is going to ruin. I do not know what we shall do. Every day things grow worse and I do not see any hope for the future." [1] Another time she disclosed "that not a single alms was coming in for the penitents." [2]

These reports weighed heavily on Mother St. Euphrasia. She was unable to aid the Angers Sister materially, but she wrote long letters of encouragement. Somehow she always said the right thing at the right time. She made it a point to minimize her own troubles but then she always had little patience with people who said dismally, "Yes, your lot is hard, but mine is worse." In her philosophy it was far better to act than to sit around bewailing one's misfortune, yet her sensitivity to the problems of others restrained her from abrupt or harsh comment. Instead she wrote to Sister St. Stanislaus, "Your sufferings should bring you close to God. . . . One must experience the cross to gain such wisdom." [3]

And so the winter wore on. One very cold morning when few people had ventured out, Count de Neuville was surprised to meet one of the *tourière* or extern Sisters in town. He greeted her cordially and inquired with interest about life at the Convent. "I hear you are doing well and want for nothing," he said.

"Monsieur le Comte, you have been misinformed," the Sister replied. "The opposite is true. We are doing badly and we need everything."

Startled by this frank outburst Augustine de Neuville questioned the Sister further and then hastened to call on Mother St. Paul. This time she kept nothing from him, spilling out bits of information which pieced together in a story of incredible hardships. Belatedly the Count realized that this good woman was woefully timid and insecure. What he had taken for her disinterest had been instead an artificial barrier of defense behind which she had hoped to hide her fears. He did not leave until he had secured a list of things most needed. This list, presented with reluctance, disclosed an appalling lack of necessities. No time was lost in purchasing supplies, the Count seeing to it that they were delivered before nightfall. A day or so later he called again and gave Mother St. Paul a most substantial gift of 6000 francs for "the alleviation of your troubles."

Ironically the francs increased the troubles for the sight of that sum of money simply terrified the poor Superior. The thought of its presence in the house brought her several sleepless nights; in her mind's eye she saw it snatched away by roaming thieves or claimed by revolutionists. At last against the protests of her associates she buried it under a big tree in the garden, working hard to break through the icy ground. Her reason was that she preferred to cope with her old worries rather than deal with financial ones.

Nevertheless new worries soon intruded themselves. With the melting of the snows the spring floods took over. The Loire overflowed its banks, inundating the gardens and fields and threatening to drive the Sisters from the Convent proper. As it was, part of the lower floor was under water. All were kept busy moving their precious effects from one dry place to another; later when the waters receded, they had to work even more arduously salvaging whatever they could and cleaning up the accumulated muck and debris. In every respect theirs was a dirty and a difficult job.

This experience was far more than an inconvenience, but it happily missed being a disaster, for no lives were lost and the chapel remained unharmed. Neither were the hidden francs washed away. At the first opportunity the Sisters wrote to Mother St. Euphrasia about their loss of supplies and enforced isolation, but they did their best to understate their troubles. However, she was quick to read between the lines, filling in what they had omitted, and her heart grew big with sympathy as she envisioned what those poor frightened women had endured. She also knew that each spring when winter was done other floods would cover their fields. For the present, though, the matter of future floods could wait while her letter to the Sisters in Angers could not. She wrote in terms of hope and reassurance reminding them that "a brighter day will come. It must come. Even the darkest night ends at daybreak."

A short time later one of Mother St. Paul's many anxieties was justified. The Revolution she had incessantly talked about broke in July, 1830. The Bourbon Dynasty was overthrown and the citizen-king, Louis Philippe of the Orleans line, brought to power. Contrary to general expectations, however, the economic situation did not improve. Poor Mother St. Paul! Whatever was she to do now? Somehow she managed, but her increasing unhappiness caused her to cry out to

Sister St. Stanislaus that "Mother Mary of St. Euphrasia is needed here; she understands M. de Neuville and would make things go." [4]

The annals of the Congregation contain an extended correspondence between Mother St. Euphrasia and Sister St. Stanislaus. More than once Mother wrote without restraint to the Assistant of the Angers House. One letter typifies others. "You ask me, if I have any feeling that I shall return to Angers. Oh, yes, that Foundation is dear to me, dearer than I can express. But what opposition from all!" [5]

Against this opposition Mother St. Euphrasia sought in vain to mend the widening breach that separated the two Communities. Although like St. Paul she might have said, "Life is become bitter by my diverse sufferings," she prayed instead to be given the strength to endure uncomplainingly her present trials.

"God moves in a strange way His wonders to perform." Now He used M. Dufêtre, the former ecclesiastical superior of the Tours Refuge, to advance His plan. Early in March (1831) Monseigneur Montault had invited Father Dufêtre, presently of Parapace, to give a series of Lenten sermons at the Angers Cathedral. Naturally this priest was eager to visit the Foundation established by his good friend, Mother St. Euphrasia. As a result of his visit he volunteered spontaneously to give a three-day retreat to the girls. Later when he remembered the many unfavorable things that he had heard about their willfulness and insubordination he feared that he had acted unwisely. Then it occurred to him that his intent was not to verify rumors but to rout them. He was convinced that he could do this most effectively by helping the girls to make a good retreat. Obviously he succeeded, for they were all unusually attentive and co-operative. Rarely had Father Dufêtre met such well-mannered, alert, and interested listeners anywhere. At the end of the last conference he congratulated the group on their excellent behavior saying, "You have surely earned a reward. Only name it and I'll be glad to get it for you."

The girls heard these words in stunned silence wondering if the Retreat Master could really make them come true.

Father Dufêtre spoke again. "What would you like? Sweets or pinafores? Or a picnic down by the river? Tell me and I'll do the rest. You'll soon find out I mean what I say."

An undercurrent of restlessness encircled the room. The priest sensed that a wordless message was being relayed from one girl to another. He had seen no signal given, yet he knew that one had been made. Just as he was about to speak again the girls called out imploringly: "Oh, please, Father Dufêtre, bring Mother St. Euphrasia back to us. We love her so and need her here."

The priest's mouth fell open in amazement. What was this they had asked? Nothing short of the impossible, that was certain. Before he could reply to their unexpected request a girl at the rear of the room stood up and said politely, "There are some of us who want to become Sister Magdalens, but we can't without Mother St. Euphrasia's help. We beg you to return her to Angers."

With reluctance Father Dufêtre was forced to withdraw his original offer. "I am sorry that I cannot do what you ask. Such a thing lies outside my jurisdiction. You all know that I am no longer stationed in Tours. Even if I were, I could not bring this about."

After that he had nothing more to say. The heaviness of the accusing silence made his chest tighten. He'd thought to make the girls happy; instead he had only disappointed them keenly.

Then someone asked hopefully, "Couldn't you at least try?"

The priest waited a long moment and then agreed. "Yes, I'll try," he promised. "But you must all understand that mine will be more or less a voice crying in the wilderness."

Father Dufêtre acted immediately. He wrote Mother St. Euphrasia proposing that she ask to be returned to Angers following the expiration of her present term of office two months hence. His letter written on the 8th of March said: "The House in Angers stands greatly in need of you. It is capable of wide development if only it could have the benefit of your spirit, your zeal, and your power of organization. . . . What would you think of making an exchange with Mother St. Paul, letting her go to Tours as Superior and you coming as Superior to Angers?" [6]

That last thought appealed to everyone. Mother St. Euphrasia longed to return to Angers. Father Alleron and Father Suchet, her former and present confessors, were in agreement with Father Dufêtre, and the Council indicated that they would withdraw their opposition to Angers provided Mother St. Paul could come back to them. They were of one mind that her irresolution and timidity would disappear with her return to the familiar surroundings of Tours. When informed of this possibility Mother St. Paul was jubilant.

Father Dufêtre had poured oil on troubled waters. At last love in the truest sense was again dominant, releasing all tensions and generating a feeling of solidarity that held everyone in warm embrace.

Personal shortcomings were forgotten as plans were set in motion to carry out the desired arrangements. The climax was reached on Ascension Thursday when Mother St. Euphrasia relinquished one charge and accepted another. This immediate reassignment was made possible, explained Father Fustier, the Vicar General, by an arrangement entered into earlier between the Archdiocese of Tours and the Diocese of Angers, whereby the Sisters of Angers had been authorized to conduct their own independent election. As had been foreseen, they had cast a unanimous ballot in favor of Mother Mary of St. Euphrasia Pelletier.

Following this decision Mother Mary of St. Paul Bodin was elected in absentia as the new Mother Superior of the Tours Refuge. Temporarily, however, she was to remain at her present post to await Mother St. Euphrasia's arrival in Angers. Later after the two Superiors had reviewed the problems pertinent to their respective Convents, Mother St. Paul would proceed to Tours. In every way the details of this double transfer were satisfactory to the persons involved.

Two days later in the presence of the entire Chapter Father Fustier, as the representative of the Archbishop of Tours, presented the official *Exeat* or *Obedience* that transferred Mother St. Euphrasia from the jurisdiction of one Ordinary to another. In a clear and steady voice he read without comment the document before him.

We, Augustine Louis de Montblanc by the Divine mercy and the grace of the holy Apostolic See, Archbishop of Tours, in order the more to second the praiseworthy and pious design of Mgr. the Bishop of Angers, establishing a House of Refuge in his episcopal city, for which purpose already we have accorded to him, in May 1829, five religious from the monastery of our Lady of Charity of Tours, we consent and command that Mme. Mary of St. Euphrasia Pelletier, our dear daughter in Jesus Christ, who began to organize the said establishment, and a few months since returned to complete the term of her trienniate in the monastery of Tours, of which she was Superioress, shall go to Angers as Superioress of the New House, known as the Good Shepherd, to govern and more fully establish it according to the form of the statutes and wise regulation approved by the Holy See for the monasteries of the Institute.

And consequently we resign our jurisdiction over the said Dame Mary of St. Euphrasia, and the five other religious of the monastery of our Lady of Charity of Tours, who already are at the House of the Good Shepherd, in favour of Mgr. the Bishop of Angers, enjoining upon them to regard him as their true and lawful superior.

This act is signed by Monseigneur de Montblanc, May 20, 1831.

By this time many of Mother St. Euphrasia's former critics had become her advocates. Tardily they recalled the parable of the mote and the beam and saw themselves as they had been—spiritually blind to the merits of one who had consistently placed their welfare above her own. Their recognition though delayed was balm to Mother's wounded heart. However, it could not lessen her distress at leaving behind the Sisters who had never wavered in their loyalty and her special protégés, the Sister Magdalens. These were friends tried and true, who like the girls in the classes revered and loved her.

The day before her departure [7] she came to the conclusion that the morrow's leave-taking would be too much of a strain on everyone. Father Suchet promptly concurred in her idea that she leave that night without making public her change in plans. Thus it came about that shortly after sunset Mother St. Euphrasia with two companions left the Tours Refuge to accept proffered hospitality at the near-by Convent of the Ursulines. Most fittingly the Superior there was her former teacher and good friend, Mother de Lignac.

Throughout the years these two friends had always corresponded. Each knew well the other's problems. But as cloistered religious of different Communities they had not met since that day long ago when Mme. Ronald de Bussy had withdrawn from the Christian Academy taking Mlle. de Lignac with her. In the meantime their patterns of life had changed considerably. Now at the sight of each other the past and the present merged. With a warm smile Mother de Lignac welcomed her beloved pupil of bygone days, assuring her of "the honor and happiness" this visit brought. Mother St. Euphrasia modestly disclaimed everything except her present need of shelter and surcease from her anxieties and misgivings.

"That was typical of her," Mother de Lignac said later. "I doubt if she ever knew how much her coming meant to me." Then she added reminiscently, "Long ago at Mme. de Chobelet's I first began to understand that a great work might be in store for Mlle. Pelletier.[8] Her brief sojourn with us convinced me that this work had already begun."

Later that same night Mother St. Euphrasia's courage weakened. Alone in her cell she went over the day's happenings and the events that had preceded them. Suddenly the strain became too great. She broke down and wept bitterly. As the clock ticked off the hours of the night her uncertainty increased. By dawn she was deep in the valley of indecision, torn with doubts concerning the wisdom of her intention to go back to Angers. Repeatedly she asked herself if she ought not stay on at the Tours Convent as a member of the Community yielding her superiority to someone better qualified than she. After all she may have taken too much for granted in thinking that she would be able to restore order and progress to the Angers House. Just when she was on the point of deciding to remain a knock came at her door. In surprise at being called so early Mother St. Euphrasia admitted the embarrassed Ursuline Sister who stood outside.

"You are wanted in the parlor, Mother," the Sister whispered.

"At this time of day?"

"Yes, dear Mother. Canon Pasquier wishes to see you. He says that his business cannot wait."

"How did he learn that I was here?"

"I do not know. He gave me no explanation."

A few moments later Mother St. Euphrasia entered the parlor to see Father Pasquier, a good friend of the Refuge, walking restlessly back and forth. Before she could speak he drew near and said with a sense of urgency, "Mother, you are about to succumb to the temptation of returning to the Tours Convent. That you must not do. God has made this known to me. The least thought of returning would be an offense to Him. He has sent me to tell you His will and to make manifest His designs over you. Go to Angers; God intends to do there a great work for His own glory by means of you." [9]

Knowing that her prayer for guidance had been answered, she was calm and certain once more and held to her earlier plans, leaving that same day in the coach for Angers. Her companions were Sister Mary of St. Philip Mercier and a devoted lay Sister whose name is not recorded. Naturally Mother was excessively weary as she started on this journey and the lurching and jolting of the coach were no aid. Fortunately the driver was trustworthy, but even his skill could not prevent the heavy diligence from rocking back and forth like a hammock. As a result the Sisters suffered from "seasickness" most of the way. When at last they reached Angers, they were unable to leave the hot and cavernous coach unassisted. However, the effects of their nightmarish trip were quickly dispelled by the solicitude and welcome that awaited them. Everyone was unspeakably happy because "our Mother" had returned. As needed rains freshen a parched countryside, Mother St. Euphrasia's presence instilled new life into the desolate and languishing Convent. With the exception of Mother St. Paul all were confident that a new era was at hand.

In good faith Mother Mary of St. Paul now told Mother St. Euphrasia that she could see no future for the Angers Convent. "Everything is in a state of stagnation," she said gloomily. "For over a year we've had practically no work of any kind for our girls. And it's been longer than that since we've had any postulants. In fact only three aspirants have sought admittance to the religious life since you went away."

Before Mother St. Euphrasia could comment on this situation Mother St. Paul continued: "Our friends and benefactors rarely come, and our chaplain is undependable. The poor man does the best he can, but he is sick and old. We never know at what time he will say Mass. Sometimes it is as late as ten o'clock when he gets here." Mother wiped her eyes and then resumed her tale of woe. "Things are really intolerable. I assure you, Mother St. Euphrasia, this place is doomed."

Hardly an encouraging report. Yet to accept it as a final evaluation meant the inevitable closing of the Convent. Instead the new Superior preferred to bide her time, finding comfort meanwhile in the fact that there had been no abuses or irregularities of the practices and observances to which the religious were pledged. Surely the Sisters had heroically withstood the attrition of unrelieved poverty and discouragement. Soon Mother St. Euphrasia concluded that the seed had not rotted despite the poor quality of the soil in which it had lain dormant. With care and skill she was convinced that it would still germinate and bear its destined crop.

Mother St. Euphrasia literally led this little group of gardeners. Her first act was to invoke God's blessings on their undertakings; her second, to dig up the 6000 francs that Mother St. Paul had long kept hidden in the earth for safekeeping. With part of the disinterred money she bought a supply of food and bedding, declaring that the Sisters must above all be nourished and rested in order to fortify themselves for the work of transformation that would follow.

Mother St. Euphrasia's superiorship had really begun.

VIII

Angers, 1831-1833

Little tribe of the Good Shepherd, so poor, so lowly, so unnoticed, you shall one day be the Church's glory! May these, my words, be fulfilled.

FATHER GLORIOT, S.J.

IN THE annals of Christianity certain names are linked together, sometimes because of a shared cause as in the case of St. Francis of Assisi and St. Clare, St. Vincent de Paul and St. Louise de Marillac. Or it may have been the prayers of a devoted mother for an errant son that won them this dual identity, as St. Monica is linked with "the son of her tears," St. Augustine. Less often, however, is the name of a layman allied with that of a religious foundress. But Count Augustine de Neuville [1] and Mother Mary of St. Euphrasia Pelletier are an exception.

Mother St. Euphrasia's return to Angers in 1831 immediately resulted in a revival of Count de Neuville's interest and support. He became her steadfast friend and counselor, attaching himself to her Community in a kind of solemn dedication, thereafter promoting its welfare consistently against every kind of reversal and misrepresentation.

Count de Neuville was seventeen years the senior of Mother St. Euphrasia. As the only child of a noble and wealthy line, he was educated by the Jesuits in Liege and later at Stonyhurst in Lancashire, England, and became a man of quiet strength and deep piety. His dignity was impressive; his generosity, almost incredible. As a young man he had seriously thought of studying for the priesthood, but had

113

finally decided that his service could best be performed outside the walls of seminary or monastery. Always after that he filled this chosen role unobtrusively, observing the Biblical injunction not to let one's left hand know what one's right hand does when giving alms.

Unfortunately Count de Neuville left no memoirs. Following his death in 1843 Mother St. Euphrasia applied to his relatives for information regarding this friend who had so generously befriended her Institute. They answered: "The Count lived such a retired life, there is nothing to record." [2]

Undaunted, Mother strove to keep alive the memory of this modest benefactor without whom the Convent of Angers might never have outgrown its swaddling clothes. As a result Count de Neuville has been given a lasting place in the annals of her Congregation. He is known "not merely as the temporal founder of the Good Shepherd, but in a sense, a spiritual founder, second only to Mother St. Euphrasia herself." [3]

Less than two weeks after Mother St. Euphrasia's return to Angers Monseigneur Montault asked her to receive twenty little orphan girls. "I realize that the care of orphans is not your specific work," he said. "But you must admit it well could be. Left alone and unsupervised these children might easily go astray."

Noting the dismay on Mother's face the Bishop explained: "For a long time I have tried unsuccessfully to start an orphanage within my diocese. But even yet many of the religious Communities dispersed by the Revolution have not reassembled. The demands upon those that are functioning far exceed their limited personnel." He went on, "For many years a group of charitably-minded women in this city have maintained an informal boarding home for dependent orphans under the kindly directress, Mademoiselle de Montergon. Unhappily for us all, she is ill and unable to continue. Frankly, I am put to it to offer a solution to this problem. Mother St. Euphrasia, will you take charge of these children for me?"

Monseigneur Montault did not plead in vain. A few days later, on June 10, Mother St. Euphrasia received these "children of Providence," accommodating them in a small house near the gate which she had hastily turned into temporary dormitories and schoolrooms. Appropriately these quarters were entirely apart from either the Community or the penitents. Her willingness to take on this additional project was widely approved. The "charitably-minded women" about whom the Bishop had spoken agreed to pay her an annual pension of fifty crowns for each orphan. Obviously the assurance of this contribution lightened the financial load considerably.

The growing infirmities of the aged chaplain who served the Convent made his visits uncertain and infrequent. According to Mother St. Euphrasia's account "there was no Mass except on Sunday and Thursday, and then at so late an hour that we could rarely receive Holy Communion. All my life I shall remember how, in that year, we were deprived of receiving Holy Communion on the beautiful Feast of Corpus Christi." [4]

Perhaps that deprivation brought matters to a head. Before long Count de Neuville with the Bishop's approval secured the services of a permanent chaplain, the Abbé Perché, maintaining him at his own expense. Abbé Perché became the stanch friend of the Congregation and under his leadership the spiritual life of the Community flourished. Voluntarily he assumed the duties of teaching the catechism to the girls and the orphans, and of instructing the novices and postulants in Church doctrine. Furthermore he taught the Sisters to sing plain chant, the normal music of the Latin liturgy sung responsively by two groups or choirs. As soon as they became adept, he formed the first choir which sang the ceremonial Office at the Convent of the Good Shepherd. He also worked for the extension of the Institute, prophesying that someday the Sisters would expand their services far beyond the confines of France. Mother St. Euphrasia smiled whenever he said these things, naturally recalling her own childhood desire someday to go as a missionary to the black children of Africa. At this time, though, she considered the Abbé's predictions unrealistic not knowing that many years later he would be the means of establishing her Sisters in New Orleans.

Meanwhile Mother St. Euphrasia longed to organize the inner Community of the Sister Magdalens in Angers. The fact that they had to have quarters of their own separated entirely from all other departments of the House delayed her action, but she continually encouraged those girls in the class who had a vocation to this life of penance and reparation to be patient a while longer. "Our Lord will show me the way. Of that I have no doubt," she said. Before long Mme. d'Andigne gave Mother St. Euphrasia a gift of 5000 francs "for the Sister Magdalens," adding, "I realize that this amount of money is only a down payment on their future home, but it will at least give shape to our dreams."

When the Count heard of what had happened, he looked about

for some means of furthering this venture and within a few days learned that a small house and a piece of land adjoining the Convent were for sale. Enthusiastically he suggested to Mother St. Euphrasia that he act at once to secure the property.

Mother wanted that property, but she could not bring herself to sanction its purchase, not wishing to impose on the Count's generosity. In her opinion his benevolence had already been excessive. But her protests were straw men which Count de Neuville knocked over easily. The important thing, he said, was not the cost of the house and grounds; it was their practicality for Mother's purpose. "Is the house adequate as to size? Are the grounds far enough removed to provide the sort of enclosure that these Sisters must have?"

Mother's reply to these queries convinced him that any further delay would be unwise, whereupon he tripled Mme. d'Andigne's contribution and closed the transaction in the name of the Congregation, Mother St. Euphrasia signing all the necessary documents. Earlier the Count had asked "that the Magdalens have half of the ground, the other half to be used as a playground for the orphans." His concern for the needs of the children touched Mother's heart; again his foresight and good will aided her immeasurably.

But certain obstacles still remained, chief of which was the woefully small number of professed religious at Angers. With the rapid extension of their work Mother St. Euphrasia saw little hope of releasing more than one Sister for the task of training the Magdalen postulants. Even an experienced person like Sister St. Stanislaus Bedouet, whom she intended to appoint as the Mistress of the Sister Magdalens, could not be expected to carry the entire burden alone.

"Mother St. Euphrasia," the Count finally suggested, "why don't you ask Mother St. Paul at Tours to lend you a few of her professed Sister Magdalens until this work gets under way?"

"I've thought of it," Mother replied. "Having a few religious who had already been formed to that kind of life would be a tremendous help. Their example and reassurance would be invaluable. Still . . . ," Mother's sentence hung unfinished in midair.

"Still what?" the Count queried.

"Mother St. Paul might not care to assist in making this foundation."

"I think she will when she understands our situation. I'll gladly go to Tours myself and present this petition to her."

At first Mother St. Paul demurred to the Count's proposals, em-

phasizing that aspect of the life of the Sister Magdalens which pre-
vents their leaving their monastery for any but extraordinary reasons.

"In my judgment, this request comes under that heading," the
Count insisted. "I'll reserve a private coach for the Sisters and make
arrangements for them to spend their nights en route at the convents
you designate. In that way they will be comfortable and will not
interrupt their regular religious schedule."

Thus it came about that two professed Sister Magdalens and one
novice from Tours were assigned to help with the new foundation.
These three religious together with four young postulants from the
local class formed the nucleus of the first Community of consecrated
penitents in Angers.

It was fitting that the new Magdalen Monastery was first occupied
on the Feast of St. Augustine, the unregenerate youth who overcame
himself and eventually attained the spiritual heights of sainthood. In
choosing August 28 for these ceremonies Mother St. Euphrasia had
not forgotten that it was also the patronal Feast of Count Augustine
de Neuville. Two months later on the 25th of October two of the
postulants received the brown habit of Carmel "having nothing so
much at heart as to be clothed in the garb of penance." To this was
added the white veil of noviceship that symbolized turning away their
eyes from the world and its vanities. From that day forward these
Sister Magdalens were unreservedly dedicated to the spirit of reparation by praying for the conversion of sinners, and particularly for all
the works of the Good Shepherd. With a grateful heart Mother St.
Euphrasia offered a fervent thanksgiving for the gift of these young
Reparatrix Religious and joined the Community in the joyful singing
of the *Te Deum*.

Before the year ended more than a dozen young women entered
the Good Shepherd Convent as postulants. This increase was heartening to Mother St. Euphrasia after the long period of sterility when
one, and sometimes none, came in the course of an entire year. Then
on the 19th of December, an older woman of breeding and distinction
asked to be received into the Novitiate.

Mme. Cesbron de la Roche at forty-nine was a socially prominent
and wealthy widow. Since her husband's death many years previous
she had divided her time among her social obligations and the care of
her invalid mother and her two little motherless granddaughters, children of her only child. But earlier that fall her mother had died. In
the days that followed she confided in her son-in-law, "For some time

I have felt the urge to enter a convent." She hesitated momentarily, then added, "But urge is the wrong word. Conviction is much better. I am certain that I have a real call to some religious undertaking."

"You are free, my dear Mother," her son-in-law assured her. "It is my responsibility and not yours to care for my children."

At that time Mme. de Cesbron knew of the Good Shepherd Convent only by reputation. Soon she became acquainted with Mother St. Euphrasia and her work. Madame listened in rapt attention as Mother St. Euphrasia explained that "we Sisters vow to continue the work the Good Shepherd came to do . . . to seek and save the lost sheep . . . the souls He died to redeem. We take three vows of religion, as do all other Orders, but we add a fourth, which obliges us to work directly for the salvation of the souls of erring girls and women." [5]

Today older applicants are very rarely admitted to a religious Order. In 1831 the admission of a person as old as Mme. Cesbron da la Roche was rare enough to evoke widespread interest and general comment. Her age together with her social position caused tongues to wag and heads to nod. The widow of a distinguished army officer and the daughter of a former mayor of Angers could not hope to take such a step in secret. However, her conduct soon quieted the inevitable discussion and caused idle comments to crystallize into praise.

At her Clothing on February 23, 1832, the Convent Chapel overflowed with the cream of Angers society. The impressive hush was broken only by the solemn words of the officiant and the low responses of the candidate. Everyone leaned forward in eagerness as Mme. de la Roche received the name of Sister Marie Chantal de Jesus in religion. In the years ahead Mother St. Euphrasia would often refer to her as one of the pillars of the Congregation.

Following her profession Sister Marie Chantal de Jesus served as the économe or business manager of the Convent, a post for which she was well qualified as the result of her natural discernment and the practical experiences she had had as the manager of her own estates. With a flexibility of spirit that belied her years this newly professed Sister adapted herself to the conventual life, sloughing off in a seemingly effortless manner her former interests and demands. In every sense she was Mother St. Euphrasia's spiritual daughter although she was fourteen years older than the Mother Superior.

One day Mother St. Euphrasia stopped by to congratulate her new appointee on the quality of her work. "You have already taken a load off my mind. Our income continues to increase, thank God, but our demands multiply. You cannot breathe life into cold figures, but I find myself relying more and more on your knowledge and competence in regard to financial affairs. Orderly and accurate records are a necessity in any successful religious establishment."

Sister Marie Chantal de Jesus smiled. She would try her best never to disappoint Mother St. Euphrasia. "Will you have time to check my records and supplies today?" she inquired.

"Gladly, Sister," Mother replied.

For a moment the turning of the pages of the ledger was the only sound in the room. Then Mother St. Euphrasia's brow wrinkled. She looked up in a puzzled manner.

"Here is one item I do not like. According to this entry you are buying two kinds of flour—white for the Sisters and a coarser quality for our girls."

Sister Marie Chantal nodded.

Mother St. Euphrasia continued, "Sister, I cannot permit such a distinction. There shall not be two kinds of bread in this house ever. The children are to have the very best. We shall manage somehow. Should our supplies sometimes make it necessary for us to use the coarser flour, then all of us will share alike. If any differences are to be made, they are to be in favor of our children."

"I am sorry I had not understood."

Sister Marie Chantal was never to forget this incident. It served as her guide of action on many future occasions. Increasingly she grew familiar with Mother's directions regarding any gifts of foodstuffs that came to them. "Give these apples to our children." "How our orphans will enjoy these oranges!"

Over and over the *économe* noted and loved the terms of affection that Mother St. Euphrasia used whenever she talked to or about the forgotten and unwanted children under her care. Less and less she used the word "penitent." "Inmate" she considered ugly and uncharitable. "We are their Mothers," she would say; "they are our dear children."

At this point one naturally assesses the present in terms of the past. One sees these principles and instructions in operation in every Home of the Good Shepherd. Rebellious, even incorrigible, girls soon find their defenses crumbling before this sincere inclusion in Mother St. Euphrasia's world-wide family. They find it difficult to hold out long against such kindly words as "the class"; "the girls"; and "the children." They need no one to tell them that these terms are unbarbed, but convey a maternal love which few of these youthful offenders have ever known.

Upon entering the convent Sister Marie Chantal de Jesus brought with her a dowry of substance including her household goods and many beautiful vestments and sacred altar vessels. Temporarily the income from the dowry proved a real boon, but even its size was insufficient to meet the needs of the rapidly growing organization. Much still remained to be done. Neglected and broken-down fences were blots on the landscape; besides they provided no protection and permitted no privacy. Uninvited vagrants and transients made it a common practice to take a free night's lodging here on the outskirts of Angers. Their uncouth and noisy conduct upset the younger Sisters and disturbed the Mother Superior. She was not frightened—one doubts that she knew the word—but she did not like the continual violation of the convent grounds. Finally when a group of boisterous anticlericals appeared, she brought matters to a head by calling in the local police captain. A few nights later he could report that all the marauders had been routed or apprehended. Mother St. Euphrasia breathed in relief, but she had already decided that sturdy and secure walls must be built as soon as possible.

With the arrival of the recurrent spring floods the matter of the walls had to wait. The year previous safe in distant Tours, Mother St. Euphrasia had associated herself vicariously with these floods; now she was kept busy directing everyone about her so that damage could be held to a minimum. With dismay she viewed the rising of the river and the flooding of the grounds, but like a captain aboard his ship in a storm at sea, she learned what must be done before the return of a similar disaster. Finally the floods receded, leaving much illness behind. Contagious colds sent many of the children to the infirmary. During the early summer an outbreak of fever grew into a real epidemic.

Mother St. Euphrasia made daily visits to the infirmary, cheering the invalids with a smile, a prayer, or a gift. One day the Sister Infirmarian met her with these doleful words: "Everyone is gravely ill, dear Mother. I do not think that many of these girls will survive."

"Don't lose heart, Sister. We shall increase our prayers." Going from one bed to another she said repeatedly to the Sister at her side, "This child will live." "This one will recover." "A change for the better is imminent." Then she lowered her voice and said very softly, "This poor child will die."

The Sister Infirmarian gazed at her Superior in startled surprise. "But, Mother, Gertrude is improving. She is ever so much better today."

Mother St. Euphrasia only said, "She cannot live."

A few days later Gertrude died.

Then without warning dread cholera struck, sending additional patients to the overcrowded Infirmary. One of the girls, an especially defiant troublemaker, became critically ill. Within a short time her writhings suddenly ceased. Seemingly rigor mortis was ready to set in. In desperation the Sister Nurse summoned Mother St. Euphrasia. Yet Mother failed to appear, sending back instead this cryptic message, "I will go, but only if she has faith." Finally she entered the sickroom and went straight to the stricken girl's bedside. "Have confidence in God, my dear. He will support you."

Kneeling by the prostrate form she started the comforting words of the *Memorare:* "Remember, O most gracious Virgin Mary, that never was it known that anyone who fled to thy protection, implored thy help, and sought thy intercession was left unaided. . . ."

Almost immediately the girl's body twitched and her glazed eyes focused on Mother St. Euphrasia. "Please, dear Mother," she whispered faintly, "make the Sign of the Cross on my forehead."

"I will do that, my child, with Holy Water."

The girl smiled and then relaxed into a natural sleep. Some time later she opened her eyes wide and sat up unassisted. She was declared perfectly cured.

About this time Count de Neuville reopened an unfinished piece of business. "You must admit, Mother St. Euphrasia," he said, "that your present chapel is completely unsatisfactory. How can you adjust its size to the needs of your growing family? I have long wanted to build a larger chapel here out of respect to my father. Must I wait indefinitely for this privilege?"

Mother St. Euphrasia smiled. The Count made it sound as though she would be his benefactor instead of his debtor. Then she recalled a sermon of Father Gloriot, S.J., in which he said, "And thou art a little one amongst the tribes of Juda, but out of thee shall come many branches, and they shall cover the earth. Little tribe of the Good Shepherd, so poor, so lowly, so unnoticed, you shall one day be the Church's glory! May these, my words, be fulfilled." [6] Even when he was preaching, Mother St. Euphrasia had looked around and wondered how she could ever hope to extend her Community without first enlarging the center of their devotional life. Now the Count's offer brought Father Gloriot's words into the realm of reality.

The Count spoke again: "May I undertake this project?"

"I shall be happy, if you will. However, you must restrict your generosity." Mother wanted to express her gratitude more fully, but she knew that the Count would turn aside any personal acclaim. In all probability he would say, "Don't thank me; it is not to you I give. It is to our Blessed Lady." "His humility was only equalled by his devotion to the Mother of God, for which he found an outlet at the Home of Our Lady of Charity." [7]

At his insistence Mother St. Euphrasia drew up a rough sketch for the proposed edifice. The Count looked at it carefully and then exclaimed, "Forty choir stalls, Mother St. Euphrasia? . . . why you must have at least two hundred. Before long even that number will be too small. This Order is a growing, not a static, thing."

Never had Mother seen her benefactor so disturbed. Why he was almost angry!

Following this interview he worked out a tentative plan on a much larger scale and brought it to her for approval. She observed with special interest that the choir had been projected so that it could be made to accommodate as many as three hundred Sisters. At the time that number seemed out of line with their humble status but she could not deflate the Count's enthusiasm, his faith that the work of the Good Shepherd would increase and multiply. "Unnumbered souls," he said, "will be salvaged and redeemed through the efforts of the Sisters trained here."

Construction was soon under way. On July 17 Monseigneur Montault blessed the cornerstone of the building that was destined to become the home base and model chapel for all future Good Shepherd Convents.

In planning the chapel Mother St. Euphrasia proposed to M. Desnoyers, the architect, that the church be built in the form of a cross with the altar erected in the center at which point four separate arms or smaller chapels would converge. The Sisters' choir was to be located at the head of the cross facing the altar with the Magdalens' chapel in the one arm and the Girls' chapel in the other. The remaining section was to be given its own entrance and exit so that the laity could attend services at will without inconveniencing the religious and the class. This cruciform church would give each department of the House its own chapel. Yet it would enable everyone to assemble for the various services under a common roof.

From then until the present this type of architecture has been used in the Good Shepherd Convents. One knows even before he sees it that the Good Shepherd chapel will be patterned after the original model. In some instances it is an adaptation, depending upon the absence or presence of the Sister Magdalens. But the chapels always radiate from the main sanctuary with the Sisters' choir and the Girls' chapel occupying separate wings.

There was one unhappy event amid the general rejoicing. Abbé Perché, at the conclusion of his first year among them, was transferred to the parish of Murs prior to his departure for an assignment in America. Although his going left a void, he would continue to serve their interests wherever he was located. In the years that followed he was to send many postulants to the Angers Novitiate and nine years later one of them [8] was to found the first American Convent in Louisville, Kentucky (1842).

Abbé Perché's successor was M. Mainguy, a friend of Mme. d'Andigne, who had known about the work of the Sisters in advance of his appointment as their chaplain. The next ten years were to find him very closely identified with the trials and rewards that lay in store for Mother St. Euphrasia and her Community.

In the meantime the building of the new chapel progressed rapidly. Whenever the weather permitted, the Sisters worked each morning as volunteer carpenters' aides long in advance of the arrival of the workmen themselves. With Mother St. Euphrasia in charge they cleared away accumulated debris, salvaged the usable parts of an old abandoned wall on the premises, and carried the stone blocks some distance to the new building site. Sometimes Mother St. Euphrasia thought of those days when she and her little friends, Clementine and Sophie, had cleaned up the neglected shrine of St. Philbert at Noirmoutier.

Often the Sisters used pick and shovel in attacking with vigor tasks that normally fell within a man's domain, but this group of ardent white-robed religious "tucked up" their skirts for convenience and pushed wheelbarrows back and forth. At first the laborers were mystified at the way in which their work sped forward. Who had come while they were gone? What did this all mean? Soon they became accustomed to seeing the task they left at dusk advance seemingly of itself during their absence. Naturally they questioned Mother St. Euphrasia, but she only smiled and made some remark about "angels." Later no one could actually repeat what she had said. But the men quickly caught the eagerness of her spirit and agreed that they would do their best to complete the chapel in record time. Their work was finished in slightly less than ten months. The dedication ceremonies held on May 14, 1833, when the chapel was given the name of the Immaculate Conception more than repaid Count de Neuville for the amount the edifice had cost him (26,500 francs).

For lack of room the Novitiate had recently been forced to discourage young women who sought to be admitted as postulants. With a total of forty persons already in residence the Convent was much too crowded and uncomfortable. The Sisters minimized their personal inconveniences, but their benefactor viewed them with distress. Once more he came to the rescue and had a two-story building erected, with cloisters and sixty cells divided by wide corridors. By midsummer it was ready for occupancy.

In the building they vacated Mother St. Euphrasia established a new branch of her work which she called the "Preservates" or the "Preservation Class." The purpose of this department was to shelter homeless young children from the perils of the world until they reached their majority or were assured proper care by responsible adults. These children ranged from three to eighteen years of age and were not necessarily orphans but unsupervised or neglected. Occasionally a parent or relative would place a child with the Sisters, but more often the children, left homeless as a result of family emergencies, were brought to the Convent by child-caring agencies. From the beginning the Preservates had no association of any kind with the older or delinquent girls, living, playing, and studying apart from them and having their own section in chapel. Like the Directress of the Girls or the Mistress of the Sister Magdalens, the Sister entrusted with their care devoted her time exclusively to them.

This department would later prove to be an active division in many of the Convents of the Good Shepherd. Today this group exists under different names according to modern parlance and the practice of the Province in which each Home is located. But irrespective of labels the work of character formation and religious training among these younger girls proceeds effectively.

In the early days Mother St. Euphrasia, looking to the future of the Institute, often received postulants without dowry once she was convinced of the stability of their vocation. Ordinarily, this matter of a dowry is a reasonable and practical requisite for membership in a religious community. According to general custom a postulant brings with her a dowry—the amount commonly specified in the official Constitutions. On or before the Clothing Ceremony these funds are deposited with the Community as the trustee. They are then invested and the interest applied to the support of the Community at large but not until the Sister dies does the title of the dowry pass to the Congregation. During her lifetime the original deposit is kept intact so that it can be returned to the individual should she leave the Community, no matter what might be the cause of her withdrawal.

Mother St. Euphrasia's willingness to admit postulants without a dowry obviously contributed to the steady growth of the Novitiate at Angers. At the same time it brought about the straitened circumstances amid which the Sisters then lived. Despite Mme. de la Roche's income and the sporadic gifts of well-wishers and kindly friends, there were many days when the menu was monotonous and the servings slim. No one was ever seriously hungry, but the devious means used to "fill the pot" could have been supplied only by a watchful Providence. More times than were tallied the Sisters in the kitchen sent word to their Superior that the larder was completely empty. "What shall we do?" they would ask. "There is absolutely nothing at all for us to eat."

Mother's inevitable answer was, "Only have faith, and the Lord will provide for our wants."

On one of these occasions Mother St. Euphrasia walked over to the Sister Magdalens' garden and greeted the Sister working there.

"How is the supply of beans today?" she inquired.

"Very low, Mother," the Sister admitted sadly.

"I'm sorry, for we must have beans for our evening meal. Won't you please go out and try to gather some for our common dish?"

"But, Mother, I'm sure there are none. I picked all we had yesterday. It will be several days before we have another crop."

"Don't think about that, Sister," Mother said. "I'd like you to look anyway. You may find enough to combine with potatoes for our supper. Otherwise, we'll have nothing but potatoes. And our supply of them is too low to feed us all."

"I'll try, Mother St. Euphrasia," the Sister Magdalen said resignedly.

Soon other Magdalens joined the search first saying a little prayer "that Mother will not be disappointed." In the beginning they could find no pods anywhere. "How could there be any," the Sister gardener mused, "when I stripped the plants bare only yesterday?" Then to her amazement she saw a full pod here and there. In excitement she cried out to her companions, "Let's each look in a different direction. Maybe we'll find enough beans after all." Their search was successful, for when they reassembled and measured their harvest, they had more than enough to feed everyone, including the girls and the Preservates. The rest of their lives these Sister Magdalens could never be dissuaded from believing that this incident had been a minor miracle.

Most interestingly this was not an isolated experience. Many other times at Mother's request the Sister gardener looked for food which she knew had not been there an hour ago. Without exception she never failed to return with a quantity of vegetables sufficiently large for the purpose at hand. No wonder she was inclined to call these happenings "Mother's miracles." Mother, however, disagreed. "It is the Providence of God," she insisted. "Without that we would have gone hungry."

Undoubtedly such experiences underlay the following entry in Mother's early writings:

"We are poor, it is true, and we have great needs, but a miraculous Providence watches over us. . . . It may be said that our Congregation is but Providence and miracles! We have no money to meet our flour bill, but God will come to our aid. I have a habit of repeating, 'Jesus, Father of the poor; Jesus, Treasure of the faithful'; and when I have said this, I feel confident all will be paid." [9]

IX

Angers, 1833-1835

*I am come to cast fire upon the earth, and what will I but that it
be kindled?*
Luke 12:49. *Also:* Communion Prayer, *Feast of St. Ignatius Loyola*

CERTAIN years in everyone's life stand out above others.
Eighteen hundred and thirty-three was one of those years for
Mother St. Euphrasia, for it was then that she reached out beyond
Angers to establish her first Good Shepherd daughter foundation.

A number of factors caused Mother St. Euphrasia to view with
increasing dissatisfaction the limitations imposed upon her as the
head of a completely independent religious organization. The concept
of adjusting the apostolate of the Good Shepherd to the changing
conditions of the times began to take form when she was handicapped by the lack of enough professed religious capable of directing
the different departments at Angers. Illness had attacked some of the
professed Sisters just when a Directress of the Class was urgently
needed. Consequently Mother St. Euphrasia was compelled to turn
for help to other Houses of the Refuge.

In vain she asked Tours for the loan of additional personnel. Then
with Bishop Montault's approval she traveled to Nantes to present
her problem to the Community Council. Nantes, however, withheld
assistance and Mother St. Euphrasia, disappointed and weary,
returned home to work out some kind of solution to her problems.

Count de Neuville found it hard to believe that Mother's appeals
had been denied. Usually calm and even-tempered he grew indignant.
"Your Order should be able to meet such emergencies," he said. "It

127

should have a Mother House to which a convent in need could turn. As I see it, an interchange of services and personnel would benefit everyone."

His words voiced Mother St. Euphrasia's thoughts. For the present, though, she had the immediate situation at Angers to resolve. She had herself taken charge of the Novitiate because she believed that the future stability of the Angers foundation lay primarily in the hands of the novices. Soon she appointed some of the most responsible among them to posts held by professed Sisters. This act released the older and experienced religious for more important assignments. After that the work grew apace. Then a day arrived when Mother St. Euphrasia was asked by Father Basil Moreau of Le Mans to establish a home in that city for wayward girls and unprotected children.

Twice before overtures for a foundation at Le Mans had been made. One had come when Mother St. Euphrasia was Superior at Tours; the second, in March, 1832. Neither time, however, had she been in a position to accept. Now with the third request she agreed to found a convent in Le Mans although she well knew that her initial efforts must necessarily be on a small scale. Father Moreau, serving for his Bishop, Monseigneur Carron,[1] understood this limitation and the negotiations proceeded.

In February Mother St. Euphrasia went to Le Mans. Satisfied with the prospects there, she returned to Angers and made haste to complete the arrangements requisite to the new foundation. On April 18 three choir nuns and a lay Sister were sent in advance; on the 29th Mother St. Euphrasia accompanied by the rest of the party followed. On May 3 the formal ceremonies of installation were held after which seven Sisters[2] officially took up their residence in a small house on Arenes Street. As had been expected, Father Moreau was named the ecclesiastical director of this foundation.

In the beginning Father Moreau was their ardent champion. A pamphlet[3] that he prepared and distributed far and wide emphasized his eagerness to make the purposes and needs of the Community more widely and favorably known.

The three classes composing the Community are entirely separated, each one having its own choir, workroom dormitory, and garden. The orphans are entrusted to Mistresses who give them special care, remaining with them day and night, forming them to a life which is simple, modest, and useful. They have no communication with the penitents who in turn are separated from the Religious by a wall; so that the penitents have no relations except with one another and with the Religious who govern them and remain with them constantly. Their occupation consists in sewing, embroidering, in attending to the orders for work received from outside, all in accordance with the ability of each one. The penitents are kept from all useless introspection by the succession of their daily exercises. Their varied activities distract them from evil and remind them of good. . . . There is not an hour of the day when the uniformity of their life, apparently so monotonous, is not broken into by prayers and hymns. All necessary religious instruction is generously given to them, and it is certain that there are but few who do not acquire a taste for a virtuous and useful life.

Such are the important services which the Sisters of the Good Shepherd render to the Department of the Sarthe,[4] services which will be appreciated more and more by noble and generous hearts. Thanks to the devotion of these truly heroic souls, when a young woman of weak rather than depraved character comes to shed bitter tears over her faults and her dishonor, she finds sympathetic and charitable hearts to weep with her, to raise her up, and to restore her to her heart-broken family whose joy and edification she becomes. Thanks also to the charity of the faithful of the diocese, to whom alone is due the success of this enterprise, poor dependent children [5] who are without means and who are exposed to the wickedness of the world will find an assured asylum against the attacks of misery and the seductions of vice.

Unfortunately a grave misunderstanding later arose between Father Moreau and Mother St. Euphrasia. Rather early it became evident that Father Moreau regarded himself as the Founder of the Le Mans Community having been designated as such in the capitulary record,[6] but Mother St. Euphrasia, having developed Le Mans from the House at Angers, naturally considered herself as its rightful foundress. Le Mans, to her, was the first-born of the many foundations she hoped to send out later from Angers. However, no serious diversity of opinion arose until after the death of the Bishop of Le Mans in late August of that same year.[7] Meanwhile several important things occurred.

In May, Monseigneur Montault wrote to Rome requesting that a Mother House for the Congregation be established in Angers with a central novitiate where young women could be trained for other foundations. His action had come about only after lengthy discussions with several of the clergy including Father Perché, their former chaplain, and Father Vaures, who held the appointment of Penitentiary for the French language at St. Peter's in Rome.[8] All of them saw eye to eye on the possibilities of service that a Generalate could provide. Once in operation the Bishop knew that a great Mother Community could distribute Sisters advantageously according to their talents and the needs of the convents that beckoned them.

In her heart Mother St. Euphrasia felt that St. John Eudes himself would approve of the expansion. She had no intention of acting for any of the existing Refuges; she only wanted to advance the common good and promote the unity of any houses that were to be founded from Angers. Consequently when the Bishop had communicated with Rome, he submitted a supplementary article to be incorporated in the Constitutions of the Sisters. Briefly this proposed article known as "Constitution Fifty-two" stated that all the houses founded from the Monastery of Our Lady of Charity of the Good Shepherd of Angers were to be subordinate to it and be administered by a Superior General, who was also to be the Superior of the Monastery and reside there. Pending an answer Monseigneur Montault recognized this provision that "all houses that shall be founded from the house at Angers shall depend on and mutually support each other."

Although this action was in the final stages of preparation during the establishment of the Le Mans foundation, it was not completed until shortly after that event transpired. The recorded evidence states that "the Bishop of Angers and the Sisters destined for Le Mans signed this article, and the Bishop of Le Mans gave his adhesion." [9] Presumedly though "Father Moreau was not made cognizant of this design." [10]

In September, 1833, Father Moreau met with Mother St. Euphrasia in Angers. In essence he approved of the idea of the Generalate, but he recommended that it be stayed until the consent of all the Refuges had been obtained. Then, he said, the Federation could be incorporated in the names of all.

Confident that such unanimity might take years to effect, Mother St. Euphrasia found herself unable to accept this recommendation. The unfortunate controversy that ensued brought travail and anguish to two devoted people. Mother St. Euphrasia called her first foundation, "My Calvary of Le Mans"; and Father Moreau, distressed at what he believed was an unjustified resistance to his rightful authority, severed his association with Mother St. Euphrasia [11] adhering thereafter to the Constitutions given the Congregation of the Refuge by St. John Eudes.

Time has proved that Mother St. Euphrasia's plan was separated entirely from selfish motives and desire of personal acclaim. Looking back from today's vantage ground her concept of securing administrative unity marks her in tune with the changing conditions of the times. In retrospect her motives cannot be doubted. Sadly, though, many of her contemporaries feared and opposed her aspirations. That Father Moreau should have been one of these persons will always be a matter of regret to three groups of religious: The Congregation of Holy Cross and the Marianite Sisters of Holy Cross, both of which he subsequently founded; and Mother St. Euphrasia's own Congregation, the Sisters of the Good Shepherd of Angers.

Meanwhile in Tours there was a growing feeling of antagonism against Mother St. Euphrasia. Many termed her a dangerous innovator bent on distorting the intentions of St. John Eudes. A number of the clergy and religious appealed to Monseigneur de Montblanc as Archbishop of Tours to end this matter before it got completely out of hand. Was Mother St. Euphrasia, they asked, not subject to him? The fact that the Bishop of Angers had already written to Rome only served as a further irritant.

Wearied and angered by these mounting complaints, the Archbishop decided on immediate and drastic action. He would recall Mother St. Euphrasia and all the Sisters who had gone from Tours to Angers. Furthermore he would go to Angers himself to deliver this ultimatum. Such defiance as theirs could no longer be tolerated.

Mother St. Euphrasia was horrified by this pronouncement. She was hurt by the epithets hurled against her and frightened by the unjust attitude that prompted them. Certainly she had never dreamed of resisting or infuriating the Archbishop. But furious he was. His wrath had reached almost a white heat by the time he arrived at the episcopal residence of Bishop Montault. Reluctantly he agreed to administer Confirmation to the children at the Good Shepherd Home. At the conclusion of the ceremony, the children having been dismissed, the Archbishop in the presence of thirty or more of the clergy including the ecclesiastical Superior of Le Mans bluntly announced his intention to recall Mother St. Euphrasia and the pioneer Sisters. Then he added that he wanted to speak to the Mother Superior in private.

With courteous composure Mother St. Euphrasia replied: "Your Excellency, I respectfully implore you to permit Bishop Montault and the members of the Council to be present at this interview."

Her statement caught Archbishop Montblanc off guard. For a time he forgot the dignity of his great office. The denunciations and false accusations he uttered were unseemly. Such terms as "schemer," "innovator," "stubborn servant," and "selfish actor" fell angrily from his lips. Everyone present sat stunned before this barrage, so unbecoming to a high dignitary of the Church. Upon the conclusion of his tirade, an embarrassed silence followed.

Then Mother St. Euphrasia begged leave to speak. Her calm manner and steady voice were in contrast to the Archbishop's impassioned attack. Point by point she refuted the charges made against her, insisting that she was convinced that it was the will of God that she should establish the Generalate and extend the work of St. John Eudes. "An interchange of subjects between the Houses will justify our training large numbers of religious, for then they can be distributed more effectively." Mother St. Euphrasia ended her defense by saying, "My final plea is that I long to labor for souls on earth. I feel consumed with zeal whenever I think of winning hearts to God. I have no desire, Your Excellency, but to do good to others and to add to the glory of God."

The Archbishop remained unmoved, declaring most vigorously that he still desired to see Mother St. Euphrasia alone.

At these words she knelt humbly before him. "Your Excellency, I will listen with submission to anything you may see fit to say, but it must be in the presence of my Bishop. I wish him to know everything."

Her words were a signal for a renewed attack. When it had subsided, Monseigneur Montault spoke for the first time, reminding the Archbishop of the *Exeat* which he had signed two years earlier. That act, he said, had automatically transferred Mother St. Euphrasia to his ecclesiastical jurisdiction. He concluded, "I beg your pardon a thousand times over, if I have offended you, but I can assure you that I never in the least intended to do that."

Temporarily the Archbishop was appeased. He admitted that he had completely forgotten about the *Exeat* and added, "Had I foreseen the question of a Generalate, that document would never have been drawn up."

But the matter did not end there. The next day Bishop Montault forwarded a copy of the *Exeat* to Archbishop Montblanc accompanied by a letter in support of Mother St. Euphrasia. Despite such evidence the Archbishop continued to oppose the Generalate in his correspondence with the Bishop of Angers.

Mother St. Euphrasia's heart was crushed by the attitude of one she had hitherto held in high esteem. For three weeks she was disconsolate. Then a letter from Monseigneur Fustier,[12] a Vicar General of Tours, written on August 10, upheld the stand she had taken. He wrote: "After having read over the permission you received on the 20th of May, 1831, we, that is Monseigneur Dugier and I, are of the opinion from its tenor that your conscience may be at rest, that your worthy Bishop is acting within his rights in keeping you in his Diocese."

This letter, coming from the Archbishop's House at Tours, preceded the arrival of Monseigneur Montblanc's historic reply to the Bishop of Angers in which he wrote: "I voluntarily renounce my rights over Mother Mary of St. Euphrasia Pelletier and the other religious who left Tours with her." [13]

Now for the first time since the Archbishop's stormy visit Mother St. Euphrasia began to feel at peace.

Six months later arrangements were made for two additional foundations. When the House at Poitiers was established on November 12, 1833, the act of Nominations specified that the Sisters sent there should remain dependent upon Angers. This stipulation formed a precedent which has remained in force ever since.

Upon their immediate arrival in Poitiers the Sisters, with Mother St. Stanislaus Bedouet as their Superior, lived at the Convent [14] of the Sisters of the Sacred Heart until their own house could be made ready. This they occupied on the 3rd of December. When the news reached Mother St. Euphrasia she wrote in happiness: "How great is God's work, and what lights He has vouchsafed to give you concerning it! O holy feast of the Apostle of the Indies! This day, feast of St. Francis Xavier, will ever remain precious to me, the day you took possession of your house. . . . Our Sisters here all rejoiced, and tomorrow, we are to make a general Communion for the dear foundation at Poitiers." [15]

Grenoble in the southeast of France was the site of the third Good Shepherd Foundation, the Sisters arriving there in bitterly cold weather on December 23. They spent Christmas with the Ursuline Sisters remaining with them until December 26. Mother St. Euphrasia's first letter to them revealed her concern for their welfare. "I went through much last night at the Crib. I did not know of your arrival. I pictured you in the midst of snow and mountains. Our benefactors and benefactresses all pray for you. Courage! Seek after God in your great work, and be free from human respect." [16]

Both of these foundations were begun in extreme poverty. In May, 1834, Mother St. Euphrasia accompanied by Mme. d'Andigne, who now made her permanent home at the Convent, and Monseigneur Abbé Mainguy, traveled to Poitiers. There Mother St. Euphrasia met a dynamic Jesuit priest, Father Barthès, who immediately became her advocate, later serving to bring about the establishment of the fourth foundation in the city of Metz.

Grenoble presented almost insurmountable problems. After six months of poverty and trials, Mother St. Euphrasia thought it wise to recall the Sisters and close this foundation. Monseigneur Montault, however, was opposed to such action saying, "The storm will pass, and then there will come a great calm." Somehow Mother St. Euphrasia managed to keep the foundation open, but she was widely berated for her rash judgment and her impractical tenacity. In one letter to the Grenoble Superior she wrote: "Many persons have said to me, 'You would make the foundation of Grenoble. So much the worse for you now.' " [17] Another letter written to the Superior at Poitiers said: "You know what sorrows we have had about the foundation at Grenoble; they have been as great as the sea. Every post brought us a journal of misfortunes and sadness." [18]

A year passed before the tide turned in favor of Grenoble. Then the Bishop tardily came to their aid. Soon Mother St. Euphrasia could write: "I assure you, I never saw anything like it. It is a marvel of love." And again, "I believe that thanks to the Cross, this house of Grenoble will flourish. . . . The Lord Himself has justified you because you do the work of His love. . . . Poor children! You might have perished, you have been saved by Jesus and Mary. Oh, it has touched me! Now I must go to bless God for His mercies." [19]

Three years had elapsed since Mother St. Euphrasia's return to Angers. In the spring of 1834 shortly before the Feast of Pentecost the Superiors of Le Mans, Poitiers, and Grenoble assembled for the scheduled chapter elections. Except for her own ballot Mother St. Euphrasia was unanimously re-elected to her second term of office. When the election was announced, she immediately dedicated her charge to the Mother of God as the real Superior of the Sisters of Our Lady of Charity of the Good Shepherd.

Two months later Le Mans withdrew from Angers to assume its role as an independent Convent of the Refuge under the direction of Father Basil Moreau. As a mother mourns over the loss of her first-born, Mother St. Euphrasia's heart was saddened by this separation. She had seen its approach, but until Le Mans actually declared its intention to withdraw she had hoped that such a finality might be avoided.

As was to be expected a torrent of opposition rained down on Mother St. Euphrasia. For a time the proponents of the separation appeared relentless in denouncing one, whose motives they had so clearly misunderstood. Later, however, a beautiful friendship was renewed between the heads of the Le Mans Refuge and the Angers Convent.

While Mother St. Euphrasia was struggling with all these major problems, she still faced the responsibility of meeting the day-by-day difficulties pertaining to the administration of her own Convent. This ongoing responsibility is exemplified in the case of Gabrielle, an especially obstreperous young woman, who was threatening to destroy the morale of the class. For several years prior to her admission Gabrielle had supported herself by theft. Cleverer than most, she had successfully evaded the law until one of her male companions apprehended by the police had named her as an accomplice. Upon investigation they had found Gabrielle's room the cache for the stolen goods. Action was immediate, and Gabrielle was soon brought to the Sisters of the Good Shepherd for help and re-education. At first she appeared to be amenable and co-operative, but when she was assigned a task she suddenly rebelled. "Do manual work? Are you crazy? Why, I haven't worked in years. Believe me, I don't intend to start now."

Patiently the Sister in charge listened and then proceeded as though Gabrielle hadn't spoken. But nothing she did could change this defiant girl's attitude.

"I'll stay here because I have to," Gabrielle cried out. "But I won't work, and that's final."

Her obstinacy held for several days during which time the ingenuity of the Directress was worn thin. Finally she consulted Mother St. Euphrasia about the girl's attitude.

A firm believer in the therapy of work, Mother St. Euphrasia smiled and said, "Let's reverse our procedure. Expose this child to work, but under no circumstances, let her do anything at all. When your efforts cease and her protests go unheeded, she will begin to adjust her thinking. Meanwhile, love her. Underneath that outer layer of self is a priceless immortal soul. Its beauty transcends its exterior casing."

When Gabrielle next saw the Directress, she called out, "You won't be able to make me work. Can't you understand?"

"Of course I do, my child," the Sister replied kindly.

Gabrielle's mouth fell open in amazement.

"You mean I don't have to work?"

"That's what I mean. In fact, I won't permit it."

"What do you want me to do then?"

"Come with me and I'll show you."

With Gabrielle frankly curious the Sister led her to the sewing room where the girls were mending the orphans' clothes. Indicating a comfortable chair near an open window she said, "Sit there, dear, and forget all about work. The other girls will do your share."

The truth of that last sentence and the contrast between her own position and that of the busy girls about her were effective curatives. By the end of the day Gabrielle was less insolent and by the end of the next, she was asking for the privilege of working too.

"Oh no, my dear," the Sister said. "Don't you remember my promise that you wouldn't be asked to do anything?"

"But I'm the one that's asking it, Sister. I'd much rather do what the other girls are doing."

For a few days longer Sister remained deaf to Gabrielle's plea. Finally convinced that this girl had learned the values of humility and industry, she consented to her doing her share of the day's mending.

This incident together with many others caused Mother St. Euphrasia to write later: "As to idlers, we must use every means to correct them—idleness is the mother of vice. We should try to discover a recompense or a punishment (the recompense is preferable) to stimulate them to work by hope or fear. It would not always be wise to correct them at once; we should rather lead them by degrees to do as much work as their companions. . . ." [20]

Throughout the summer of 1834 Mother St. Euphrasia was alternately an object of attack and defense. Many letters and petitions were sent to Rome, their contents depending upon the writers' convictions. Feelings ran high and even one of the Vicar Generals of Angers found himself allied with the opposition. Adroitly he secured Bishop Montault's permission to demand the return of the newly drawn Constitutions. Sister Marie Chantal de Jesus, serving as Sister Assistant during Sister St. Stanislaus' absence, thwarted this action by giving the precious document to a trusted friend outside the Convent. Then she could say in all honesty, "The document you seek is no longer here."

This episode inspired Sister Marie Chantal de Jesus to write to Cardinal de Gregorio, then the Prefect of the Roman Congregation of Bishops and Regulars, portraying in minute detail the situation as she knew it. In addition, she wrote a series of letters to other eminent ecclesiastical personages in Rome, many of whom knew her directly or by reputation.

On July 17 Cardinal de Gregorio's reply reached Angers, bringing hope and encouragement to the distraught Community. Although he suggested that a happy solution would eventually be reached, he reminded Sister Marie Chantal de Jesus that any action taken by the Holy Father would be deferred until he had studied all the pertinent evidence. That would, of course, require time. Rome, he wrote, acts slowly and wisely. Meanwhile the Cardinal saw no reason why the Sisters should not establish convents depending upon Angers. Their Bishop's permission, he reminded them, was sufficient authorization.

Fortified with that permission Mother St. Euphrasia went ahead with the preliminary arrangements for a foundation at Metz, an old walled city located on the banks of the Moselle River. She gave credit to Father Barthès, S.J., for this particular foundation for immediately upon his transfer from Poitiers to Metz he had actively espoused her cause, convincing Monseigneur Besson, the Bishop of Metz, of the efficacy of the work of the Sisters of the Good Shepherd among women offenders and juvenile delinquents. This work Father Barthès knew well. Only a short time before he had conducted a retreat for the religious of the Good Shepherd at Angers. During his visit to the Mother House he had an opportunity to observe the skillful organization and operation of five different departments working together in harmonious unity.

On the eve of the Assumption three Sisters [21] left Angers for Metz, arriving there four weary days later. To this foundation Mother St. Euphrasia wrote many times saying, "You, I think, will dry our tears and bring to pass the triumph of the Generalate." And again, "Preserve our holy work of the Generalate . . . make this foundation succeed, my dear daughters."

The day following the departure of these Sisters Mother St. Euphrasia was overcome by an urge to write to Rome in her own defense. Until now she had suffered in silence, but on this occasion she could not quiet the idea that possessed her.

The entire Community was gathered in choir for the Solemn Vespers on the Feast of the Assumption. Just as the *Magnificat* was intoned, Mother St. Euphrasia found herself unable to hold back her tears. Leaving the direction of the Office to the Sister Assistant, she hurried to her cell and wept unrestrainedly. This experience dismayed her, for never could she remember having similarly lost control of herself. But she continued to cry on until she was emotionally and physically exhausted. After a brief period of rest she felt refreshed and wonderfully renewed in hope. A peace, unlike any she had known since Archbishop Montblanc's dreadful denunciation a year ago, now descended upon her. That peace gave her the strength she needed to write the most important letter of her life. It was as though a voice within her was saying: "You must pen this letter now—today. Time is of the essence. Do not wait." Stirred by these words of command, she sat down at her desk and poured out her story humbly and concisely.

She directed her message to a Cardinal, knowing that his office would bring him in frequent contact with the Pope, but she had no particular Cardinal in mind. Although her acquaintance with Rome and the Curia was almost nonexistent, she wrote from her heart, beginning her letter with the same words of praise which only a short time before had sent her from the chapel: "My soul doth magnify the Lord; and my spirit hath rejoiced in God, my Saviour." "Your Eminence," she concluded, "I desire nothing but the greater glory of God. Should the Sovereign Pontiff and your Eminence perceive that there are obstacles to the erection of a Generalate, I most humbly submit."

Such were the opening and closing thoughts of this important missive, the body of which explained her conviction that a Generalate would result in a greater opportunity to help save the lost ones of the earth. She realized, she said, that the concept of a Generalate would not appeal to everyone—many religious would prefer the anchorage of one convent for their entire lifetime—but she outlined in ordered detail the manifold advantages she believed a Generalate to hold, emphasizing her desire to make the goodness of God known beyond the borders of any one convent or city. Every word that she wrote revealed her singlehearted desire to labor for others.

At last the letter was finished, but she wondered to whom it should be sent. Some particular Cardinal had to be selected, but Mother St. Euphrasia had no idea how to go about choosing one from many. Leaving her cell, she sought advice of the first person she met. This happened to be Abbé Jules Morel, who came weekly to instruct the Novices.

"Good afternoon, Father. Perhaps you can help me."

"What is your problem, Mother St. Euphrasia?"

"I need to send a letter to the Cardinal who is in closest contact with the Holy Father. Do you know which member of the Sacred College that would be?"

"Yes, Mother, I do. His name is Cardinal Odescalchi."

"What is his position?"

"He has lately been given the post of Cardinal Vicar to Pope Gregory XVI."

Once more an indescribable feeling of peace filled her heart. Now she knew beyond doubt that her letter should go to the Vicar General of His Holiness.

Later when her good friend Monseigneur Regnier called and heard of Mother's temerity, he said abruptly, "What folly! Women know nothing of the Roman Courts. Your letter will go from bureau to bureau, and at length come back to you looking like a rag. . . ." [22]

Mother St. Euphrasia refused to be discouraged, for an extraordinary thing had occurred only the day before. Upon awakening that morning she had shared this comforting experience with the Sisters; and more than a score of years later she recorded it for posterity.

"One night I had just fallen to sleep, much more quietly than usual, when it seemed to me I saw a prelate whom I did not know. He was dressed like a Cardinal. His countenance was gentle and holy; his whole person inspired respect. He said to me: 'Fear nothing, my daughter; your work will be approved. God has chosen me to be its protector.' After these words he disappeared, leaving me full of trust, filled with confidence and consolation." [23]

Two months later Cardinal Odescalchi's reply reached Angers. Dated October 28, 1834, it brought the good news that, "while awaiting the time when your petition will be presented to the Pope for his decision—after which you will hear from me—I can say with certainty, that you will obtain what you ask. Get your Bishop to write immediately to the Holy Father. On receipt of this letter, I will at once communicate to the proper quarters on your behalf. After that I assure you, the business will soon be concluded." [24]

When the Congregation of Bishops and Regulars met later in Rome, it was in unanimous accord to approve the petition that had been received to establish the Generalate in Angers and agreed that the petition should be sent to the Cardinals for their approval. At the final meeting of this Council, Cardinal Odescalchi read Mother St. Euphrasia's letter aloud. Everyone was deeply impressed by its clarity and charity. At no time had she mentioned any of her adversaries by name. Such an omission spoke eloquently in her favor.

Impressed by Mother St. Euphrasia's letter, Father Anthony Kohlman, S.J., a consultor privileged to be present at these deliberations, spoke forcefully in support of the petition saying, "The truth is here."

Later when the Cardinals had acted favorably on the petition "that all the Houses of the Good Shepherd founded in France should be under the authority of a General Government," Father Kohlman was heard again. Turning respectfully to Cardinal Odescalchi he requested, "I humbly beg your Eminence, to change the word 'France' into that of the 'Universe.' "

"Do you wish to make of this Congregation another Society of Jesus?"

"Yes, Your Eminence, you have expressed my views."

"So shall it be," the Cardinal answered. "A work such as this should indeed be universal."

Shortly after this decision the Cardinals met with the Sovereign Pontiff for the purpose of petitioning him to approve their recommendation that the Generalate be officially ratified.

"Most Holy Father," the spokesman said, "we are of one heart and one voice in favor of the Congregation of the Good Shepherd."

"Then I also give it my heart and my voice," Pope Gregory XVI declared.

That same day in Angers the Sisters were chatting amiably at their noon recreation when they were startled by a stroke from the great bell that hung in the chapel tower. They looked at one another in open amazement when a second stroke was heard, and then a third. The reverberations of the bell hung in the air as they sought to learn why it had sounded at this unusual hour. What was its message? Everyone was mystified—the Angelus was over; the first Office of the afternoon not yet due. Mother St. Euphrasia questioned the official bellringer, but she could offer no explanation. In bewilderment she wondered who had interfered with her assigned task. A thorough investigation proved fruitless. Clearly no one at the convent had rung the bell and no stranger had been seen thereabouts.

Later it was learned that at that very time on January 16, 1835, in distant Rome, Pope Gregory XVI had affixed his signature to the

Brief establishing the Generalate of the Congregation of the Good Shepherd of Angers—and of the Universe.

Both Father Kohlman, S.J., and Father Vaures of the Conventuals, immediately informed the Bishop of Angers that the Decree had been approved. Father Vaures wrote: "It will console Your Lordship and those poor Sisters who have had to suffer so much. You will see that not only are they being granted the solemn Brief for which they ask, but there is talk of their being called here, to Rome." [25]

Bishop Montault lost no time in sending this news to the Convent where the rejoicing was unanimous. Indeed, Mother St. Euphrasia was in "an ecstasy."

Father Vaures, being a friend of both Sister Marie Chantal de Jesus and Mme. d'Andigne, kept them advised in regard to subsequent happenings in Rome. In one letter to Sister Marie Chantal he wrote: "God be praised! My dear Sister, sing to the Lord a new canticle; bless His Holy Name for He has granted your desires. . . . The question is settled: you will have a General, and nobody will be able to trouble you any more. One of the most influential of the Cardinals told me that he considered it a real miracle that we should have obtained so advantageous a decision in so short a time,[26] and so promptly, in spite of the great opposition."

On February 18 the Decree was forwarded to Bishop Montault, reaching him a week later. Father Regnier was now chosen to serve as the Bishop's courier. The Sisters found it hard to control their inner excitement as they assembled in the choir to hear what Father Regnier would say. They leaned forward expectantly as he read aloud the words of the Papal Decree. His voice was choked with emotion; their eyes were flooded with tears. As one they felt inclined to say with the Psalmist, "Clap your hands, all ye peoples, shout unto God with the voice of joy." With happy and grateful hearts they pledged a continuing thanksgiving to the Giver of all good gifts, who had bestowed this special gift upon them. Later in the Community room gathered around Mother St. Euphrasia, they gave way to their own personal delight. The words spilled from them spontaneously as they repeatedly exclaimed, "Isn't it wonderful?" "Can this really be true?" "It has actually happened at last!" "God be praised!"

Even as the Sisters rejoiced, their opponents were busily rallying their forces against them, for they knew that until the Apostolic Brief was signed and dispatched to the Bishop of Angers, the Generalate would not be able to function. Consequently they were determined that the proceedings should not advance beyond the preliminary stage. Aware of their actions, Father Vaures informed the Sisters that additional letters had arrived from their adversaries and that as a result, a French ecclesiastic in Rome had asked for a delay until further evidence could be obtained. Most of the Bishops in whose Dioceses the Refuges were located protested to the Holy Father urging him to postpone issuing the Apostolic Brief, which would legalize his approval expressed in the Papal Decree. Apparently they feared that such legislation might affect the Refuges adversely. Added to the Bishops were outstanding members of the clergy, including Monseigneur Dufêtre who had returned to Tours. Strangely enough this was the same Father Dufêtre who not so long before had promised the class at Angers that he would help bring Mother St. Euphrasia back to them. Since then, however, he had become an uncompromising critic of her aspirations. One searches in vain for the cause of his change of heart.

In the face of such concerted opposition, Pope Gregory deemed it wise to reconsider the entire issue, instructing Cardinal de Gregorio to suspend the sending of the Apostolic Brief to Angers. In spite of this enforced delay the matter was brought to an early conclusion when the Cardinal assured His Holiness that all objections had been carefully reviewed by the examining committee. Item by item, he said, they had been judiciously evaluated. "Your Eminence," the Cardinal asserted; "we believe that this Brief should not be withheld. In our opinion we hold that Mother St. Euphrasia is a woman of abounding charity. Although violently attacked, even calumniated, she has not uttered one word of protest or denunciation. On the contrary, she has excused her adversaries by saying that undoubtedly their motives are pure and their actions consistent with their convictions."

The Pontiff was deeply impressed. "How many letters are there against the Mother Superior of Angers?" he asked.

"Thirteen, Most Holy Father."

"And she says nothing at all in reply to her accusers?"

"Nothing, Your Holiness."

"Then," Pope Gregory spoke with finality, "the truth is on her side."

Accordingly he authorized Cardinal Gregorio to dispatch the Apostolic Brief [27] to Angers immediately.

This was done on April 3, 1835.

X

1837-1838

As the ivy clings to the oak, and by this means grows and thrives, so must we in like manner attach ourselves to Rome. . . . As the sunflower, so named because it ever turns toward the sun, and the mariner's compass always points toward the pole, so should you look continually towards Our Lord, towards Rome and towards your Congregation.

ST. MARY OF ST. EUPHRASIA

*P*OITIERS, Grenoble, Metz, St. Hilaire-St. Florent, Nancy, Amiens, Lille, Le Puy-en-Velay, Sens, Strasbourg, Rheims, Arles. Within eight years Mother St. Euphrasia had seen twelve foundations of the Good Shepherd established beyond Angers. With the Mother House they made a baker's dozen. Such growth surprised the public, but not Mother. In and out of season she strove incessantly "to help in the preservation of innocence, to contribute to the purification of the common morality, and to the elimination of a vice supremely detrimental to society," adding that these aims really meant working "for the peace and happiness of family life, the salvation of innumerable souls, and one's personal sanctification." [1]

Naturally she had looked forward to the day when she could open a convent in Rome. Cardinal Odescalchi had the same idea but presently he preferred to wait. In the meantime the controversy over her Institute was losing its bitterness, and many of her critics were less vocal, doubtless abashed by the success of her accomplishments.

Then one beautiful autumn day in 1837 she received an invitation from Cardinal Odescalchi asking her to establish a foundation of the Good Shepherd within the Eternal City. "Come, my dear daughter and bring several of your religious—to assist those poor souls who groan beneath an iron yoke and have so long needed your maternal care. . . . It is my wish to receive you myself at the monastery which I have had prepared for you, according to your rules and constitutions. Come then, my dear daughters, and fear no obstacles." [2]

Some moments passed before Mother St. Euphrasia grasped the full significance of this message. Among other things it meant that for the first time the Sisters of the Good Shepherd would go outside France. In the light of her lifelong loyalty to Rome, it seemed to her "a peculiar grace" that her spiritual daughters should now be called there. She also realized that her Congregation was fortunate in having Cardinal Odescalchi as its counselor. For more than two years he had been their Cardinal Protector. In the beginning Mother St. Euphrasia had taken for granted that the Bishop of Angers, in whose diocese the Mother House was located, would be named to this post. However, others including Father Anthony Kohlman, S.J., did not agree. From Rome he had written, "Your present venerable Bishop is in harmony with you, but can you be sure that his successors will be? . . . For religious Orders with a wish to extend, there is no better Superior General than the Sovereign Pontiff with a Cardinal delegated by him to act in his stead. . . . It is under the immediate jurisdiction and protection of the Holy See that they prosper most. . . . The Ladies of the Sacred Heart, so organized, give evidence of the wisdom of these statements." [3]

Father Vaures of the French Conventuals, the Community's close friend, had endorsed this proposal and the Bishop of Angers himself concurred. As a result Pope Gregory XVI promptly appointed Cardinal Odescalchi as Protector of the Good Shepherd Congregation. Because the Cardinal believed that he and Mother St. Euphrasia held common views in regard to the salvation of individuals ordinarily considered beyond reform, he was happy to be associated with her work and confident that someday her Sisters would go beyond their national borders.

Among the first to send his congratulations was Count de Neuville. "Madame, like another Hannibal, you are preparing to enter Italy, but not like him to enrich yourself with gold; you go to seek nothing but neglected souls. May our Lady bless your peaceful conquests!" [4]

With careful deliberation Mother St. Euphrasia chose the Sisters for Rome, naming Sister Teresa of Jesus de Couespel as Superior of a group of five, all of whom were flexible in meeting new situations yet unswerving in their stand against the forces of evil. Hereafter the name of St. Teresa of Jesus, like that of her fellow townsman, Sister Marie of St. Chantal, was to be closely linked with that of the Mother Foundress. Formerly a prominent member of the social and military life of Angers, Melanie de Couespel had in her widowhood been drawn to the religious life. Following the advice of Bishop Benedict Flaget of Bardstown, Kentucky, then on a prolonged visit to the land of his birth, she had entered the Good Shepherd Novitiate, later receiving her religious habit from this same intrepid American missionary. That event had occurred only eighteen months previous.[5]

Following Sister Teresa's profession Mother St. Euphrasia had initiated her into the intricacies of administering the expanding Community, and a fortunate appointment it proved to be, for thereafter Mother St. Euphrasia thought of Sister Teresa as one of the pillars of the Institute and did not hesitate to entrust her with the responsibility of the Roman mission. Arrangements for their departure were practically completed when an epidemic of cholera broke out in Italy so that there was nothing to do but wait. By the time the dread disease had run its course spring had arrived.

In a letter written to the Superior of Sens Mother told of her intention to spend a month in Rome: "Good, kind Madame d'Andigne takes us there in spite of her great age. . . . It is arranged that we start [from Angers] on Easter Tuesday sailing from Marseilles [a month later]. . . . I shall return by Paris, for Madame has business there. While she is occupied, I will visit . . . Sens." [6]

They broke their journey by visits to a number of the convents, spending the first night en route at St. Florent de Saumur and going on the next morning to Tours where Mother St. Euphrasia spent two days with Mother de Lignac, the Superior of the Ursulines. Through letters Mother de Lignac had kept in touch with the growth of the Good Shepherd Congregation but she found it much more satisfactory to hear about it directly. "And now you have been summoned to the Holy City itself. God is surely smiling on your work for souls."

Mme. d'Andigne's affairs called her to Paris earlier than she had at first expected. Mother St. Euphrasia went on but with a heavy heart after deciding it was better not to call at the Tours Refuge. She had one exciting experience: the party traveled a distance by

train, a primitive conveyance but at that time hailed as a great
scientific advance.

In Paris the Sisters enjoyed the hospitality of St. Vincent de Paul's
Daughters of Charity. At Bourges Mother St. Euphrasia promised
Bishop Villèle that she would soon make a foundation in his diocese.
At Lyons she was entertained in the home of her fellow compatriot,
Mlle. Pauline Marie Jaricot, who had won the appellation of
"admirable" from Pope Gregory for her effective work in founding
the Society for the Propagation of the Faith and the Association of
the Living Rosary, both of which projects had caught the spiritual
imagination of the land. Mother St. Euphrasia was particularly
interested in hearing the story that lay back of the Propagation of the
Faith, an enterprise which eventually grew into a great international
missionary organization maintained by steady contributions of the
laity everywhere. The two women proved to be kindred spirits and
exchanged reminiscences of their early attempts to organize and
stabilize their societies.

Mlle. Jaricot explained, "One autumn evening in 1819 when my
family was playing cards and I was sitting near by praying and seeking
help from God, the idea of the Propagation came to me. It was
simplicity itself. I would ask each person I knew to give a halfpenny
for Missions and find ten others who would likewise give a halfpenny.
This money would then be deposited with a group leader who would
unite with other leaders to receive the funds from a hundred, and
then from a thousand persons. Then it would become the responsibility of an accredited central agency to receive and distribute the
money collected. Just think, Mother St. Euphrasia, the state of the
foreign missions before they were assured regular support!"

With that clarity of vision given to those who espouse human
projects for spiritual ends, the two talked on into the night. Each was
a child of her times—practical, compassionate, and intensely aware
of the social problems left in the wake of the Revolution. Both then
and later Mother St. Euphrasia believed that their meeting had been
providentially arranged, for when she left Mlle. Jaricot she carried
with her an awakening hope that someday she could send her
daughters on missions "everywhere, to the ends of the globe."

Meanwhile Sister Teresa de Cousepel and a companion had left for
Bourg to examine a proposal to establish a Home there. Missing coach
connections at the junction point of Macon, they stayed overnight at
the Hospice of the Sisters of Providence. There a local group met

with them while Father Larcher, their leader, questioned Sister Teresa searchingly. Satisfied with her answers he then enthusiastically recommended that she petition her Mother General in behalf of a Home in Macon. The result was that both cities later became members of the Good Shepherd family.[7]

The trip continued with visits to the Good Shepherd Convents in Puy, Arles, Clermont-Ferrand, and Grenoble. Mother St. Euphrasia also detoured to the provincial township of Billom where her good friend, Bishop Flaget, had gone in search of health. Billom was currently enjoying special recognition as the birthplace of Benedict Joseph Flaget, the "Wilderness Bishop" justly acclaimed as one of the Founders of the American Church. An unexpected sidetrip to Chambéry in Savoy, only thirty miles from Annecy, completed the French itinerary. "In a way," Mother St. Euphrasia commented, "that gave me the most inspiring experience of all. Words could never express my satisfaction in seeing places hallowed by St. Francis de Sales and St. Jane de Chantal whose Order of the Visitation has contributed much to our Institute. The prospect of a foundation in their neighborhood appeals to me very much."

Then on to Marseilles from which city she wrote back to the Mother House, "I have not yet begun my journey and already I am wishing I were back, so much do I love you all. . . . My heart is at Angers. I assure you of my tenderness." [8]

This bustling seacoast city with its incessant activity, its maritime sounds and smells, seemed an enlargement of Noirmoutier. Yet it was a strange and unfamiliar world which Mother St. Euphrasia found both fascinating and frightening. Its industry won her admiration but its fearful potential for evil left her desolate. The girls of the docks seemed to her even more pitiable than the girls of the streets. Everywhere she looked she saw nature's beauty recede before the heavy shadow of sin and misery that stalked the waterfront.

Aboard the steamer both crew and passengers proved respectful and generous traveling companions. Men's voices lowered whenever Mother St. Euphrasia and her party appeared and general solicitude was expressed when she became seasick. Fortunately, her illness was short, and each day she reveled in the wide panorama of sky and sea, blended at sunset into a magnificent and colorful tapestry. There were moments when the changing lights and shadows brought tears to her eyes. Such beauty filled her with awe at the majesty of God's handiwork.

After two days at sea the Sisters reached Leghorn in time to cele-
brate the Feast of the Pentecost, proceeding by boat to Civìtà Vecchia, one of the Papal States. At this point they engaged a coach for
Rome, thirty miles beyond. The Italian scene is always at its best in
June with spring enhancing the small farms and pastures. The sight
of shepherd lads tending flocks, one of which included both black and
white sheep, reminded her of "the little black girls" she longed someday to receive into her flock, for she had never forgotten her childhood dreams of helping African children sold into slavery.

Shortly before sunset St. Peter's dome appeared in the distance,
looming high above the city. As was the custom the driver immediately halted the horses and flourished his whip in the direction of
the towering edifice, announcing impressively, "*Ecce Roma!*"

Mother St. Euphrasia, moved to tears, alighted and knelt in silence,
kissing the soil hallowed by the blood of countless martyrs. It was
nearly ten o'clock when they reached the gates of the city. Sentinels,
suspecting they were French spies disguised as nuns, held up their
lanterns and thundered at the latecomers, threatening to deny them
entry until morning. Only Mme. d'Andigne knew any Italian and her
vocabulary was too inadequate to make clear why a group of religious
and an old woman had arrived at that unseemly hour.

Impatiently the mistrusting men pushed aside the Papal Brief
Mother St. Euphrasia produced, assuming it to be a forged document.
Just as they were on the point of locking the gates, they begrudgingly
granted the nuns permission to proceed to a hospice near St. Peter's.
However, as guardians of the law, the gendarmes took the precaution
to accompany them the rest of the way.

In view of what happened next it seems certain that the police left
as soon as the little group arrived at its destination. No one came to
the door to admit Mother St. Euphrasia and her party; no amount of
knocking and ringing brought any response. Weary and frightened,
they asked their driver to take them to the residence of the Jesuit
Fathers located near the famous Church of the Gesu where they
hoped to be directed to some shelter. But the driver must have grown
weary too for upon reaching the Piazza of the Gesu, he curtly deposited his passengers and their effects and drove off in exasperated
dudgeon. Women were bad enough but French Sisters were even
worse—he'd never before heard of a group of religious wandering
about unescorted in the middle of the night. The clocks about struck
twelve, bringing home to the forlorn women huddled together with

their luggage that theirs was indeed a most awkward situation. Fortunately a passer-by pointed out the home of the Jesuit Fathers and the sleepy porter there carried Mother's request to her friend, Father Rozaven. He hastened to send them to a reputable hotel not far away. "One kept in the French manner," he said.

Almost a century later following Mother's beatification a Jesuit priest stirred his listeners at the first Triduum of the new Beata held in the Church of the Gesu by recalling Mother's unheralded arrival in Rome. Then she had sought assurance from the Jesuits; now [9] they were privileged to proclaim her glory publicly almost on the same spot at which her driver had abandoned her. Another evidence of the way God tests His own in time and rewards them in eternity.

Early the next morning Father Vaures came to the Sisters to explain that he had gone to Città Vecchia to meet them but had arrived too late. In haste he had returned to Rome only to learn of the discourteous treatment that had been accorded them. "Now things will be different, my friends. I have already informed Cardinal Odescalchi that you have arrived. He is sending two of his carriages to take you to St. Peter's for the solemn High Mass at eleven o'clock, at the end of which you will receive the Pope's blessing."

Everything else was forgotten in the face of such wonderful news. As long as she lived Mother St. Euphrasia treasured the memory of that Whit-Tuesday, particularly her first visit to the basilica of St. Peter, the personal blessing of the Holy Father to whom the Sisters' presence had been made known by Father Vaures, and her meeting with Cardinal Odescalchi, Vicar General of His Holiness and Cardinal Protector of the Sisters of the Good Shepherd. Following the services at St. Peter's, Father Vaures took the Sisters on to Cardinal Odescalchi's residence. "Only a brief call today, Mother St. Euphrasia; a longer one will come tomorrow."

In high expectation Mother St. Euphrasia waited to greet the Cardinal. Despite his palatial quarters she found herself completely at ease for the stories about his holiness and his simplicity were legion. Everyone agreed that his learning and piety took precedence over his exalted rank.

All these things Mother St. Euphrasia knew, but one thing she did not know until she saw him. Cardinal Odescalchi was the "prelate in the garb of a Cardinal" she had beheld in her dream that auspicious night three years previous. He was the same person who had then said: "Have no fear, my daughter: your work will be approved. I am chosen by God to be its protector." [10]

This interview made an indelible impression on both the white-robed religious and the gracious churchman. Sensing that she was deeply affected by the situation—she remained strangely quiet almost the entire time—he set her at ease by outlining his reasons for wanting her to assume the administration of the Convent of the Santa Croce so sadly in need of reorganization. Presently it was a detention center for girls brought to him by their disturbed parents. "This institution is under the direction of the Parish Priests but it is managed by a small number of seculars—good women in every respect but lacking in training for this vitally important work. However, I have continued to assign wayward and insubordinate girls there in preference to the women's prison where the range of misconduct is wider and more serious."

The Cardinal prolonged the audience, reasserting his firm conviction that the hand of God rested on the Sisters of the Good Shepherd. "Why, otherwise, did you address yourself to me without knowing that I was judge of the penitents? Why did the Holy Father charge me with your affairs? Why did he appoint me, without any knowledge of mine, to be your Protector? Why did your Bishop view the appointment with pleasure? Many similar coincidences prove that it was God's will, and that this work of the Generalate is His." [11]

Later when the Sisters were alone, Mother St. Euphrasia said, "Oh, my dear children, I am so overwhelmed I can scarcely find words to tell you. . . . That holy Cardinal is the same that I saw in my dream when the business of the Generalate was going so badly." [12]

The next day Mother St. Euphrasia told the Cardinal about her dream. He then told her that before the arrival of her first letter he had been seeking for an Order of religious whose chief purpose was to labor for the conversion of sinners. One morning while celebrating Holy Mass he had petitioned that he might soon find this Order. "Later that same day, Mother St. Euphrasia, your letter reached me. It seemed particularly significant coming as it did on the Feast of the Annunciation and starting with the words of Mary to the Angel Gabriel. I had no doubt that God had directed its writer to me."

Upon Mother St. Euphrasia's return to Angers she elaborated upon this interview. "His Eminence related to us that one day, after celebrating Mass in St. Peter's . . . he was meditating on the immense good accomplished by the Society of Jesus, and he said to himself,

'Why should there not be a Religious Order of women to effect in due proportion the good done by the Jesuits, who would in addition take charge of prisons for women?' That very day the Cardinal received our letter beginning: 'Behold the handmaid of the Lord; be it done to me according to Thy word.' Deeply moved, he understood at once that the request for a Generalate was according to God's will . . . from that moment he formed the resolution which he has now executed of founding a House of our institute in Rome." [13]

The House to which Mother St. Euphrasia referred was located on the western bank of the Tiber almost at the foot of the famed Janiculum Hill. The building though gloomy and forbidden from the outside, was spacious, well-ventilated, and pleasant within. Built originally as a convent, it was well-suited for a reconstruction center. To be sure, some remodeling was needed, but surprisingly little for a structure over two hundred years old. Its wall were thick, its corridors wide, its chapel, choir, and cells entirely adequate. The physical aspects of the house satisfied Mother St. Euphrasia; the human aspects, however, pleased her not at all.

Twelve listless young women under the direction of two good but inept matrons slouched about at will, lacking order, discipline, and interest in themselves or their surroundings. Idleness ruled the place and its handmaids; slovenliness, apathy, and ennui were everywhere. The girls looked at the Sisters with complete indifference. A heart less stout than Mother St. Euphrasia's might have been discouraged. But she knew that these undisciplined girls would respond in time to kindness, physical comforts, and an ordered life. Meanwhile the Sisters would pray for them, beginning where they were to train them. With Mother St. Euphrasia cleanliness and kindness always preceded religious instruction. From the beginning she had stressed the rule, "Let kindness be the rule of our conduct, of our language, of our manner; thus the children may render testimony that we are, as we ought to be, true Mothers." [14]

A few days were required to effect the transfer of Santa Croce, sometimes called La Scalletta. "I desire to remove its jurisdiction entirely from the College of Parish Priests," Cardinal Odescalchi said. "They may still place girls with you but you Sisters of the Good Shepherd will have the care and direction of them. In that way there will be no conflicting duality of management."

Mother St. Euphrasia and her companions made good use of their time visiting many of the basilicas, churches, and shrines of the

Eternal City—St. Paul's without the Walls, St. Mary Major, and St. John Lateran in turn. They ascended the twenty-nine steps of the Scala Sancta upon their knees as an act of devotion to the Son of God who was said to have descended these same steps then part of Pilate's praetorium after receiving His death sentence.

In the Maritime or Tullianum Prison they drank of the spring which had reportedly sprung up in answer to St. Peter's prayer for water with which he might baptize his converted jailers, and they went deep into the Catacombs of St. Sebastian, subterranean burial ground of the early Christians. At times Mother St. Euphrasia stopped to exclaim in whispered tones, "Here in this very place the divine mysteries were celebrated. How insignificant are our poor sufferings alongside those of the holy Apostles and Martyrs!" In addition she made pilgrimages to the rooms of St. Ignatius, St. Aloysius, and St. Stanislaus Koska, all of whom held a warm spot in her heart as Jesuits and as patrons of Catholic youth. Her letters to her daughters at Angers and to the various foundations abounded in detailed accounts of the impressions made upon her. "Beautiful Rome, holy Rome, journey a thousand times blessed," she wrote to St. Mary of St. John of the Cross at Nancy.

Before long Mother St. Euphrasia was notified that her audience with the Holy Father was set for Friday, June 15. Its early inclusion on the Pope's agenda emphasized his keen personal interest in the Sisters of the Good Shepherd. For loyal Catholics nothing can quite compare with a visit to the Head of all Christendom. No one goes casually to an audience with the successor of Peter; few, if any, leave his presence unmoved. For Mother St. Euphrasia the approaching audience with His Holiness was easily the high spot of her life. She felt lifted almost to the portals of Heaven itself.

Wearing their long white mantles over their white habits encircled by the blue girdles peculiar to their Congregation, the Sisters in the company of Cardinal Odescalchi and Father Vaures entered the presence of the elderly and kindly Gregory XVI. They were happily surprised by the gracious and human welcome accorded them. The Pope left his red and gold chair and advanced midway of the room, speaking in a compassionate and friendly manner, "This is my Good Shepherd. Come, Reverend Mother; come, my dear daughters." Then he returned to his Papal Throne, insisting that his visitors also be seated. Mother St. Euphrasia demurred but His Holiness would not have it otherwise. Consequently the Sisters acquiesced and listened attentively as Pope Gregory expatiated on his awareness of their aims and purposes and the difficulties that they had had to overcome in order to achieve their present status. His knowledge of Mother St. Euphrasia's hopes and problems astounded her. Later she commented that it was as though he had actually been at Angers. Without any notes to guide him he asked pertinent questions about the various Bishops with whom she had dealt. She answered directly and charitably, speaking ill of no one and praising those who had sustained her.

"A magnanimous soul!" was the Pontiff's verdict. Before the interview concluded he thanked her for assuming the administration of Santa Croce, promising to visit the Sisters there once they were settled. This promise he made good in due time. "Now indeed I can support your Institute," he reiterated.

The audience concluded, he stood and bestowed the Papal Blessing on his visitors. Afterward in speaking of Mother St. Euphrasia's attentive spirituality he remarked to Cardinal Odescalchi, "I do believe the good Mother took me for our Lord in person."

Mother St. Euphrasia used her remaining time visiting and receiving calls from many churchmen and superiors of religious houses and continuing her sightseeing and devotional trips to the shrines with which Rome abounds. Two visits stood out above others: her call on Cardinal Lambruschini, the learned Papal Secretary of State, and her reception by the Sisters of the Sacred Heart whose Superiors had earlier called upon her. Mother's visit to the Sacred Heart Convent of Trinita dei Monti epitomizes the warm relationship that has always existed between these two great religious Congregations, one serving children favored by birth, wealth, and social advantages; the other dedicated to the welfare of orphans and girls whose problems bring them into conflict with God and society. Of this visit Mother St. Euphrasia wrote: "I shall always preserve the most delightful memories of the Trinita dei Monti and of the worthy Superior of the House (Mme. de Caussans). What a religious spirit! What perfection in all those Ladies!"

When invited to speak to the students, Mother St. Euphrasia hesitated momentarily and then won their friendship with her straightforward stories. Among those present that day was young Constance Bonaparte, a niece of the Emperor. Later as a religious of the Sacred Heart she recalled: "When our Reverend Mother pressed the Mother General of the Good Shepherd to speak to us, she excused herself, saying she was quite incapable of doing so, as she was only accustomed to speak to orphan children, or to women who had grievously offended the good God. But when Reverend Mother again urged her, she did so, simply, charming us all by the interesting facts she told as well as recalling some touching conversions that had come within her own experience." [15]

Through Cardinals Lambruschini and Odescalchi, Mother St. Euphrasia became acquainted with a number of socially prominent gentlewomen, most of whom became her ardent advocates. With few exceptions they enrolled themselves voluntarily as benefactresses of the new Convent of the Good Shepherd, aiding it materially in numerous ways. To a degree its success was due to their sustained interest and support.

The transformation of Santa Croce presented many problems. The girls looked with disfavor at the changes under way. They stubbornly refused to clean up their persons and their surroundings and were adamant in clinging to their idleness. "Why should we work?" their attitude said. "Let others do that. We haven't come here for any such purpose and we don't intend to start now."

In the beginning the language difference was also a formidable barrier but the Sisters rapidly acquired Italian, although during the first troublesome weeks the directions from "those foreigners," as the girls dubbed the Sisters, were ignored. During all of these difficulties Mother St. Euphrasia remained undiscouraged, smiling upon the children, arranging for a special dinner by way of a small celebration and distributing little gifts among them. On the surface these attentions went unheeded but the day came when the girls spoke in generous terms of Mother St. Euphrasia's kindness, admitting regretfully, "Then we wouldn't say so, but we knew better times were in store for us."

Meanwhile hard work and patience were required. It was the old story of clearing out a brier patch before planting a garden. Mother St. Euphrasia never doubted that under Sister Teresa's direction the situation would gradually improve.

Before leaving Rome, Mother St. Euphrasia took the Sisters to visit the dismal old St. Michael's Prison. The sight of two hundred women behind bars filled her with regret at her present inability to aid them, especially as the women begged the Sisters not to pass them by, imploring them to come nearer so that they might touch their rosaries.

"If only we had some Mothers in white like you, they would love us and make us happy. Won't you stay?"

Obviously, that was not possible, but not too many years would elapse before she could found a prison for women on Via Francesco di Sales. On her first visit to St. Michael's, however, that likelihood seemed remote. Still Mother carried the thought deep in her heart, for guilty or not, those women had souls.

Her stay was now fast drawing to a close. Two visits weekly with Cardinal Odescalchi had enlarged her concept of the work of her Congregation. More and more she viewed it as a missionary Order destined to work for the salvation of souls throughout the entire world. The little mustard seed she had planted in Angers would become a great tree under whose branches many would find rest and solace. Throughout the rest of her life she was to be guided by the practical and inspirational ideas given her by the first Cardinal Protector. Whenever things became especially burdensome she would remember that he had said: "Of the more than twenty offices I hold from the Pope, the one I esteem the most is that of serving as your Protector."

A final brief audience with the Holy Father preceded her departure, his paternal interest expressing itself in the generous acclamation, "I consider your Congregation the brightest diamond in my crown."

On the 4th of July Mother St. Euphrasia with Mme. d'Andigne bade farewell to Sister Teresa and her associates. Hearts were heavy as she entered the carriage that was to take her away. "Good-by, my daughters. Do not grieve. Although time and space separate us, our love bridges the gap. We came hither to win souls for God. For that purpose you remain. I depart confident that you will draw down many graces on our work."

Perhaps Mother St. Euphrasia thought back to a day many long years previous when roles were reversed. Then it was she who stood on strange ground and watched her own beloved mother ride off, leaving her to solve her problems unaided. In any case, she understood well the challenge and the loneliness that lay ahead for the Sisters.

All of this time Mme. d'Andigne had been Mother's companion. As an experienced traveler she assumed entire responsibility for their return, routing them directly to Paris where they met Abbé Mainguy who escorted them home. The little party of three reached Angers on the morning of July 17, some days earlier than they were expected.

Less than two weeks on the road! In 1838 such a rapid journey was something to talk about. It made Rome seem ever so much nearer.

On the succeeding days a train of well-wishers called. But on that first evening before the news got about that Mother had returned, she was made happy by a message from Count de Neuville. Its words, she soon discovered, were held in common by many of the town's citizenry.

"Madame, . . . it is very sweet to think of you at the Good Shepherd of Angers at last! Now the mind is quiet, the heart satisfied. No longer does the imagination see you far away in the dim distance, beaten about by waves, or jolted roughly along roads, tired out, in heavy miserable diligences. Thanks be to our Lady for protecting you and giving you back to your flock." [16]

Good faithful friend—where could his like be found?

XI

1839-1841

The patient suffering of afflictions that come to us from God and neighbor gains us more merit than we could acquire by ten years of self-imposed mortifications.

ST. FRANCIS DE SALES

BISHOP Montault was now an old man. In his mid-eighties, he admitted that he was no longer able to participate in the lengthy and elaborate ceremonial functions of his office. However, he still came to the Good Shepherd regularly, commenting, "I esteem myself happy in having been chosen by God to help in establishing it [this work]."

One day he had just arrived at the Mother House when he suffered a sudden fainting spell. Upon recovering consciousness he said, "This, I fear, is to be my last visit to the Good Shepherd but I shall not forget you. When I reach Heaven, I shall be better able to intercede for you." Only the day before his death on July 29, 1839, he ratified the Rule for the Consecrated Penitents, an act giving official status to the organization of former members of the class who had worked long and diligently to prove themselves worthy to have their own special association within the family of the Good Shepherd.

The formation of the "Consecrates," or Auxiliaries as they are often called, came about spontaneously. In the early spring of 1835 Mother St. Vincent of Paul Cornet, then Mistress of the Class at Angers, found herself pondering over the future prospects of certain young women in her care. Because they were older than the other children, she had purposely given them tasks in keeping with their age and

157

ability and the way in which they discharged their tasks proved that they were dependable and trustworthy. Consequently she had extended their freedom, permitting them to serve as pages or couriers, passing freely among the various departments of the House. When no liberties were violated, she assigned them to other posts, gradually increasing their responsibilities. Without exception all were devoted to the Institute. "It's the only home I know," one after another would say. "Surely you won't make me leave it."

Finally this state of affairs came to a head. The girls came to her with a request. "Won't you please ask Mother St. Euphrasia if we might not have an organization of our own? It would be small but it would grow for there will always be people like us, who had never known God or had completely forgotten Him until they came here. We're too old to be with the children as classmates but we could supervise their daily chores. By showing them how to do things the right way, we think we could make their tasks less irksome. Besides, we could take care of the children when they're sick. We could keep the mending in order. We could help in all sorts of ways."

Mother St. Vincent agreed. Discussion further defined their request. The young women made it clear that they did not aspire to become Sister Magdalens, but they did want to wear a distinctive uniform and to obligate themselves by annual promises which could be renewed at the end of every twelve months. "In that way we can remain or leave. Such freedom would rule out any discontent that might otherwise result."

The idea appealed strongly to Mother St. Euphrasia. "This sort of association would be similar to the medieval guilds with the difference that these women would not bind themselves for wages, but for love of God. Certainly they deserve to have a trial at this voluntary Christian service. If it works out here, we can extend it to our other foundations."

Consequently Mother St. Euphrasia and Sister St. Vincent gave thought to the organization of the Consecrates. They agreed that no one would be eligible until she had completed two years in the class after which she would be requested to spend another two years on probation. If she had met these requirements satisfactorily, she would then be permitted to consecrate herself to the Mother of Sorrows, the chosen patroness of the Consecrates, this consecration to take place each year on the Feast of St. Mary Magdalen. Each Consecrate would wear a plain black dress, a white head covering, and a silver cross hung around her neck. Thereafter, she would be affiliated with the Order of Servites, reciting daily the Little Office of Our Lady of Dolours.

This first little group was much more than another department in Mother St. Euphrasia's organization. They served as extra hands and feet, eyes and ears, and hearts too, for the Mothers. Having once been in a comparable situation, they were able to understand the problems that accompanied frightened and belligerent new girls. One commentator likened them to good noncommissioned officers in a regiment.

With great interest Bishop Montault had watched their progress. Because of his paternal interest, the young women were happy that he lived long enough to ratify their Rule, composed and perfected by Mother St. Euphrasia and acclaimed and blessed by Pope Gregory XVI in January, 1845.

Ever since their inception, the Consecrates have been useful adjutants to the Sisters of the Good Shepherd. In Europe and in some other localities this semireligious Congregation has remained strong but in the United States its appeal has lessened, due perhaps to the differences in national attitudes and customs. The average American girl does not seem drawn to this restricted life. Her choice is usually clear-cut: she has a real religious vocation or she does not; if not, she prefers marriage or a career in the world. Exceptions do still exist, however, and Consecrates or Auxiliaries are to be found in some American Convents, including those in Baltimore, Omaha, and New Orleans.

Four months after Bishop Montault's death, Mother St. Euphrasia suffered another loss. In November Cardinal Odescalchi carried out a personal decision that had long lain hidden in his heart. Its open declaration startled all Rome and the adjacent countries as well, pushing other news into the background and causing people to shake their heads in disbelief. Men did not do such things, they cried, but here was the indisputable evidence that one man had. Cardinal Odescalchi, Vicar of Rome, and holder of numerous honors and titles, resigned all of his high offices and withdrew quietly from the Papal Court to enter the Novitiate of the Jesuit Fathers in Verona. The Cardinal's family and intimates recalled that as a lad he had longed to enter the Society of Jesus. Clearly that desire had never left him for now at the height of a great career in the Church, he had doffed his scarlet biretta and mantle as a member of the Sacred College of Cardinals to seek hidden membership among a group of lowly novices wearing the plain black habit of St. Ignatius. Mother St. Euphrasia was stricken at the loss of the Cardinal to the Good Shepherd. Who would support her now against the attacks and defamations of those die-hards who even yet seized any opportunity to malign her? The Cardinal had always recognized her fervor and humility for what they were, because these same qualities were an integral part of his own heritage.

From Florence he wrote a letter of farewell to the Sisters in Rome. Knowing how much this letter would mean to Mother St. Euphrasia, the Sisters had it framed and sent to her. Upon its arrival she hung it on the wall of her cell where it remained as long as she lived, a reminder of the wise and holy man who had penned it. Later when the Cardinal's estate was distributed among many deserving charities, the Sisters at Santa Croce were included among the beneficiaries.

In the summer of 1840 Cardinal della Porta Rodiani was named as the second Cardinal Protector of the Congregation. Although overshadowed by his noted predecessor's personality and accomplishments, the new appointee was earnest and sincere, making a constructive, though not a brilliant, contribution to the progress of the Good Shepherd. Quite early it became evident that he could be depended upon to support the Sisters in weal or woe, an assurance which set Mother St. Euphrasia's mind at ease.

Early in 1840 Louis Robert Paysant was named as Bishop Montault's successor. At the Mother House this news was received with apprehension for Monseigneur Paysant had the reputation of being austere and cold. But dismaying as these facts were, they seemed insignificant alongside one that came much closer to the Sisters of the Good Shepherd. The Bishop-elect had been the ecclesiastical Superior of the Refuge of Caen, the "Cradle of the Institute" founded by St. John Eudes. As the original foundation it had strenuously opposed Mother's idea of the Generalate. Under those circumstances Mother St. Euphrasia thought that Bishop Paysant might naturally prefer the concept of autonomy in operation at Caen to that of the continuing growth and unification in existence at Angers.

On March 12, 1840, the new Bishop was acclaimed officially by the entire city and four days later he called informally at the Mother House. None too well after an arduous visitation to a number of her Convents, Mother St. Euphrasia had returned only a few days previous. Still pale from her travels, she received Bishop Paysant with a cordiality that hid her lurking doubts. Hospitably she first welcomed the Bishop in private, attended only by Sister Marie de St. Chantal and the local Superiors, after which she escorted him to the Community Room where the rest of the Sisters were gathered in nervous trepidation. Contrary to their expectations he was genial and friendly, swiftly laying at rest any rumors that had preceded him.

"It pleases me to see so many Sisters assembled here. The growth of the Generalate in the five years of its existence stands as a tribute to Mother St. Euphrasia's foresight and perseverance. Far from wishing to retard that growth, I shall do all I can to favor it. In my opinion, the Generalate responds to the needs of the times."

Everyone immediately relaxed. To be sure, there would be occasions when Monseigneur Paysant would thwart some of Mother St. Euphrasia's cherished plans. But everything considered, theirs proved an amicable relationship.

Meanwhile Mother St. Euphrasia was meeting the trials and joys that went with every new foundation. Already she had established Homes at Chambery in Savoy and at Mons and Namur in Belgium. In each case the Sisters, like the disciples of old, had departed without scrip or purse, trusting in Divine Providence to aid them. The first religious of Namur took this injunction almost literally, for their combined capital amounted to only forty-four francs.

Mother St. Euphrasia was often berated for her foolhardiness in sending the Sisters out on these unsubsidized ventures but she was never intimidated by the ogre of possible failure; she believed implicitly in tilling the fields offered her, awaiting the day when the harvest of souls would be a rich and mighty one. How otherwise, she reasoned, could she justify her work? "The Son of God came to redeem sinners. He did not permit the lack of personal comforts to turn Him aside. Neither shall we. To wait until there are no problems of maintenance might deter us forever. As Good Shepherd Sisters we dare not risk that."

It is not hard to understand why her Congregation continued to grow. Rome was again to beckon her. Munich, London, and Paris would soon follow.

Within two years the Convent of Santa Croce in Rome had increased its population from twelve to seventy, and extended its services to include a Novitiate for Italian girls. No longer was there any language problem or lack of familiarity with national customs. Consequently when the directors of La Lauretana, a convalescent home that provided for the care of unmarried mothers, decided to transfer its management to a group of religious, they turned as a matter of course to the Sisters of the Good Shepherd. For some time La Lauretana, so called after Our Lady of Loretta, had been the responsibility of the Loretta Union, an association of women, many of whom were members of the Roman aristocracy. Their motives were the best but their results far from satisfactory. It was only natural for them as women to think that they understood the problems of other women, but those to whom their charity was directed knew that they and their benefactors had no common meeting ground.

Finally one of the patronesses put her finger on the crux of the matter. "We have tried with little success to improve the morals of the women who come here. They listen passively but are not impressed, primarily because we do not get through to their inner selves. Many of us remember Mother St. Euphrasia Pelletier, and all of us are familiar with the work her Sisters are doing at Santa Croce. I think we would do well to ask her to take over the operation of La Laurenta."

As a result of this suggestion plans were set in motion to effect the transfer, and on June 1, 1840, the Sisters of the Good Shepherd assumed charge of La Laurenta. This time Mother St. Euphrasia did not go to Rome. Instead she delegated Sister St. Celestine Husson to act for her. Although a Frenchwoman, Sister Celestine was well acquainted with Roman life, having made her novitiate and profession at Santa Croce.

Sometimes the most simple deeds have far-reaching effects. Certainly that was true in the case of Mlle. de Baligand, a postulant from Treves, who innocently set in motion a chain of circumstances that ended only when the King of Bavaria invited the Sisters to come to Munich. Mademoiselle's letters to her uncle in Ratisbon told him of the social service she would engage in once she was professed. She wrote enthusiastically about Mother St. Euphrasia and her Novice Mistress, emphasizing that all of the girls who came to the Good Shepherd had immortal souls "just as precious in God's sight as yours or mine."

Her uncle became fired with the idea of bringing the Sisters to Germany. The Bishop of Ratisbon was most sympathetic but could not act without the King's approval since only the ruler himself could authorize the introduction of an organization originating in another country. However, he consented to seek the necessary permission with the result that Ludwig I became interested. Later when the Sovereign had read the Constitutions of the Good Shepherd, he sent the Abbé Eberhard, Court Chaplain, on a visit to the Good Shepherd in Strasbourg. Father Eberhard returned to Munich an advocate and friend of Mother St. Euphrasia's Congregation. The King caught his enthusiasm and expressed his desire to meet "some of these good ladies." Accordingly his request was forwarded to Mother St. Euphrasia.

In the past many unusual things had happened at the Mother House but never before had a royal summons penetrated the cloister. Startled, Mother cried, "Can it be really true that the King of Bavaria bids us come?" It was not easy for her to remain at home when such a project beckoned but her earlier commitments could not be set aside. In her place she sent the Superior of Nancy, Sister St. John of the Cross, commissioning her and her companion "to assess the field carefully as to the prospects for the success of our work there." Before long the Sisters reported that Bavaria was a promising mission field. Their interviews with the King had resulted in his insistence that they settle forthwith in his domain, establishing their first German foundation.

When Sister St. John of the Cross returned to Angers, she carried with her the royal authorization and in addition brought the daughter of a Court official, Fraulein Augustin von Müller, the first postulant to come from Germany. Through the years she was to be followed by an unbroken line of stanch religious, many of whom gave comfort and solace to Mother St. Euphrasia during her lifetime.

Events now moved rapidly. In early June Father Eberhard came to Angers to escort the newly appointed Superior and her assistant, Sister Mary of St. Helena, to his homeland, Mother St. Euphrasia promising to send three more Sisters within a short time. Not long afterward Father Eberhard became gravely ill. Denied his help, the Sisters were compelled to support their new work alone with only sporadic outside aid for the King had by then turned his attention elsewhere. Eventually the long delayed installation ceremonies were set for November 9, a celebration which brought Sister St. John of the Cross deep satisfaction. Mother St. Euphrasia wrote to her, "You do nothing by halves, either at Munich or Nancy. . . . We rejoice in God, who has broken the chains of your captivity."

One morning Mother St. Euphrasia entered her office at Angers, shutting the door behind her, glad that until Sister Marie de Chantal came, she would be alone. In her cell and at private devotions she was often alone but in her office someone was usually waiting to see her or

Sister de Chantal had ready a matter of finance to discuss. Of late there seemed to be less and less money for more and more demands. Mother St. Euphrasia sighed and sat down heavily. She was tired through and through, there was no denying that. Sometimes her bones ached far into the night as she stared into the darkness identifying herself with her dear daughters carrying on so valiantly in France, Alsace-Lorraine, Saxony, Italy, and Germany. All of them had met calumniators, people who stubbornly clung to the distortions and recriminations that had accompanied the birth of the Generalate. That these troublemakers were misinformed did not prevent their convincing others.

Sometimes Mother St. Euphrasia wondered how much longer she could endure. Covering her eyes with her hands she bowed her head and wept silently. The clock ticked the moments away. Before long she smiled to herself, "Were things otherwise, I'd be suspicious for God's work is never easy. And I know that the work of the Good Shepherd is God's work. He wants us to seek out and reclaim the sinners that society rejects. Poor misled and disillusioned girls, young in years and old in vice, what would be their lot, were we not at hand to lead them to Our Lord?"

A light tap came at the door. "Yes?" Mother answered. The door opened ever so slightly to admit a bright-eyed, alert-looking young woman in her early thirties.

"What is it, Clara dear?"

"Mother de Chantal will be detained a while longer, perhaps fifteen minutes or so."

Alone once more, Mother's thoughts followed Clara. "A beautiful and a happy woman now, but only a year ago she was far from that. I'll never forget her bedraggled state when the gendarmes brought her to us."

Then a huddled pitiable creature had sat tensely on the edge of the chair, her bloodshot eyes shooting hither and yon in frightened bewilderment. What were these people going to do to her? Beat her? Lock her up? She would fight if they tried any of those things. She did not have much strength, though, that was certain.

Ten years ago Clara had come to the city in search of a job. First, she had worked as a domestic; later, she had gone into a factory, attracted by higher wages. At the factory she had become friendly with two older women, Kate and Mamie, who saw in the farm girl a gullible innocent. "Too good to be true," they told themselves. Their attention and flattery made Clara think they were the two nicest persons she had ever known. Naturally she had agreed when they asked her to wait outside a certain building while they went inside to visit a sick friend. Before long she was accompanying them regularly on similar visits. Sometimes she wondered at the number of sick friends Kate and Mamie had but she kept faithful watch with their parting words ringing in her ears, "Let us know at once if anyone is about."

Then a day came when Clara was taken into custody, charged with having served as a front for thieves. The more she protested, the sillier her story appeared. When her sentence expired, she had no job, no friends, and no place to go. Soon she was forced to steal in order to live. Once she was put behind bars for a loaf of bread; another time for a slab of meat. Hungry, lonely, and untrained, she heard herself denounced as a vagrant. She grew defensive and difficult. After all, a girl had to live.

The night when the gendarme picked her up and brought her to the Good Shepherd, she was in a fighting mood. How dare they fool her by bringing her to this place?

"What kind of a place do you think it is?" Mother St. Euphrasia had asked quietly.

Clearly Clara did not know and the lack of information caused her to scream wildly, "Get it over with. I don't want to wait here forever."

"You won't need to, my dear. A hot bath and a drink of warm milk will make you feel much better. After a night's sleep, things will look brighter." Mother St. Euphrasia's kindly voice calmed Clara's near frenzy.

"But aren't you going to punish me?" she asked in bewilderment.

"Not at all. I think you've had enough punishment. We don't punish girls here; we love them."

"Love?" Clara blinked in wide-eyed astonishment. "I don't understand what you mean."

"You are one of God's children. He loves you dearly and so will we."

In the months that followed Clara slowly lost her resentments and mistrusts in others. She was working hard to qualify herself for membership in the band of Consecrates.

Reviewing Clara's story had healed Mother St. Euphrasia of her weariness. It had also given her the courage to act on Monseigneur Paysant's directive that she close the embryo London foundation.

Given time, she had hoped that the Sisters working there might be able to resolve their difficulties.

Two months previous the London foundation had begun with Father Eberhard's telling Mother St. Euphrasia that his friend, Father Jauch, desired to have the Good Shepherd Sisters settle in England. Having recently visited in London en route to Angers, Father Eberhard spoke with some authority about the conditions there. "Although England is an overwhelmingly Protestant nation, the lot of Catholics is destined to improve now that the Emancipation Bill has gone into effect. However, no religious attire can be worn publicly and all religious who live there are forced to carry on their work quietly and unobtrusively. But the underground Church is doing a splendid work. At this moment Father Jauch has a number of young girls in his parish who wish to become Sisters. He would send them to Angers but they are in no position to bring even a slight dowry."

Mother St. Euphrasia did not know that Father Eberhard had already told his friend and fellow pastor that she would accept these English candidates, lack of dowry notwithstanding. Accordingly he felt almost clairvoyant when he heard her say: "These girls will be the first fruits of a great country that has produced many martyrs for the Faith. Under the circumstances, they do not need a dowry to be assured a welcome here."

In view of later events it appears evident that Father Jauch was talking wistfully rather than realistically about wanting the Good Shepherd in London. He had not asked Father Eberhard to act for him, but Father Eberhard had pleaded the English cause so effectively that Mother St. Euphrasia mistook his words for an official summons. As a result she had sent Mother Mary of the Angels, the Superior of Lille, and one other religious to London to acquaint themselves with the prospects there.

The Sisters felt ill at ease in secular dress. They knew no English and they were unprepared for the strangeness of the huge city to which they had come. Father Jauch was dumbfounded at the unheralded arrival of the French Sisters. He looked at his credulous visitors and tried to remember what he might have said or done that had led to this awkward situation. However, this was no time for recrimination. He rallied his wits and sent the Sisters on to Father Voyaux, a French priest located in another section of London. Father Voyaux was equally surprised when he learned that his unannounced callers were two Good Shepherd Sisters from Angers. Without their white habits he had not recognized them.

"My dear, good Sisters, you cannot hope to make a foundation here. The 'No-Popery' element, as it likes to call itself, would never permit that. Once your presence became known you would be subjected to indignities, stoning among them. Leave, I beg you, before any kind of untoward incident occurs."

The Sisters thanked Father Voyaux for his friendly advice but made it clear they could not accept it. Mother Mary of the Angels explained that she and her companion had been sent here for a particular purpose. To return home without Mother St. Euphrasia's permission would be a serious violation of their vow of obedience. Such being the case, would he not be so kind as to arrange for a meeting with the Vicar Apostolic, Monseigneur Griffiths, leading Catholic churchman in the nation, pending the day when the Hierarchy would be established?

Father Voyaux accompanied the Sisters to this interview. Monseigneur Griffiths was most unsympathetic, looking upon the Sisters as impostors and forbidding them to receive Holy Communion until he had written to Angers and verified their story. Almost beside themselves, they also wrote in haste to Mother St. Euphrasia. Some weeks passed before the situation was resolved. Although Mother St. Euphrasia blamed herself for having subjected the Sisters to such hostility, she had an intuition that there would soon be a turn for the better. Monseigneur Paysant disagreed, saying that "this most unfortunate situation" left no doubt as to what Mother should do. "Recall the Sisters and forget London as quickly as you can. With my permission they cannot return there until they go fortified by definite assurances and ecclesiastical approbation."

Mother St. Euphrasia wanted to wait for another letter from Mother Mary of the Angels but Monseigneur Paysant was unwilling to wait. Mother knew she was acting against her better judgment when she sent her letter of recall. A few days later a letter arrived from London bringing more encouraging news. Father Voyaux had offered the Sisters a furnished home at St. Leonard's by the Sea and Monseigneur Griffiths had withdrawn his opposition and offered his friendship. He had also agreed to their starting a foundation whenever they could ensure its solvency, expressing regrets at his inability to help them financially. In the meantime the Sisters were being aided by the wealthy Marchioness of Wellesley who had offered to provide for their immediate needs. Furthermore, she had promised that she would enlist her friends in their behalf. "Things could be ever so much worse, dear Mother," they wrote. "We are trying to forget our first unpleasant experiences here."

Then Mother St. Euphrasia's letter of recall arrived, bringing with it both disappointment and satisfaction. Mother Mary of the Angels was sorry to leave her task unfinished but glad that she could take six English girls back to the Angers Novitiate—an English pilgrimage to the Good Shepherd that has continued to the present day.

Through these newcomers Mother St. Euphrasia gained the lasting friendship of Monseigneur de Hercé, Bishop of Nantes. Having heard of his lingual accomplishments she solicited his spiritual direction for the postulants from England for they did not speak French and the local clergy did not speak English. Bishop de Hercé agreed to instruct "this colony of young English ladies" and later to officiate at their clothing ceremony. "The ceremony and discourse will be partly in English, partly in French, with a little Italian, if you wish for it. . . . Together at one altar, with one heart and soul . . . we shall all unite in praising and blessing the Lord."

In November the prospects in London had improved sufficiently to warrant the return of the Sisters. At first Monseigneur Paysant was adamant in his opposition but gradually he relented and then consented. Mother St. Joseph Regaudiat, formerly the Superior of Arles, was assigned the obligation of building on the base her predecessors had laid. She was to have as her Assistant, Sister Mary of St. Celeste Fisson. Obediently but timorously the Sisters made ready to leave France. They feared the unknown and yet desired to conquer it for God. Shortly before their departure on the 11th of November, Mother St. Euphrasia looked at the two religious dressed in plain black secular attire and smilingly remarked: "I am black but beautiful." A little ripple of laughter broke the tension; then Mother continued in a more serious tone: "The ashes of the martyrs seem quickened to call us to that city."

With these words ringing in their ears the two Sisters left Angers in the company of Abbé Mainguy and an English novice-interpreter. It took them seven days to reach London. At St. Malo they missed connections, although they could never explain why for they were waiting on the quay listening for the signal that was to summon them aboard when suddenly they saw their ship leaving the harbor. The ship was wrecked off the coast of Jersey, costing the lives of several passengers. After a two-day wait they made the rest of the crossing in a crowded cargo boat loaded with hides. The miserable weather and the offensive odors made everyone seasick. The captain fought the storm as far as Guernsey but could not risk going further with his lumbering old craft. His decision meant that the last lap of the trip had to be made overland. The next morning the little group of four resumed their travels in a coach that Abbé Mainguy had secured to carry them to their destination, a small family hotel in the West End of London. By the time the weary group completed their journey, night had fallen, bringing heavy fog and penetrating cold.

Only the grace of God and the determination of Mother St. Joseph sustained them during the winter months, for their misadventures started at once with the untimely death of Father Voyaux. True to his word he had not forgotten to will the Sisters a home at St. Leonard's by the Sea but they learned that as aliens they were not eligible to inherit property in England. They realized too that St. Leonard's, sixty miles distant, would not have been a suitable location but its denial meant that they had no place of their own. When informed of this fact Monseigneur Griffiths arranged for them to stay indefinitely with the Benedictine Sisters at Hammersmith.

Three months later the Sisters were still wanderers, striving unaided to achieve their goal. For some reason the Marchioness of Wellesley had not resumed her earlier benefactions. The records are not clear, but in a letter sent to Mother St. Euphrasia (from Nantes) on February 9, 1841, Bishop de Hercé wrote: "She [the Marchioness] had written me a long letter, which I enclose, telling me she will take no part in the good work. . . . You will be struck, as I have been, with the coldness of its tone." [1]

In spite of this disheartening news Mother St. Euphrasia found the courage to write: "London is our daughter. We shall no doubt pay dearly for its foundation but we must not give up, even if it were necessary for us to work by night as well as by day, and to make great pecuniary sacrifices." [2]

With the approach of spring the world seemed less forbidding. Evidences of quickening life were everywhere, bringing hope and promise to the Sisters. Looking back they could see that they had chosen the worst season of the year to start their project. They now redoubled their efforts to find a suitable house.

About this time Monseigneur Griffiths was involved in a lawsuit, the outcome of which was in doubt. He asked for the Sisters' prayers, promising them a gift of substance should things be resolved in his favor. When they were, he gave Mother St. Joseph the munificent sum of 1000 English pounds. The Sisters simply could not believe their good fortune. With tear-filled eyes Mother stood mute before the Bishop. The shock of release from her heavy cares had taken away her voice. "It robbed me of my courtesy as well," she said later. "However, Bishop Griffiths understood. He also had borne the cross of poverty."

On the 10th of March the Sisters started a Novena to St. Joseph, begging him as a householder and Mother St. Joseph's patron to help them find a proper home. Nine days later on his Feast Day they learned that a house on near-by King Street could be leased for two years. Naturally they accepted that news as an answer to their prayers.

In Angers Mother St. Euphrasia rejoiced when she learned that the English foundation was finally under way. On March 24 she told the entire Community of the progress of affairs as reported to her by Mother St. Joseph. "Tomorrow, my dear daughters, on the Feast of the Annunciation, the English Sisters will at last have a house of their own. . . . We may say, therefore, that this much-desired foundation is about to be born, but it will sorely need our help, for a child just born is yet far from being able to walk alone."

On May 3 the Sisters moved into the first London House of the Good Shepherd, there to inaugurate a work that would spread like pollen into the far places of the British Isles. The coming of three additional Sisters early in June and the receiving of their first penitents later in the same month proved that Mother St. Euphrasia's daughters had come to stay. Sometimes the going would be rough and the feelings against them bitter, but no kind of attack could dissuade them from their mission of accepting and caring for the strays of the Good Shepherd's flock.

During this same period Mother St. Euphrasia had somehow found time to encourage the foundations already in operation and to add two new ones to the growing roster. On New Year's Day the Paris Home was opened on the Boulevard de Gobelins with a staff of six Sisters. This foundation had been made possible through the zeal of Mme. de Lamartine, wife of Alphonse de Lamartine, the great romantic poet of France. On earlier occasions Mme. de Lamartine had given assistance to the Good Shepherd foundations in the south. Now as president of a Parisian association directed to the care of girls and women leaving the great prison of St. Lazaire, she turned to Mother St. Euphrasia for help. Greatly interested, Mother St. Euphrasia went at once to Paris. What she found there caused her to say: "Girls released from prison need friends badly. It is then that they are most responsive to outside influences. Lacking a more promising alternative, they naturally tend to return to their old haunts and acquaintances."

Now was the time to provide that alternative but both civil and church authorities were united in their opposition. Knowing that no progress of any kind could be hoped for without their good will and support, Mother St. Euphrasia set about to win them over, explaining her principle of giving each girl a definite responsibility in a well-ordered environment as a means of aiding her to break completely with the disordered environment from which she came. And equally important, Mother insisted, was the emphasis on moral and spiritual training without which delinquency grew like an ugly weed on an untended city lot.

In spite of conflicts of personalities, serious misunderstandings, and mounting expenses, she held on tenaciously, managing always to retain her equanimity and clearheadedness. By June, twenty-nine children and two women had been given shelter by the Good Shepherd. As statistics those figures were impressive but as opportunities for God's grace they were even more meaningful.

That same year also brought the establishment of a House in Toulon, reputed to be the most wicked spot in all of France. When Father Marin, a navy chaplain, learned of the Sisters through a nephew of Mme. d'Andigne, he spearheaded a movement that resulted in bringing them to that maritime city. His efforts were so heroic that an eminent biographer referred to the Toulon enterprise as "a terrible and uneven struggle." [3] Identified closely with this undertaking were Mother St. Euphasia and Mother Teresa of Jesus,[4] the new Superior. More than any other foundation Toulon can offer no logical reason for its survival.

In August the Mother House was favored with a visit by the Bishop of Montreal. Despite the lack of modern media of communication all France knew of Monseigneur Bourget and his exploits in the new world. At Angers the name of this pioneer Bishop was held especially dear. In a sense his endeavors were similar to those of St. Francis Xavier, for like the great Apostle to the Indies, he too had carried the love of Christ to a distant and strange land, his labors extending far beyond Montreal into the Canadian wilderness.

Soon it became known that Monseigneur Bourget desired to take some of the Sisters back with him. The stirring accounts of his travels by horse, sled, and canoe in order to reach his scattered flock of French "habitants" and North American Indians fired the Sisters to volunteer for work in his diocese, in spite of the prospect of bitter-cold winters and the necessary privations of pioneer life.

Mother St. Euphrasia shared their enthusiam but Monseigneur Paysant discouraged it, saying that the Good Shepherd Order was still too young and insecure for expansion abroad. In the face of his opposition Mother St. Euphrasia regretfully postponed taking any action on Monseigneur Bourget's invitation. However, less than three years later (June, 1844) she was able to send four Sisters on the long journey to Montreal.

Meanwhile Mother St. Euphrasia was busy with plans to make the Angers Novitiate international in character. Under Bishop de Hercé's direction courses in English were being offered along with the European languages to prepare the novices for whatever fields might beckon them upon the completion of their training. Mother's foresight was soon to be rewarded.

Only a few weeks after Monseigneur Bourget's visit, a letter from Bishop Flaget in America brought the news that his jurisdiction had been rechristened. Instead of being known as the diocese of Bardstown, it would now be called the diocese of Louisville, a vast area, subsequently to be subdivided into numerous daughter dioceses. Bishop Flaget, an old friend of the Congregation, encouraged Mother St. Euphrasia to make early plans to send him a nucleus of her Sisters. He dispelled any doubts that such a move might be premature by writing that one of his priests who knew Louisville well "is convinced that such an Institution, the only one in the United States, could not fail to be popular, and for that reason would be sure to succeed. . . . Let me, therefore, encourage you to make this attempt; . . . on a small scale, say with five or seven religious, of whom three or four ought to be young enough to be able to learn English.[5] They should also be filled with the Spirit of Him whose name is theirs . . . they will have a very abundant harvest to gather in . . . out of a population of 28,000 to 30,000, of whom only 5,000 are Catholics."[6]

Had it not been for Monseigneur Paysant's attitude toward Montreal, Mother St. Euphrasia would have immediately shared Bishop Flaget's letter with him. Instead she preferred to wait a while, writing first to Cardinal della Porta. Her action in this regard was not unique for it was her custom to keep in close touch with Rome at all times. To her great delight, the Cardinal Protector readily approved of the Sisters' settling in the United States. In addition he made it clear that he did not consider the Montreal issue closed. "I permit the Foundation of Montreal, Canada, as well, and will gladly lend my assistance when the time shall come for it." [7]

With this official approbation Mother St. Euphrasia was free to act without the permission of her Bishop, but she had no desire to do that. Instead she hoped to persuade Monseigneur Paysant to withdraw his objections, but her plans were cut short by Monseigneur Paysant's unexpected death from apoplexy on the 6th of September. The entire city was stunned and no one's grief was more real than Mother St. Euphrasia's. More than once she and the Bishop had disagreed on policies and procedures but their differences had not diminished their regard for each other. "The Good Shepherd has lost a good friend. We shall miss Monseigneur Paysant sorely."

Three months later Cardinal della Porta also died. Apart from her personal sorrow, Mother St. Euphrasia faced the fact that these two deaths coming so close to each other checked any plans she held for early action on Bishop Flaget's proposal.

Disappointed but undaunted, she surveyed the size and state of the Good Shepherd Institute, now completing its first decade under her direction. At the close of 1841 it numbered 26 Houses in all, 20 in France and 6 in other countries. Distributed among these were 500 religious, exclusive of 126 novices, working zealously to remake the lives of the girls entrusted to them. But Mother St. Euphrasia was quick to add that impressive as this inventory appeared, it should be looked upon only as a beginning.

XII

1842

There is no sin, however great, that others have committed of which I am not capable, if God did not support me by His grace.

St. Augustine

THERE were signs of approaching spring everywhere. The air was fresher, the sky clearer, and the days brighter. Crocuses carpeted the ground and daffodils were beginning to show their saucy yellow heads. Spring was definitely Mother St. Euphrasia's favorite season with its constant rebirth and renewal. She could apply its message to every aspect of her work.

One morning she was occupied with such thoughts when suddenly she heard a human cry, a whimpering followed by a steady moaning. She opened the window and looked about. At the far side of the building some Sisters were bending over a prostrate child, then two Sisters carried the crying child to a chair and others helped to carry the burden into the Infirmary.

One of the group joined Mother St. Euphrasia. "It was Janie Scott. She'd taken a notion to run away and had made a rope of sheets and pillowcases and slid within a yard of the ground. When she jumped she twisted her foot badly."

"I do hope she hasn't broken any bones. Ah me, she's homesick, no doubt. We must be very kind to her, poor unhappy child."

Had it not been for some passers-by this incident would have ended with Janie's return to health. Instead it became an occasion of widespread ill will, for it was reported that the Sisters had carried a screaming child forcibly into the house. Before long rumors were rife that the Sisters punished the children corporally, even binding them with chains in an effort to break their will. Soon the wild reports got out of hand. A number of local papers fanned the blaze by printing bizarre stories. One editor became so vindictive that Mother St. Euphrasia, acting under advisement, instituted a suit of libel against him, going into court to defend herself and her associates from the untrue and malicious charges that this unscrupulous man had perpetrated. The coolheaded manner in which she met her accusers and the direct and ingenuous way in which she presented her side of the case disarmed her opponents and left them her reluctant admirers. Even the editor who had maligned her admitted begrudgingly that he had been wrong. Later he became a supporter of the Institute.

This event was a forerunner of similar unfriendly attacks which have broken out intermittently in other places. Whenever they have occurred they have caused the Sisters deep distress but in the end have won them wider and more favorable recognition.

In 1842 Mother St. Euphrasia realized one of her lifelong dreams with the opening of a House in the bustling seacoast city of Genoa. At last she was to have "little black girls" among her flock. To the people of Genoa and vicinity the name of Father Oliveri, a former sailor, was synonymous with the ransom of "children-slaves" sold at public auction in the main square of Alexandria in Egypt. He had dedicated his life to raising money with which to purchase these children whom he then brought back to Italy for placement in approved institutions and occasional private homes, instructing them in the basic truths of Christianity.

The bruised and broken bodies of these boys and girls bore witness to the brutality of their former masters. Tirelessly Father Oliveri worked to collect sufficient funds to justify his trips to Alexandria; then happy and penniless he would return, bent on finding good homes for the frightened waifs he had rescued. When he learned that the Good Shepherd Sisters had settled in Genoa, he hastened to them, confident that they would help him. Happily Mother St. Euphrasia was there at the time. She listened to his story, observing the entreaty in the eyes of the children he had brought along. She saw them as gifts from God and instructed the Sisters to do their utmost for them. No doubt the early problems experienced by the Sisters and the children were mutually difficult, but before long the Sisters could report that two twelve-year-old girls had been baptized by Father Oliveri and that others were to follow. Mother St. Euphrasia then asked that some of these children be sent to Angers, whereupon Father Oliveri lost no time in journeying to Angers himself, bringing with him a number of the ransomed children. The advent of little black girls in the classes was historically significant although numerically the group was small alongside those who were to come later to the Sisters at the Convent of El Biar in Algiers and other subsequent foundations.

Bishop de Hercé of Nantes was familiar with several Arabic dialects and made it a point on his frequent visits to the Mother House to converse with Father Oliveri's protégés. In turn they quickly learned the French language and were able to teach it to later newcomers. With the reception of these black children Mother St. Euphrasia set a precedent that the Sisters of the Good Shepherd have never violated: there is no discrimination in the Good Shepherd fold on grounds of race, creed, or color. Whenever segregation exists, it is dictated by the customs of the locality. In some places, the Sisters would not be permitted to operate their Homes if a color barrier was not observed. Hence there are parallel colored and white classes in the Homes at New Orleans, Louisiana, and Memphis, Tennessee, and separate Homes for colored children as in "Calverton," Baltimore, and Germantown,[1] Pennsylvania.

Like St. Paul, Mother St. Euphrasia was "in journeyings often." Remembering her aversion to travel one marvels at her endless peregrinations. Apart from the official visitations required canonically, she made numerous trips to potential convents or those already in existence. Until 1842 she had never had a serious illness. But after an accident that occurred that year she was never again to be free of pain. In October she left for Angoulême in answer to an invitation from Bishop Regnier that she open a Home of the Good Shepherd within his See. With a companion she had set out happily, viewing this venture as an opportunity to repay the Bishop, partially at least, for favors he had extended her in the past. Often her mind went back to a day early in February, 1835, when Monseigneur Regnier, then a member of the Cathedral staff in Angers, had celebrated the Solemn High Mass that marked the birth of the Generalate. Later upon the arrival of the Decree of Authorization from Rome, it was the Monseigneur who had presented it officially to the rejoicing Community.

The day was clear and the stage in perfect condition. The horses

were fresh and the road smooth and level. Three passengers, two of
them religious, had settled themselves for the long journey ahead
when suddenly, and for no known reason, the horses stumbled and
fell, overturning the carriage and scattering the baggage in all directions. The travelers were thrown violently into Mother St. Euphrasia's
corner, probably breaking some of her ribs. Fighting for breath she
had to wait until helpers came to right the coach. She was then taken
into a near-by house and given first aid. The physicians called to
examine her diagnosed her injuries as minor, but as a precautionary
measure advised her to rest in bed for several days.

Diagnosis to the contrary, Mother St. Euphrasia had evidently
received a severe contusion which was to cause her constant and
increasing pain, developing eventually into a malignant tumor. As
soon as possible after the accident she set out again and effected the
arrangements to send the Sisters to Bishop Regnier.

Early in January, 1842, Constantin Cardinal Patrizi had been
appointed the third Cardinal Protector of the Sisters of the Good
Shepherd. As a close friend of Cardinal Odescalchi, he always held a
warm personal affection for the Good Shepherd, having visited the
Houses in Rome a number of times. Consequently his appointment
was received at Angers with great joy. Fortunately he was to hold
this position for thirty-six years, a fact that augured well for the
inviolability of the Institute. Had a less stanch personality been its
defender, Mother St. Euphrasia might not have been able to weather
the storms ahead.

Encouraged by Cardinal Patrizi Mother Euphrasia lost no time
in resuming negotiations for the first American foundation, and then
in making the involved and extensive arrangements required for this
mission far across the sea. "Come, come, Sisters," wrote Bishop Flaget
of Louisville. "The work I offer is worthy of your vocation. . . . All
of you, by the union of your prayers and co-operation, will be baptiz-
ing with your Sisters in America; you will be with them in those great
forests where they will seek wandering souls." [2]

Mother St. Euphrasia's enthusiasm ran high but her practicality
restrained her. She was careful to outline the hardships that would
be the lot of the Sisters who volunteered for America, among which
would be their enforced absence from the Mother House. "Someday
I may be able to arrange for your periodical return to Angers but at
present that prospect does not exist."

At the Chapter called for the purpose of nominating the Sisters

for the American mission, Mother St. Euphrasia likened this opportunity to Our Lord's injunction to His apostles: "Go ye, therefore,
and teach all nations." Then she recalled the words of St. Ignatius
when he had bemoaned the small number of laborers that he had
available for service in the foreign field: " 'Oh, why have I not many
more faithful servants to immolate to the glory of God?' Today, my
daughters, the same invitation comes; the same words are spoken.
It is . . . now that the glorious plan of your future labour is to be
unfolded to you."

Five young Sisters,[3] each of a different nationality, were finally
selected for this expedition. "I give you Sister Mary des Anges
Porcher as your Superior," Mother St. Euphrasia said in a tear-choked
voice. Sister Mary was then only twenty-four years old. "Love her and
serve her well for the Good Shepherd's sake. With her as your leader
you should do great work for souls."

This little band laid the path for those who were to follow, leaving
the Mother House on October 10 and stopping briefly in Paris before
their scheduled departure from Le Havre on the ship *Utica*. From
the start the voyage was rough and unpleasant. Between their bouts
with seasickness and an acute shortage of pure drinking water, the
Sisters sometimes feared they might not survive the trip. Had it not
been for the kindness of their fellow passengers, four Sacred Heart
nuns and their Superior, Mother Aloysia Hardey, the lot of Mother
Mary of the Angels and her companions would have been even
harder. At last on the 17th of November they reached New York
where they spent five days at the Sacred Heart Convent on Houston
Street before they resumed their journey.

Mother Mary of the Angels made use of this delay to write Mother
St. Euphrasia. "Our voyage across the ocean is at an end. It took
thirty-one days. This is considered short for the season, which is
always unfavourable. We have passed through great perils and attrib-
ute our safety to the fervent prayers offered for us at Angers. The
terrible storms of the first few weeks at sea were followed by intense
heat. On the first evening of this sultry spell, the ship's officer called
us on deck to see the phosphorescences. The night was a dark one,
which made them appear the more brilliant. It was a magnificent
sight.

". . . When our arrival in New York was announced, we had numerous visitors. Some came out of mere curiosity and seemed to look
upon us as peculiar specimens of humanity! As our religious habit at-

tracted unpleasant notice on landing, we are, by order of Archbishop Hughes, to change into secular dress. Reverend Mother Hardey is adding to her other kindnesses by providing this for us. His Grace in blessing us said he admired our courage in coming so far in search of the lost sheep of Israel. He is procuring a guide for the remainder of our journey. We have yet many hundreds of leagues before us." [4]

At Philadelphia the Sisters visited the Sisters of Charity, then proceeded by train to Chambersburg where they made connections with the stage for Pittsburgh. In describing their coach one of the Sisters wrote: "Picture to yourselves a piece of scarlet stuff spread on four boards and you have the interior of one of those dreadful stages." The trip across the Allegheny Mountains in subzero weather proved even worse than the heavy storms at sea. The Sisters were not dressed warmly enough to protect them from the wintry blasts and they found no suitable places along their route at which they could stop for food and shelter. They reached Pittsburgh in a near state of exhaustion, but the Very Reverend Father O'Connor, Vicar General of the Diocese, met them and took them immediately to the Convent of Mercy, where the warm hospitality helped them to forget their physical discomforts. A short time later they boarded a steamer that carried them down the Ohio River to "Our Promised Land," as one of the Sisters dubbed their destination.

On December 1, after seven weeks of travel, the pioneers reached Louisville, the first stronghold of the Good Shepherd Sisters in the United States. Bishop Flaget awaited them at the Convent of the Loretta Nuns where they were to stay temporarily. He welcomed them in a ringing voice: "I bless the day of your arrival in my diocese."

From the beginning people everywhere had shown great interest in the success of the American enterprise. The secular press in Angers acclaimed it with enthusiasm; the other Convents of the Good Shepherd sent the Sisters small gifts; Count de Neuville and Mme. d'Andigne contributed money and furnishings for the Sisters and their new chapel; and the Bishops of New York, Philadelphia, and Pittsburgh proved hospitable hosts, urging them to settle in their respective dioceses as soon as possible. As Monseigneur Pasquier has written: "The seed was cast into the furrow; soon the harvest would ripen." [5]

Not until the following September would the Sisters be able to carry on their work from their own headquarters. "Mesdames,"

Bishop Flaget had said, "you must have patience for a little while in the modest house which is all we can now place at your disposal; but we will use the money we had set aside for the Cathedral to make you a monastery [6] and the Cathedral will come later on with the help of God."

Before the Sisters' letters had time to reach Angers, a letter written on November 11 arrived from Mother St. Euphrasia. "My beloved children . . .: You are in America, that Divine Mission, the object of our heart's love. Zeal, obedience have carried you 2000 leagues away from us! It is now 25 days since you left, and oh, my poor children, how many more before we hear from you. . . .

"Were you ill on the way, my angels? I am afraid Sister St. Louis of Gonzaga and Sister St. Joseph will have gone through much suffering, and perhaps all five of you at the same time; but the love of Jesus will have made everything sweet. Our prayers, good wishes, and Communions have followed you continually. We have been counting the days and watching the weather. Ah, how we have besought Him who calms the troubled winds and waves, to save you from storms. How thankful we shall all be to hear about your voyage—your holy voyage, during which I am very sure, my dear daughters, God gave you great graces. He would surely speak to our Xaviers when leading them to distant shores." A little more than a century later there would be a total of 55 chapters in the United States.

In February, 1842, Mother St. Euphrasia learned with pleasure that the late Monseigneur Paysant's successor was to be Monseigneur Louis Angebault, the Vicar General of Bishop de Hercé of Nantes. Some months later, on the 10th of August, the colorful ceremonies of consecration took place in the Cathedral of Angers, followed the next day by an imposing reception at the Mother House of the Good Shepherd.

Mother St. Euphrasia reasoned that Bishop de Hercé's Vicar General would naturally share his own Bishop's enthusiasm for her apostolate. With that in mind she wrote Bishop de Hercé of her joy in the appointment of Monseigneur Angebault. He replied under date of March 17: "Your German and English novices, . . . I shall always call daughters of mine. But I must no longer speak in this way of your Italian daughters, for Monseigneur Angebault has traveled in Italy, and if he does not speak the language, he at least understands it. . . . He and I will come to you together someday, my dear

Mother, and for me it will be a gala occasion. You will have a good
Bishop. . . ."

Meanwhile Cardinal Patrizi had offered to confer on Bishop Angebault the powers vacated by Monseigneur Regnier, recently appointed
Bishop of Angoulême, authorizing him to serve as his delegate and
personal representative in reference to the Good Shepherd located in
Angers. In answer to an inquiry from Monseigneur Angebault, the
Cardinal explained that each Convent had its own ecclesiastical
Superior whose powers are held to the House or Houses within his
own jurisdiction. This ruling known as the 32nd Constitution had
been officially incorporated in the Statutes of the Good Shepherd and
approved by the Holy See. Already it had turned out to be a wise
inclusion, assuring universal progress and harmony among the various
Convents.

In due time Mother St. Euphrasia was informed of this correspondence. To a large degree Cardinal Patrizi's pronouncements would
serve as her future bulwark of defense. In the past at Angers she had
not always been able to follow her own judgment in the matter of
foundations and problems of administration. Naturally the rejection
of the Montreal invitation was foremost in her mind. But everything
considered, she had to admit that even when Bishop Mountault and
Bishop Paysant had interfered in the government of the Congregation,
they had always sympathized with her work. Criticisms notwithstanding, they had never withdrawn their friendship.

Remembering these things Mother St. Euphrasia reasoned:
"Bishop Angebault will be well disposed too. Should a difference ever
arise, I shall be able to justify my actions in the light of Cardinal
Patrizi's adherence to our Constitutions. I must never permit anything to weaken our allegiance to Rome. However, I shall always take
pains to instruct the local Superiors to co-operate fully with their own
Bishops."

As the time drew near for the Reception of Bishop Angebault the
Sisters found themselves busier than ever. Special verses of welcome
were composed, illuminated, and hung in the Community Room.
The chapel was polished to high resplendency, and the flowers reserved for the altar cut at the last moment. Everyone was happy and
proud to have even a small part in the welcome of the new prelate.
How significant, the Sisters said, that his first official call should be on
the Good Shepherd. Mother St. Euphrasia, overhearing this remark,

was quick to say, "The Bishop honors us, that is true, but he comes here primarily on account of Bishop de Hercé, our mutual friend."

August 11 dawned bright and clear. Bishop Angebault accompanied by an entourage of visiting clergy arrived at the Mother House to be received with simple dignity. Bishop de Hercé, who had served as the Consecrator in the previous day's moving ceremonies, was once more the person in charge. But he made it clear that he was acting in the Sisters' stead. "These good Sisters are your rightful hostesses, Your Excellency. In the name of their Mother General, Mother Mary of St. Euphrasia Pelletier, the Good Shepherd salutes you."

The event proceeded to a satisfying climax. Everyone hoped that Bishop Angebault, then in his early fifties, was destined for a long and rich life. All prayers held the common refrain that God would bless him and his efforts as the leader of this diocese. Had it not been for one incident that occurred just before the prelate's departure, Mother St. Euphrasia might not have known that he entertained any antagonism toward her.

"Your Excellency, I am overjoyed at the honor you have paid us today. I have already written the Cardinal Protector telling him of the great happiness that is ours. From the time of your nomination he has known of our joy."

Bishop Angebault spat out rather than spoke his words of sarcasm. "Am I to understand then that it is you who are to be my protector at Rome?"

The silence was deafening. Mother St. Euphrasia had no words. She had thought to please her Bishop. For the next twenty-six years this offense was to be held against her. Whatever she did or did not do would displease the Bishop of Angers. A good and righteous man, he was inclined to be a nationalist in religion and an autocrat in his personal manner. In a crisis he accepted the decisions of Rome and bowed to its universality but he was an unreasoning defender of the rights and privileges of the French Church. Undoubtedly his attitude came about indirectly as a result of the long controversy between the French monarchs and the papacy in regard to the question of papal jurisdiction. The teachings of Gallicanism, or absolutism, exalting the prerogatives of the French Church at the expense of the authority of the Holy See had developed centuries earlier. Like every movement of protest it had weakened itself by its excesses. During the Reformation era the Gallican theory that both the Church and the State in France had ecclesiastical rights of their own, independent of and exclusive of the jurisdiction of the Pope, held sway. Later Bossuet incorporated this theory in a solemn declaration of the French clergy made in 1682. This declaration led to a serious quarrel with Rome and was officially withdrawn in 1693 though it died hardly among many of the French clergy, continuing to flourish until the Revolution. Shortly thereafter the Pope had condemned its chief concepts, refusing to confirm the nomination to French bishoprics of those who had signed or approved the Gallican Articles formulated by the French clergy in 1681. Despite this action the remnants of this philosophy lingered in the hearts of many.[7]

Monseigneur Angebault, although not a Gallicanist, found it hard to believe that the Church in France was not really superior to the Church in any other nation. He was jealous of his rights as a Bishop, going beyond the defined powers of his office in refusing to tolerate anything that he considered an infringement of his authority. Whenever such a challenge arose, it immediately became the object of his antagonism. In his eyes no project could have real worth unless he had instituted it and found it amenable to his jurisdiction.

At the same time Monseigneur Angebault was a man of piety and zeal, possessing the qualities of an excellent organizer and administrator. These qualities had already shown themselves in his interest in social and educational affairs. At Nantes he had founded the College of St. Stanislaus for the education of young men and had also reestablished the ancient Order of St. Gildas for the education of girls. His success in directing other religious Congregations [8] qualified him, so he naturally assumed, to direct the Good Shepherd similarly. In his mind, the fact that he was the Ecclesiastical Superior of the Angers Convent automatically meant that he was also the Superior General of the Order. When informed that this was not the situation, he insisted that Mother St. Euphrasia's authority was subject to his, refusing to make any distinction between ecclesiastical jurisdiction and the domestic power of internal authority. He was convinced that it was his legitimate right to have the determining voice in the affairs of the Good Shepherd as they affected all of the Houses of the Congregation. Consequently he found it impossible to accept the idea that cloistered religious, dedicated to works of charity, should hold primary allegiance to a Superior General in Rome, as did the Jesuits and Dominicans.

A short time previous Bishop Angebault had indicated that he planned to change the Constitutions of the Religious of the Cenacle, whose Mother House was in Angers. "The Bishop of Angers," he had said, "is *ipso facto* the Superior of this Congregation. He governs it directly or through an ecclesiastic whom he names and delegates to direct it in his place." Having taken this point of view, he objected even more vigorously to those sections of the Constitutions and Rules of the Good Shepherd which restrained him from being the Superior of the Order.

The crux of the matter lay in the Bishop's opposition to a Cardinal-Protector's having absolute jurisdiction over any Congregation whose Mother House was located within his diocese. With undiminished vigor he fought this ruling, considering it a personal affront and disobedience on the part of Mother St. Euphrasia that she should support such an arrangement. One would like to say that these misunderstandings were ephemeral and that the light of truth soon flooded Bishop Angebault's soul, but the record stands. On many occasions this ecclesiastic excoriated Mother St. Euphrasia publicly. As the years progressed his antagonism increased, causing friend and foe alike to declare: "Can not the Bishop realize that he persecutes an innocent person?"

More than a quarter of a century later he admitted that he had come to Angers with the intention of forcing Mother St. Euphrasia to return to the obedience of the Rule of the Refuge. The reports he had received from her adversaries at the time the Generalate was formed had led him to believe that she was an ambitious and determined person bent on promoting her own cause at the cost of an honored institution. In the light of his actions, it appears doubtful that he ever modified this belief.

Mother St. Euphrasia suffered the assaults her Bishop unleashed against her in silence. "God permits these things for His own reasons," she told herself. "Otherwise I could not endure them."

God's reason, it now seems, must have been to test Mother St. Euphrasia's sanctity—her patience, her forgiveness, her fortitude—for through her acceptance of her daily trials and tribulations, she won eventual sainthood. During her Beatification Process Bishop Angebault was represented by various witnesses as "willful," "impressionable," and "severe beyond reason." Even his close friends strenuously opposed his treatment of Mother St. Euphrasia. Monseigneur August Saudreau [9] wrote: "I owe Bishop Angebault a personal debt of gratitude, because on April 22, 1869, he became the impelling influence of my priestly vocation. Nevertheless, it is impossible to grasp fully the patience, humility, and heroic charity of Mother Mary of St. Euphrasia without considering how much this prelate made her suffer."

Canon Portais [10] also held the same point of view in his writing about Mother St. Euphrasia. "Bishop Angebault was so attached to his own ideas that he thought he was rendering a service to the Institute by attacking its fundamental Constitutions. The suffering caused by this attitude on the part of the venerable prelate was doubled by the impossibility of enlightening him. Opposition such as that which broke forth at the attempt to establish the Generalate was renewed in a very painful manner. All those, however, at Tours who knew the good Mother most intimately, . . . remained unshakeably faithful."

Beginning that August day in 1842 and continuing until Mother's death, Bishop Angebault exceeded his rights in every matter that pertained to the Good Shepherd. Like a hurricane he would make a surprising descent upon the ordered serenity of the cloister, summoning the Sisters before him while he assailed their Mother General, standing defenseless before him. After one such uncalled for attack Mother St. Euphrasia passed a small group of Sisters gathered together whispering their protests. She interrupted their little drama of indignation by saying most earnestly: "Sisters, you must not say anything about Monseigneur; it would not be right. Remember he is our Bishop."

Only in the vital matter of her allegiance to Rome did she oppose her diocesan Superior. That allegiance could not be weakened by threat or intimidation, attack or excoriation. As long as she lived Mother St. Euphrasia suffered anguish and humiliation for the sake of the stability of her Congregation. Such suffering constituted her martyrdom.

XIII

1843 - 1846

We need crosses and humiliations; if they were wanting we should perish. When we truly love God, nothing seems hard to us where His glory is concerned.

St. Mary of St. Euphrasia

MOTHER ST. EUPHRASIA made her second visit to Rome in the spring of 1843 at the insistence of Cardinal Patrizi who believed that certain problems affecting the Italian Houses should be resolved by personal conferences. Originally she had thought to make this visit the preceding fall but at that time Bishop Angebault had objected on the grounds that the weather was uncertain and there were pressing problems at home.

On the 18th of April Mother St. Euphrasia and Sister Elizabeth Renon left Angers, stopping first at Le Mans and then proceeding to Paris where they were joined by Sister Mary of Nazareth Drach. At Marseilles they learned that their companions aboard ship were to be three secular priests and four young Jesuits en route to India, together with M. Boré, noted traveler and orientalist, later to become a priest, and still later, the Superior of the Missions. Fortunately for posterity M. Boré wrote delightful letters about this pilgrimage. For her part Mother St. Euphrasia listened attentively to his vivid accounts of the Asiatic Mission Field. "These neglected countries cry out for a service such as yours," he said. "Mother St. Euphrasia, will you not send your Sisters to them?" She indicated her willingness to do so as soon as feasible.

After three calm and happy days at sea the party arrived at Cività

Vecchia where the French and Austrian consuls awaited them. Of the consuls she said, "They so overwhelmed us with kindness and attention we were quite confused." As she re-entered Rome the towering basilica of St. Peter rising high into the heavens seemed to her a welcoming beacon, both testimony and pledge to the great apostle for whom it was named. Later she told her daughters in Angers, "Nothing can equal the devotion one feels on entering St. Peter's. Those are indeed happy who live in this Holy City."

Mother St. Euphrasia spent a busy fortnight in Rome. On two occasions she was received by the scholarly and gentle Pope who repeated with emphasis his heartening words: "I consider the Order of the Good Shepherd as one of the most precious ornaments of my crown." She found Cardinal Patrizi's intimate knowledge of her work and aspirations equally heartening. He encouraged her to expand the work at every opportunity. "It is noble and it is important," he said, "and it must go on regardless of all obstacles." With such an advocate Mother St. Euphrasia found herself renewed in strength for the problems that lay ahead.

On the 1st of June she left Rome satisfied with the work that was being done at the Convents of Santa Croce and La Lauretana and determined that come what may, she would extend the services of the Good Shepherd. A statement she made one evening to the Sisters at Santa Croce was the wellspring of her apostolate. "My children, the good God has given me two special missions: to work for the penitents and to favor religious vocations."

On her return trip to Angers she visited fourteen Good Shepherd Convents and made arrangements for a new foundation in Turin. On the overland trip from Leghorn to Turin she found the mountainous terrain steep and dangerous, and the conduct of the drivers most alarming. They were scoundrels, no less, who attempted to extort money by threatening to abandon the Sisters on the lonely highway. Although that possibility terrified Mother St. Euphrasia she refused to pay more than the regular fare. Happily Sister Mary of Nazareth could speak Italian and when she told the drivers that their passengers were traveling to Turin at the personal invitation of the young monarch, Charles Albert of Piedmont, they gave no further trouble.

Mother St. Euphrasia reached Angers on August 11, having been away four months. Listening to the accounts of her trip, the Sisters appreciated more fully the vocation that was theirs. "Wherever I went," she told them, "I reminded our beloved Sisters of these words spoken by our Venerable Father Eudes: 'They should employ mind, heart, and diligence in making themselves the worthy coadjutors and co-operators of Jesus Christ, Our Lord.' "

Until recently she had always appeared to have endless energy, although those who knew her best realized that it was as much an achievement as an endowment. She planned her work, both at hand and ahead. However, of late she felt her physical limitations and would occasionally say, "When, oh when, shall I be able to rest?" But she knew that her question was merely rhetorical for each mail added to her responsibilities. With the departure of five Sisters for Turin on the 1st of November, she hoped to have a brief respite. Count de Neuville heartily approved of a respite, constantly telling Mother St. Euphrasia that she should give more time to rest. Ever since her accident on the way to Angoulême he had been concerned about her health. "What would the Order do without you, dear Mother?" he asked. In turn she smiled and said, "What would it do without you?" Before long she was to learn the answer to her question.

On December 3, 1843, following a serious illness aggravated by his self-imposed fastings and penances, Count Augustine de Neuville died, impoverished by his benefactions to the Order. However, he objected to being called poor, remonstrating, "I consider myself wealthy beyond measure for the part I have been privileged to play." Even when his generosity had reduced him to straitened circumstances, he still insisted on contributing five francs each week. When Mother St. Euphrasia had protested, he silenced her by saying: "How can you who are a Religious of Our Lady of Charity of the Good Shepherd deny me the gift of charity?" His last words revealed his happiness in the knowledge that she considered him the Founder of the Mother House in Angers: "How glad I am! How happy I am! . . . I have founded the Good Shepherd. I die in peace." The small residue of his estate enabled Mother St. Euphrasia to enlarge the Novitiate and to add to the main church the Chapels of St. Augustine and St. Philomena. If she had built them with her own hands, which no doubt she would have attempted if necessary, she could not have been more pleased with them as tributes to "our good father, M. de Neuville, who gave us everything and made such great sacrifices for our sake. I hope there will never be a Religious of the Good Shepherd anywhere, who could forget his name."

Since then the young women who have come to the Angers Novitiate have sought to make his spirit a reality far beyond his native Angers. As a result the Count de Neuville, the father of the Good

Shepherd, has a place in memory near to St. John Eudes, the original founder of the Institute.

For a long time the Sisters in London had been urging Mother St. Euphrasia to visit them but she preferred to wait until English custom would permit her to wear her religious habit in public. "I have worn this holy habit for thirty years," she said, "and I cannot make up my mind to put it off. I will go to London when I can dress as a religious." In the spring of 1844 Mother St. Joseph Regaudiat reported that prejudices were slowly dying and the Sisters themselves were appearing less frequently in secular garb. They had even put up a cross over the Convent gate, probably the only one in all of London, and the fact that it had caused no trouble encouraged them to believe that Mother St. Euphrasia could come in safety to England.

She left Angers on the 19th of June, arriving at Dover six days later. With her were Mother Teresa de Couespel, now the Second Assistant to the Mother General, and a novice interpreter. In a leisurely manner they proceeded to London by way of Kent and Surrey. Later she reported, "The beauty and the orderliness of the countryside and the similarity of the small brick homes interested me extremely. I longed to speak the language of these people and to become acquainted with them. Then I recalled St. Evermond's observation that 'the French speak too much and think too little,' and I comforted myself with the thought that under those circumstances it was probably just as well that I had to depend upon our little interpreter for communication." Actually a language barrier was scarcely a detriment to her because instinctively she spoke the common language of the heart.

It was ten o'clock in the evening when they reached London and as they were not expected until the next day, they went to a near-by French hotel where M. Pagliano, the proprietor, proved a gracious host. By a happy coincidence he was a benefactor of the London Good Shepherd. In the morning Mme. Pagliano took the nuns to Hammersmith where the welcoming Sisters were still putting last-minute touches to their preparations in honor of their Mother General's visit. For a few minutes joyous confusion reigned. Tears flowed freely, tears of real happiness.

The next ten days were busy ones. Mother St. Euphrasia was pleased with affairs at the Hammersmith Convent, knowing well what they had cost in labor, disappointment, and sacrifice. Thirty children in the Class had embraced the Faith, a record that would be hard to match anywhere. The children entertained the Head Mother from

France with a little play, "The Story of Ruth." She watched attentively, noting particularly a girl named Agnes who played the part of Ruth. Unaware that Agnes aspired to become a Consecrate, Mother observed that this child gave herself wholeheartedly to her part. Upon the conclusion of the program Mother St. Euphrasia rose and smiling at the children, especially Agnes, motioned them close to her. Then she spoke slowly and distinctly the English sentence she had learned for this occasion: "The more I see you, the more I love you, my dear children."

The children clapped their hands. The Sisters glowed. Until the present day, these words of Mother St. Euphrasia have been perpetuated at Hammersmith, serving as a kind of accolade to the children when they have succeeded in some important task.

As was her custom Mother St. Euphrasia visited many of the local churches. When she found that the Blessed Sacrament was not present on the altars, she cried out softly: "Where are you, my Divine Master? The sanctuary lamp is not in its rightful place. Does that mean that You are not here?" The priest at her side answered her whispered question by saying, "The Blessed Sacrament is not here. It is still hidden as One proscribed." Then he led her quietly into the sacristy where a little night light burned before a wooden cupboard, indicating that the Blessed Sacrament was reserved there, locked securely behind its doors.

Mother St. Euphrasia fell to her knees, promising her Lord that she would direct her efforts to raising chapels in His honor in the land she was then visiting. She made her promise good by establishing Convents in Bristol, Glasgow (Dalbeth), Liverpool (Ford), East Finchley, and Manchester, later succeeded by others throughout England and Wales.

One of the first things Mother St. Euphrasia did was to call on the Benedictine Nuns to express her appreciation to Abbess Selby for the hospitality extended her spiritual daughters during their first months in London. After that she was kept busy greeting important visitors. Monseigneur Griffiths, the Vicar Apostolic and Head of the Catholic Church in England, conferred with her on a number of occasions; the Marchioness of Wellesley renewed her interrupted benefactions to the Hammersmith Convent; Lady Peel, wife of Sir Robert Peel, then Prime Minister of England, came to pay her respects. Never had Mother St. Euphrasia's catholicity of interests been more apparent.

So occupied, the days passed too quickly. When Mother St. Euphrasia left on July 2, she carried with her the satisfaction that old and new friends were drawn to the work of reclamation. As one commentator has remarked: "Mother Pelletier by the mere fact of her presence, not only stirred up her daughters' zeal, but excited charity in their favor, and attracted alms and warmer interest in their work." [1]

On her return trip she visited the Convents at Lille, Amiens, Rheims, Sens, and Paris, arriving at Angers on July 26. The rest of the year found her extraordinarily busy. Letters from Louisville, Kentucky, told of many stirring conversions among the penitents and reported the charity the Sisters steadily dispensed. They wrote about the Bishop of Texas, Rt. Rev. J. M. Odin, having been set upon by Indians and forced to flee his poor mission in the middle of the night, arriving in Louisville in a near state of exhaustion, clothed only in goatskin. En route to the residence of Bishop Flaget he had stopped to rest at the Convent of the Good Shepherd where the Mother Superior hastily made a cassock for him out of the cloaks the Sisters had worn on their voyage from France. The Bishop's gratitude was unbounded. "Someday, if God so wills, I shall report this act of kindness to your Mother General." A year later while on a visit to France he was able to do that, bringing Mother St. Euphrasia a firsthand account of the work being done by the Louisville Sisters.

One of Mother St. Euphrasia's most satisfying experiences occurred in the summer of 1844 when a native Vendean, Monseigneur Soyer, Bishop of Luçon, visited Angers. As a young priest Father Soyer had experienced the rigors and dangers of the Revolution, carrying on his pastoral duties in hiding under the protection of native Vendean soldiers. On a certain spring night in the valley of the Hirome, he had administered First Holy Communion to a large group of children whose parents had risked their lives to bring them there. As she listened, Mother St. Euphrasia recalled the days of the Vendean Wars when she was obliged to say her catechism in private and to await visits of the clergy who came intermittently at the peril of their lives.

She was happy to have a class of five postulants ready to present to Monseigneur Soyer for clothing in the habit of the Good Shepherd. This impressive ceremony never failed to touch her heart but it assumed an added significance as she watched this favored group receive the white veil of noviceship from the prelate whose jurisdiction included her own birthplace, the beautiful isle of Noirmoutier.

The year ended with two new foundations added to the roster. One was in Montreal, June 11, 1844; the other in Dôle in the Jura, on the border of Switzerland adjacent to the Diocese of Genoa, December 18, 1844. For a time this latter foundation appeared marked for failure, denied the support and resources it had been promised. Mother St. Euphrasia felt compelled to disperse the Sisters, reassigning the Superior to Perpignan. However, the dispersal did not materialize because Mother Rogerson, the Assistant Superior, begged to be given the opportunity to continue the work. Later when Mother Rogerson's efforts had met with success Mother St. Euphrasia gratefully acknowledged the "zeal of this English daughter."

Meanwhile the relations with Monseigneur Angebault had become more strained. In the early spring of 1845 he took umbrage at a letter written by Sister Teresa of Jesus de Couespel in which she had beseeched His Excellency not to seek to change the statutes of the Good Shepherd, an intention he pursued with undiminished determination. The Bishop's reaction to that letter had far-reaching consequences. In no uncertain terms he informed Mother St. Euphrasia that she must banish Sister Teresa of Jesus from Angers at once, allowing only five days for her transfer to another foundation. He permitted no negotiations regarding his order, adding that unless Sister Teresa of Jesus were sent elsewhere immediately, he would withdraw his permission for the approaching ceremony of clothing and profession.

Who can describe the cost at which Mother St. Euphrasia carried out this direction which forced separation from her beloved spiritual daughter? She named Sister Teresa the Superior of Amiens but she wrote in confidence to Mother Mary of St. John of the Cross, presently in Munich, "Except that I am not in prison, I am suffering every sort of sorrow without any support or aid. The Bishop has just banished our dear Sister Mary of St. Teresa of Jesus from his diocese because of her loyalty to Rome. He wished to expel me also. The tears of the Council, however, prevented him."

To understand Monseigneur Angebault's next act one needs to keep in mind the fact that Canon Law, the official statutes and rules of the Universal Church, had not yet reached its present concise codification. As regulations then stood, the Bishop of Angers could refuse to accept Cardinal Patrizi's interpretation of his diocesan authority in regard to the Good Shepherd, appealing directly to the Roman Congregation of Bishops and Regulars, the same body that had earlier approved the Generalate. In April, 1845, he was answered by a decree of that Congregation, forwarded simultaneously to the Bishop's Residence and to the Mother House of the Good Shepherd, in which Cardinal Contini, the Prefect of the Congregation, granted Monseigneur Angebault certain privileges, including the naming of the confessor for the Community and the appointing of his own personal representative as well as the delegate of the Cardinal Protector. All other regulations, however, were to remain unchanged.

"If their Eminences the Cardinals," Cardinal Contini wrote, "have preserved intact the authority of the Cardinal Protector, they have done it solely for the good of the pious Society. In fact it is under this patronage that it has taken its immense extension, and the unity which is necessary to it would greatly suffer if the Sisters, especially in matters that concern the entire Society, should not be able to appeal to him as Superior in last report, dispersed as they are in many places and dioceses. And it would not be with good reason that local Superiors should complain of a diminution of their authority. That of the Cardinal Protector himself is confined within given limits and he only exercises it as delegate of the Holy Apostolic See. That is why their Eminences, trusting in the veneration which Your Lordship professes toward the Holy See, trusting in Your zeal for this pious Institute, rest assured that Your Excellence will receive with joy and respect a decision of their Congregation, confirmed by His Holiness, and that You will give all Your care in order that, with the blessing of God, the said Institute shall increase yet more in Your diocese." [2]

For six weeks following the receipt of this communication Bishop Angebault stayed away from the Good Shepherd, neither visiting it himself nor appointing a representative to serve for him. Under these conditions all matters which required the sanction or the presence of an ecclesiastic were blocked. One can scarcely envision this state of affairs in a house of religion. Without an authorized ecclesiastic to minister to them, the Sisters and the children were spiritually bereft. Among other things Mother St. Euphrasia was powerless to make arrangements for the necessary ceremonies of clothing and profession.

At last Monseigneur Angebault relented and named Father Augustine Joubert, his Vicar General. This appointment, dated June 1, 1845, was received with joy for Father Joubert had many times voiced his understanding of their work. Now he pledged his allegiance to the Cardinal Protector, assuring the Sisters of the Good Shepherd of his humble desire to serve them well. "I place myself at your disposal for whatever services you might designate, and I solemnly promise that nothing shall interfere with my satisfactory performance of those services. I shall always strive to advance the welfare of this holy Institute. If the duties of my present office ever encroach upon my duties as your Superior, I shall not hesitate to ask to be relieved as the Vicar General. Such is my given word and intention." For the next thirteen years he kept that promise admirably but he was not able to eliminate wholly Monseigneur Angebault's prejudices toward Mother St. Euphrasia.

Mother St. Euphrasia's term as Superior General expired in 1843, but the Holy See, recognizing the state of tension in Angers, recommended the postponement of the elections until a more propitious time, meanwhile authorizing Mother St. Euphrasia to remain temporily in office. By the summer of 1845, however, it was thought wise to conduct the overdue elections. Cardinal Patrizi himself then invited Monseigneur Angebault to preside over the Assembly of the Chapter set for August 26. In spite of this invitation Monseigneur Angebault was not to be appeased. He refused to attend the elections, informing Father Joubert, who was to preside, that he did not want Mother St. Euphrasia re-elected. "It is my desire that the Sisters nominate Sister St. Euphrasia von Pechman, the Superior of the Convent at Turin. For them to disregard my wishes will be a direct and disobedient act."

The Bishop's order was in violation of integrity of a religious congregation. Consequently the eighteen Superiors who had come from afar felt justified in obeying their own consciences, supported stanchly by the other Superiors who were unable to be present but had sent their votes under seal. Tears of joy ran freely when Father Joubert announced the outcome of the election. Everyone present knew that Mother St. Euphrasia alone was their true leader and to have chosen any other would have been an ungrateful repudiation of one who loved and suffered much in their behalf.

As had been foreseen Monseigneur Angebault protested the re-election of Mother St. Euphrasia, but Rome stated tersely that "the election had been made strictly according to the Rules, and as it presented no irregularities, it was maintained and should be exercised in full." Silenced on that issue, the Bishop opened another, forbidding the re-election of the absent Sister Teresa of Jesus as Assistant General. Sister St. Euphrasia von Pechman was his candidate, and he indicated that he wished her to serve additionally as Mistress of Novices. Although he was again violating the Constitutions, Mother St. Euphrasia proposed the name he suggested to the Chapter for approval. She alone could name her as the Mistress of Novices. She knew that Sister von Pechman was a devout nun but believed that she lacked the very special qualities needed to deal with aspirants to the religious life. However, she appointed her to the post the Bishop had designated, hoping to win his good will for the Community by means of this act of co-operation.

For six years Mother regretted having made this appointment because she found that the Bishop's favor was fleeting and that Sister von Pechman's inefficiency was lasting. Her inadequacies as Head of the Novitiate resulted in general dissatisfaction which continued throughout her term of office. Had it not been for Mother St. Euphrasia's counsel, the Novitiate might have completely disintegrated.

Mother St. Euphrasia's re-election brought a touching letter from her good friend, Monseigneur de Hercé, the Bishop of Nantes. Having expressed his joy over "the good Mother General's re-election" he offered his respects and congratulations to her "for whom I feel an attachment and reverence that can know no change." Then he added his felicitations to "you, my good Mothers, whom I congratulate upon her continuing to be Superior. It would have been a terrible misfortune for the whole Congregation to have been deprived of such a Head—so skillful, so prudent, so filled with the Spirit of God." [3] He added that he would come to "comfort, exhort, and converse with all the dear children from distant lands" but only when Father Joubert deemed it necessary to request Monseigneur Angebault to invite him for that purpose. His inference was that his presence was no longer considered useful. He did not elucidate, but Mother St. Euphrasia could read between the lines. Clearly Monseigneur Angebault did not approve of Monseigneur de Hercé's continuing his visits to the Mother House, useful linguist though he was. Consequently, the foreign Sisters and novices were denied his help.

Two years passed before Monseigneur de Hercé visited the Good Shepherd, briefly, on his way to Rome. After his arrival there he wrote Mother St. Euphrasia that the Holy Father (Pius IX) had told him "that when a foreigner asks for my aid, either for confession, or to receive her vows in her native language, I should not hesitate about the matter when informed of her wishes through you, Madame, the Superior General; but save in such cases, he gave me to understand that I ought to decline so as not to embitter the misunderstanding existing between your Bishop and your pious Community." [4]

Under these conditions Monseigneur de Hercé again resumed his visits, often saying he wished he could spend the final years of his life, following retirement, at the Mother House and use his talents in the service of the members from England, Germany, and Italy. However, his death in 1849 forestalled such a fortuitous arrangement.

During 1845 foundations were made at Loos, France, April 4, 1845; Saint-Omer, France, September 22, 1845; and Imola, Italy, October 20, 1845. At Imola, the Bishop was Cardinal Jean Marie Mastai, prince and churchman of merit and destiny. Probably he had first heard of the Sisters of the Good Shepherd through their first Cardinal Protector, Cardinal Odescalchi, his close friend. In any case he invited the Sisters to come to his diocese, his invitation reaching Angers in May. Two months later, on August 17, three Sisters with Sister St. Irenée Bellanger as Superior, left Angers for Imola by way of Genoa where they were joined by another Sister. From Genoa the little party of four proceeded by boat to Imola, located on the peninsula in the Papal States.

Upon their arrival they were taken directly to the Cardinal's Residence where he greeted them most hospitably in French, "At last, I can welcome my dear daughters of the Good Shepherd." His informal manner set the Sisters at ease. Later they said they found it hard to believe that their host was really the Archbishop of Imola for he possessed a natural simplicity they had not expected to find in one of his exalted rank. Subsequently they judged all great men by this gentle ecclesiastic. Soon he told them that it would give him pleasure if they would disregard his titles in favor of the one he loved most. "That is the beautiful title of 'Father.'" At first the Sisters hesitated, but at the Cardinal's insistence they complied.

The Sisters were informed that their Convent was still in the process of reconstruction. "It had neither a chapel nor a parlor," the Archbishop said, "and of course that would never do. Until the workmen have supplied these and the enclosure grille as well, I would like you to remain here in my palace. Apartments, shut off from the rest of the house, are at your service. I hope very much that you will do me this honor."

At first the Sisters were embarrassed at the idea but reluctantly consented to be the Cardinal's guests until their Convent was ready for occupancy. Thereafter at the Cardinal's invitation they attended daily Mass in his private chapel and ate breakfast and the midday meal at his table, usually having their supper alone in the privacy of their own quarters. During the next few weeks Cardinal Mastai learned to know them well, often visiting them at their evening recreation when they talked to him freely about their beloved Mother General. When the news of her re-election reached Imola, the Sisters' evident joy caused the Cardinal to exclaim: "Your union with your Foundress is a visible mark of the Presence of God in your midst. As long as this perfect harmony reigns, your Congregation has nothing to fear. It will grow and thrive increasingly."

One day Cardinal Mastai asked to read the Rules and Constitutions of the Good Shepherd, afterward declaring that they were most excellent. "The exact observance of Rules and Constitutions contributes effectively to the perpetuation and prosperity of Communities," he said, adding that lashed to the bark of Peter, the Institute would survive whatever storms lay ahead.

In mid-October the remodeling of the Convent was completed. Prior to the Sisters' departure, the Cardinal assembled them in his chapel to ask the blessings of God on their work. "The time you have spent here in this house has not been wasted. It has helped me to become better acquainted with you before confiding to you a mission which, beautiful as it is indeed, is still a thorny and difficult one. Now I feel sure you will fulfill it with zeal and with prudence. I bless you and your work. I wish you every blessing of Heaven, that you may work bravely for the souls confided to you." [5]

The formal blessing of the Convent took place on the Feast of St. Teresa of Avila, October 15, the Sisters taking possession five days later. His Eminence, the Cardinal-Archbishop, presided at the ceremonies which included blessing and consecrating the church and monastery, the house and grounds. The Sisters entered upon their work with zest, despite political unrest in the Romagna and the actual outbreak of war in Rimini, only 18 miles distant. Cardinal Mastai instructed them that should a revolt occur they must be prepared to flee to the Convent of the Dominican Nuns. For a time he moved to the safety of his country home on the outskirts of Imola.

Then just as a general rebellion was about to erupt in the Papal States Gregory XVI died on the first day of June, 1846. There was widespread grief over the death of the eighty-one-year-old Pontiff, but Mother St. Euphrasia and the Sisters of the Good Shepherd felt a poignant and personal desolation. Not only did Mother St. Euphrasia realize that she had lost a warm friend and treasured counselor but she had enough common sense to value a highly placed protector. No doubt she would have said that to feel assured of God's own leading was her greatest desire and consolation, the Light in which she walked daily, the Staff on which she leaned. But it was also sustaining to have His Holiness, than whom there was no higher on earth, making known that she *did* walk in the Light and lean on the staff. It gave her a certain stature both among her friends and among those who could scarcely be called her ardent well-wishers. Now the future loomed uncertain again, except as faith gave it validity. In grateful acknowledgment of his many kindnesses she had his name written on the first page of the Annals of the Good Shepherd as a perpetual testimony to his memory.

As she mourned the passing of the learned Pontiff she had an insistent inner intimation that his successor was to be the Cardinal Archbishop of Imola. She made haste to write this growing conviction to Sister St. Irénée and her associates. Greatly impressed by such a possibility the Sister Superior shared Mother St. Euphrasia's letter with His Eminence as he made ready to leave for Rome to participate in the Conclave that would elect Pope Gregory's successor. He smiled. "I quite believe that your Mother General is a saint but I cannot believe the prophecy she has made. Do not fear; I shall be back within a month's time full of plans for the future; your Bishop intends to build a large convent here to hold one hundred penitents."

But Jean Marie Cardinal Mastai of Imola did not return. On June 16, 1846, he was elected the Sovereign Head of the Roman Catholic Church by the majority vote of the assembled Cardinals. When the bells in Rome and the cannon of Castle St. Angelo proclaimed "*Urbe et Orbe*" (to the city and to the world) that a new pope had been chosen, the word was given out: "*Viva Pio Nona!*" "Long live Pius IX!" So began a pontificate that was to be one of the longest in history (1846–1878).

His close interest in the Good Shepherd was made manifest almost immediately when the new Pope sent one of the Noble Guard to Imola. At the request of His Holiness, this ambassador included the Good Shepherd in his itinerary, going there to announce officially the election of the former Cardinal Mastai to the chair of Peter. Some eighteen years later, at the time the Holy Father revisited his former See of Imola, he paid a visit of state to the Sisters of the Good Shepherd. In recognition of this very special honor, they had a marble slab laid in the entrance of the building.

But the high point of this relationship came at the time of the definition and dogma of the Immaculate Conception of Mary. On December 8, 1854, Pius IX, surrounded by a vast retinue of cardinals and bishops, defined, pronounced, and solemnly promulgated this particular tenet of Catholic doctrine.[6] For the execution of that historic act he used a quill pen that one of the Good Shepherd Sisters in Imola had cut and decorated for him. On earlier occasions this nun had served as his secretary when he was a Cardinal, making his pens and keeping them in a state of repair. At her request the Pontiff used the pen she had sent to sign the Bull. Later His Holiness presented this pen to the Sister who had made it. It might well be that this is the same quill preserved in honor at the Chapel of the Immaculate Conception [7] at the Mother House in Angers. All of these things were duly recorded in the archives of the Community by order of the Mother General.

Since 1825 Mme. d'Andigne had been closely associated with Mother St. Euphrasia. For thirteen years she had lived at the Angers House as a paying guest and during all of that time had expressed her gratitude by contributing regularly to the improvement and expansion of the Convent. Naturally her death, on July 8, 1846, saddened the entire Community. Mother St. Euphrasia realized how much she owed the older woman, how dear to her Mme. d'Andigne had been. Some time previous she had expressed her appreciation for this friendship by proposing to the Community the following engagement, which was then officially inscribed in the Book of the Chapter [8]:

LIVE JESUS AND MARY!

The Superior-General and the Religious of Our Lady of Charity of the Good Shepherd, in Chapter assembled, have, in consideration of the benefits bestowed upon them by Madame d'Andigne, drawn up a formal document on the 13th of November, in the year of Our Lord 1836.

The Community promises to have one monthly Mass said in perpetuity for the Countess d'Andigne, our worthy benefactress (after her death), and also to educate two orphans for the same intention, in perpetuity.

The year and date given above,
At our Monastery-General of Angers.

There were times when Mother St. Euphrasia sorely missed these two friends, the Count de Neuville and Mme. d'Andigne. All grief may be selfish, as many a saint has pointed out, and perhaps Mother St. Euphrasia was grieving for her own loneliness, as do we all, as—

apparently—did the apostles also when their Friend and Guide was taken from them. The stanchest heart needs counsel; needs, too, the feeling of being sustained by the mere presence and empathy of a long-time friend. In a sense these two had been the more valuable to Mother because they were outside her life of vows and renunciation of the world. They kept their worldly contacts but moved serenely unshaken by worldly temptations. Their Center and hers were the same but theirs was a different perspective. After they were gone she had other friends to whom she could turn but these were the oldest friends; they had known her from the days of her young ardor, throughout her long struggles, and had shared each joy as it winged into the expanding life of the Order.

In spite of a persistent sense of their absence, however, she had a growing sense of their presence. They were not forgetting her in their new state. For them she could have only joy and in their joy she was lifted. That thing was happening to her which happens to all as the decades unfold: her fulcrum was shifting from the childhood end of life's plank, when the loved ones on earth far outweigh the loved ones in the heavenly state, to the adult end of this span when the loved ones gone ahead outweigh those at hand. She made room in her mind and her days for the change. And so she matured.

Before that year came to an end Mother St. Euphrasia herself became gravely ill, presumably from overwork and the continued misunderstandings directed against her by her Bishop. Stricken on December 22 as she worked at her desk, she fell into a deep faint from which she was restored only with great effort. For weeks she was confined to bed with a persistent fever and a series of complications. The Sisters were desolate at the thought that their dear Mother might not live.

Happily the time came (1846) when Mother St. Euphrasia returned to her pressing administrative duties. To the protests of her nurses she answered: "I cannot rest with all the Houses depending upon me. Especially do I wish to help our newest foundations in Cairo and Moulins. My illness will depart more quickly when I know that I am of some service to them."

Mother St. Euphrasia had spoken truthfully; the Houses did depend upon her. Cairo, Moulins, and all the others were fortified to know that she was once more at the helm of affairs.

XIV

1847-1848

When everything unites to try us, when we have not a moment of repose, when each hour brings a fresh trial, our watchword must be FIAT. . . . *Our Lord in giving us trials proportions them to our weakness.*

St. Mary of St. Euphrasia

A HALF century and more had gone by since the close of the French Revolution without bringing the promised political and economic millennium. In politics the pendulum had swung to and fro between republicanism and royalism resulting in periodic outbursts of popular revolt. True, the wars of the empire had raised the *bourgeoisie* to new power and wealth but the great masses of the French people were toilers and peasants still dependent upon the work of their hands and the products of the soil. Consequently the transition from an agricultural and commercial society to a growing industrialism produced serious social derangement.

In the cities the proletariat toiled long hours at starvation wages— the average wage was 1.78 francs for a thirteen-hour day. The ruling classes talked nobly about improving their economic position without accepting responsibility for that improvement. Theoretically, the worker could become an elector but practically he found it difficult to surmount the hurdles in his way. Standards of living fell and costs of government mounted, making wider the gap between the workers and the middle class. Everyone was becoming exhausted in a struggle that few understood and many resented. Each man's plight seemed more grave than his neighbor's. Conditions were further worsened by a succession of poor harvests that caused the price of food to soar. In

1845 wheat sold for 19.75 francs a hectoliter; two years later for 29 francs. Potatoes and cereals rose proportionately. These harvest failures meant hunger and death for many; famine and misery walked hand in hand.

Mother St. Euphrasia grieved over the poverty and trials of her Houses, fearing that some of them might have to close. Paris especially was faring badly. Early in 1847 she decided to visit that harassed Convent herself. There, as in Angers, the economic situation was made worse by the inundation of vast areas of farm lands by floods. She shared the weight of these hard times, for ever since the failure of the previous year's harvest she had been obliged to pay out 3000 francs monthly for flour alone.

The possibility of having to discharge some of the girls and women tormented her. Memories of the stories told years ago by the old Sisters at the Tours Refuge came back to her now. Would she, too, be forced to watch the dispersion of the classes? If the price of wheat continued to increase, she did not know how they would be able to keep their poor penitents. The feeding of eight hundred persons at the Mother House was an enormous task in itself but somehow she had managed.

Without the handwork formerly given the Good Shepherd by the Parisians the Sisters in Paris had no means of support. All avenues now appeared closed to them with the possible exception of laundry work. Might they enter this field in competition with local laundresses? "Our Ecclesiastical Superior approves. What, dear Mother, shall we do? Please advise us."

Upon her arrival Mother St. Euphrasia studied the local situation carefully and then asserted her well-known policy: "Unless there is work for all, we do not engage in it, despite the pressure of circumstances. We must earn our livelihood but not at the expense of the livelihood of others. Where there is not enough of the same kind of work for all of us, we shall turn our attention to a new field. Such practice, my daughters, is wise and charitable." That she discovered some such new field is certain, although its nature is not indicated in the record. The Paris Sisters were heartened by their Mother's common sense and understanding. As practical as she was zealous she succeeded in reconciling their physical hardships with their avowed obligation to heal the sick souls of the girls who came to them. By words and deeds she reiterated that their fourth vow—to labor for the salvation of souls—was the very essence of their religious vocation.

Her days in Paris, though arduous, brought some compensations. One of them was a visit with Mother Madeleine-Sophie Barat,[1] Foundress of the Religious of the Sacred Heart, whose spiritual daughters had often helped various Good Shepherd foundations. With high anticipation Mother St. Euphrasia sat awaiting Mother Barat in a small reception room of the Sacred Heart Convent. Before long the door opened to admit a sprightly little woman dressed in black. Mother St. Euphrasia arose and stepped forward, falling on her knees in reverence. Mother Barat immediately returned the courtesy and kneeling, these two women embraced. Another of the Sacred Heart Sisters [2] who was present later wrote to Angers: "Ever since our holy Foundresses met and gave one another that holy kiss which we think of as the kiss of St. Francis of Assisi and St. Dominic, our two religious families are forever united as are the Franciscans and the Dominicans." [3]

Mother St. Euphrasia begged Mother Barat to bless her, but Mother Barat demurred. "It is you," she said, "who ought to bless me, you who bring back so many souls to the Divine Master."

Then for more than an hour they sat beside each other, exchanging confidences. Although Mother St. Euphrasia was usually reluctant to talk about her troubles, she found it easy to tell Mother Barat about some of her most vexing problems, including not only those which had brought her to Paris but also the difficulties that faced her in other places. At one point she paused to inquire: "But you, *Ma Mère,* in your holy vocation, you do not meet with crosses of this kind?" Without hesitation Mother Barat replied: "Crosses, Mother St. Euphrasia? Crosses? Why, I am sewed up in them from my head to my feet!"

Mother St. Euphrasia left Mother Barat, confident that she had talked with a saint, while Mother Barat was convinced that she had entertained one.

A few days later Mother St. Euphrasia called on Mother Javouhey, Foundress of the Sisters of St. Joseph of Cluny, whom she had met earlier on a visit to the south of France. From the beginning these two women were attracted to each other. Mother Javouhey's work had already won her recognition at home and abroad, centered, as it was, on the education and evangelization of slaves in the French colonies. Far in advance of their liberation she had begun to prepare the slaves on the West Coast of Africa and in French Guiana for the new life that would be theirs, starting with the creation of farms and the teaching of agriculture and handicrafts and proceeding to their moral stabilization by means of the schools, hospitals, and asylums.

In some ways the sorrows that these two religious had experienced bore a striking resemblance. Like Monseigneur Angebault, Mother Javouhey's Bishop had sought to change the Statutes of her Order. In this he had been supported by the Civil Authorities. Despite these pressures, however, Mother Javouhey had refused to comply unless her entire Community was given a voice in the decision. Her insistence had drawn forth epithets designating her as stubborn and recalcitrant. In addition she was denied the Sacraments for a period of time. "The prohibition imposed upon me in reference to the reception of the Sacraments," she said, "has been the worst of my many afflictions. To be denied the solace of Penance and the Eucharist is the heaviest load I have been asked to carry. May you, dear Mother, be spared that kind of grief."

Mother St. Euphrasia attempted to console Mother Javouhey, reminding her that at some time everyone must travel the Via Dolorosa. Such suffering, she said, was hard to bear, but they both understood what Christ had meant when He said: "Take up your cross and follow me." As a result of this visit, Mother St. Euphrasia felt better prepared to endure whatever burdens lay ahead. In the light of future events it was well that she was so fortified.

The death of Sister Marie Chantal Cesbron (de la Roche) on May 10 brought Mother St. Euphrasia another sorrow. Old friends were indeed going on, and with the passing of each of them a part of herself seemed also to go. But this was not all loss for the part of her that went with them shared their joy. She hoped they could also share their wisdom in this time of her need, for Sister Chantal's death entailed a financial loss difficult to meet. From the beginning of her religious life in 1831, Sister Chantal had given to the Good Shepherd all of her worldly goods. The fact that she had been able to provide for a number of the improvements at the Mother House had pleased her exceedingly. "I'd like you to use my annuity, too," she had said. "It will end at my death, but until then it will bring in 10,000 francs each year." The loss of this regular income made it necessary for Mother St. Euphrasia to borrow money for the support of the establishment. She loathed the thought of debt, but had no alternative.

Food was increasingly difficult to obtain. Each morning Mother St. Euphrasia went over the list of supplies, praying as she estimated the day's needs. The Sisters ate less that the children might be fed. Still the ogre of hunger stalked near, waiting to enter and take charge. Constantly Mother St. Euphrasia assured them all: "If we trust in God's benevolence, He will not abandon us. Of that I am sure." A rumor arose that she had her own way of stretching the food and the fact that the supplies, though low, were never exhausted gave credence to this report.

At Bourges in the fall of 1847, rumor that the supplies were unaccountably augmented was even more persistent. Mother Mary of the Heart of Jesus, like the Superiors of all the French Houses, was feeling the bite of hard times. All work orders had been canceled because people had no money to pay for either fine sewing or laundry; wheat was scarce and prices exorbitant. With mounting concern the Mother Superior checked the diminishing supply of flour, conferring with the Sisters who did the baking. For some time they had used only twelve measures every fifth day, this providing twenty large loaves with which 116 persons must be fed. As the supply grew lower, the Mother Superior turned in confidence to the Venerable Germaine Cousin whose beatification was then under consideration. (Germaine Cousin died in 1601.) As a poor shepherdess of Pibrac, near Toulouse, Germaine had often shared her last crust with the poor, denying herself for those in greater need. To her surprise the amount of bread she had in her kerchief always remained the same. Such inexplicable happenings increased her humility, for she knew that such a gift could come only through the hand of Providence. Remembering these things Mother Mary of the Heart of Jesus prayed to the little French shepherdess, begging her to provide bread for the children at Bourges. In addition she asked all of the classes to join with her in a novena—a prayer of nine days—for this same intention. Stories of the shepherdess' life were read and a wave of devotion followed.

One night the Mother Superior instructed the Sisters to use eight instead of twelve measures of flour for their next day's baking and to pray that this amount would produce the needed twenty loaves. The Sisters did as they were told, but the bread was in direct proportion to the recipe, no more and no less. In spite of her disappointment Mother's faith remained unshaken and she insisted that these short measurements be repeated on several successive occasions. However, when nothing came of them, she decided that she must tell the Sisters to return to the usual twelve measures of flour. But because she would not break the rule of silence until morning, she spoke only in prayer to the little shepherdess. "Evidently I have been premature or arrogant. I meant to be neither. I believed that you who had been known sometimes to multiply bread on earth might be permitted to feed our poor children. For days they have not had enough bread. Soon they will have none at all. Will you not please put in the extra four measures of flour that I meant the Sisters to add?"

The next day the eight measures produced more than twenty loaves with enough dough remaining for a second baking which filled the big oven to capacity, and in addition left a large lump of dough to be used at a later time. The excited Sisters sent in haste for the Mother Superior who knelt in thankfulness on the kitchen floor.

From then on the astounding multiplication of loaves continued. In November the Sisters had thought they had only enough flour on hand to care for their needs until the first of the year. When that time arrived, however, the flour in the granary stood at the November level, despite the fact that they had drawn from it steadily. In January they weighed the flour and at the end of a fortnight, after three intervening bakings, weighed it again. The weight remained unchanged. No one could explain this paradox but no one could deny that the children had been well nourished throughout the winter.

Meanwhile Mother St. Euphrasia had been kept informed of these strange events. She advised decorous silence until the ecclesiastical authorities had had an opportunity to study them. In the beginning the authorities were dubious, withholding judgment until additional evidence could be secured. When their queries failed to shake the testimony, they began a formal investigation. Midway of this investigation another of the mammoth bakings resulted from eight measures of flour which the investigators themselves had carefully weighed and recorded. This occurrence was considered of sufficient importance to be submitted to the Congregation of Rites in support of Germaine Cousin's claim to beatification. Later at the time of her beatification by Pope Pius IX on May 7, 1854, two paintings representing the events that had transpired at Bourges were hung in the transept of the Vatican Basilica. One of the miracles required for the beatification [4] had been performed at the Convent of the Good Shepherd.

Most fittingly Mother St. Euphrasia suggested that the youngest class in the Bourges House be named after Germaine Cousin, a custom often perpetuated in Good Shepherd Homes. In addition many of the Sisters, as well as the children, carry the name of Germaine in gratitude to the little shepherdess who fed the hungry flock at

Bourges. Each day after that Mother St. Euphrasia made it a daily practice to invoke Germaine's help in providing bread for all her children.

Meanwhile other Convents were being subjected to tribulations. The year 1848 was one of great disquiet throughout all France, the ferment extending itself to Italy and other European countries. When Louis Philippe of Orleans fell and the Republic was proclaimed, nation-wide unrest resulted in widespread riots and revolts. For a time it seemed that the French Revolution had returned to scourge the people. Violence raged everywhere and once again religion became the target of attack.

It is hard to understand the hatred and fury that popular revolt engenders in the hearts of men. When compassion is most needed, bigotry asserts itself and human beings turn from ordinary decencies to inhuman brutalities. Then religious houses appear to represent temporal power and become the objects of violence. And the people angered by their impotence to seize power become through their anger the instruments of evil, defeating their own ends.

With increasing frequency Mother St. Euphrasia experienced attacks on the Convents of the Good Shepherd. At Angers an angry mob surrounded the Mother House shouting: "Down with the nuns! Down with the nuns!" Finally the outbreak was brought under control through the impassioned plea of an old man who begged the mob to cease their assaults on "these pious women whose lives are given wholly to the relief of the sufferings of their brethren." [5] Some months later, following riots and disorders in town, Angers found itself again threatened. This time Mother St. Euphrasia knew that the mob would not listen to reason, and so she prepared in advance by appealing to the recently appointed M. Bordillon, Prefect of Angers, who responded by posting a guard of fifty soldiers and fifty national guard. Some years previous this gentleman had been Mother St. Euphrasia's avowed enemy, but after his election to public office he had learned that the Good Shepherd was a force for good throughout the entire community. Repeatedly in crises he had been struck by Mother St. Euphrasia's good judgment and levelheadedness, on one occasion praising her publicly to his fellow citizens assembled at the City Hall. "There is only one man in all of Angers," he had cried, "and that is the Superior General of the Good Shepherd." Mother St. Euphrasia smiled in amusement when this news was relayed to her. What a curious thing for Monsieur to say!

Elsewhere the Convents fared poorly. The House at Bourg was sacked and the Sisters forced to put off their religious dress and flee into hiding, taking with them the Sister Magdalens and children. At Macon thirteen nuns, forty-eight penitents, and forty-five Preservation Children were driven out by a group of hungry laborers, goaded by unscrupulous instigators who fanned the flames of religious intolerance. "The Sisters and their charges eat while you go hungry," the leaders shouted. "Why should this be? On to the Convent for flour and meat!"

Mother St. Euphrasia found it hard to reconcile these outbursts of the working people. In more than one discourse to the Sisters she had said: "When you are sent for, go quickly, in order to avoid giving cause for impatience or insult. A poor laboring man will sometimes go without his food to get time to come and see his daughter at one of our houses; and if you keep him waiting and make him lose his day's wages, how is he to provide bread for his other children that evening?" [6]

In Italy, Genoa was attacked and the Sisters forced to flee for their lives while the Convent there was completely demolished. Dôle, too, was closed and the religious escorted to safety under the protection of the National Guard. Lyons, although often threatened by a mob at the gates, was spared destruction through the combined efforts of the chaplain and a band of loyal peasants. Not until the Convent was searched thoroughly by the Government Commissary did the ridiculous rumors of hidden stores of food subside. When it became known that the Sisters of Lyons were also hungry, abuses ceased.

Early in the spring of 1848, Mother St. Euphrasia dispatched a circular letter to all of her daughters, urging them to preserve their Houses by putting on secular dress when necessary, and to till the land until the time when they could once again resume their work of reforming girls to a new and honored life. Whatever they did, she said, they were to follow as closely as possible the advice of their ecclesiastical superiors. Should their best efforts meet with failure they were to try to reach the nearest Good Shepherd Convent, but if that, too, had been destroyed, they were to head toward Angers. Difficulties might intervene, Mother St. Euphrasia knew, "but . . . our Mother House of Angers will always be open to you. You will find here the tenderest of Mothers who loves you dearly, affectionate Sisters who will share with you whatever is left to them, and who will endeavor to dry your tears while they weep with you over your misfortunes and your losses." [7]

That many Sisters were able to reach Angers in safety was shown in a letter written by Mother St. Euphrasia on April 28 to the Superior at Munich. "My beloved daughters, we pray very much for you. Angers is Mary's town. Your Sion [8] is calmer than ever, and is respected and beloved by all shades of opinion. . . . There are several hundreds of us here without work or gifts, and deprived of benefactors; but we have great peace and perfect union. Already 400 penitents have been driven out of our houses; we have lost 500,000 francs, have been robbed, have suffered loss by fire; 60 of our professed have been sent into exile; day and night they arrive here."

As the months progressed radicals prominent in the provisional government proved themselves unable to cope with the political forces set in motion by the February Revolution. In the struggle that followed the bourgeois revolutionists triumphed over the Leftist working men's group, cutting deeper the chasm between these two factions. Although neither side could claim a victory, both sides manifested a growing leniency toward the things of the spirit. To some degree this was due to the tragic death of the Archbishop of Paris, Monseigneur Denis Affre, who was killed by a stray bullet as he sought to bring about peace between the contending parties. In any case, the Second Republic was gradually being leavened by the elements of conservatism. Throughout the summer and fall the outbursts against the Church were sporadic, and once more there was hope that the forces of anarchy and irreligion might possibly have been brought under control.

In Italy, however, no such hope was felt. A violent revolution broke out in Rome bringing with it the assassination of Count Pellegrino Rossi, the Papal Minister of State, and the shooting of Monsignor Palma, the Pope's private secretary. The Pontiff himself (Pius IX) was besieged in Quirinal Palace. On the night of November 24 His Holiness agreed to flee Rome and make his way to Gaeta in the Kingdom of Naples, where he remained until the following spring.

When the news reached Angers that the Holy Father had been forced into exile, Mother St. Euphrasia was shocked. With the Pope in hiding she was like a mariner who had lost his way. In the face of the great desolation that now enveloped the Catholic world she found her personal sorrows more poignant. Greatest of these personal sorrows was the death of her beloved spiritual daughter, Sister Teresa of Jesus de Couespel.

Since her clothing as a religious in 1836 Sister Teresa had been Mother St. Euphrasia's other self, fulfilling all of Mother's expectations for her. From the beginning the older woman had admired the manner in which the former Melanie de Couespel had sought the spirit of detachment and humility, never referring to her natural or acquired gifts but using them simply in the service of God. At the time of her death she was again living at the Mother House, Bishop Angebault having sanctioned her return. She served as an unofficial administrative assistant, lightening Mother St. Euphrasia's heavy load by carrying on much of the complex business involved in the day-to-day running of the Institute. Theirs was a rare and precious friendship and a happy mother-daughter relationship, both sharing the gifts of quick minds and winsome personalities which made others glad to work with them for common ends.

During the weeks succeeding Sister Teresa's death the Community feared for Mother St. Euphrasia's health. Added to the strain of cumulative attacks on herself and her Convents, this personal loss seemed to take some of the heart out of her. A circular letter of November 4 prepared by the Council Sisters portrayed the general participation in Mother's loss. "Our dear Sister Mary of Teresa of Jesus shared in all the trials and anxieties of our beloved Mother General. In thought, desire, and action they were entirely at one. We cannot at the moment dwell upon the heroic virtues of our departed sister, nor upon her unbounded generosity towards our Institute from the day she entered. . . . Her memory will ever live among us, and our gratitude to her will be lasting." [9] On November 11 Mother St. Euphrasia wrote, "I mourn for a daughter of exceptional holiness, affection, and loyalty. Could you but realize the support I found in her! I shall never be able to meet her equal in this world." [10]

But dark as that year was, it brought two new foundations into the Good Shepherd fold—Limerick, Ireland, and Aix-la-Chapelle, or Aachen, situated on the border of Germany between Holland and Prussia. To be sure, two foundations could not compensate for those that had been destroyed but they did serve as encouragement to Mother St. Euphrasia since she had been unable to open any new houses in 1847—the only year since the Generalate that had not seen an increase in the number of Good Shepherd Convents.

Bishop Ryan of Limerick had requested the sending of a group of

Sisters to take charge of a local Home for Penitents. He had learned that Miss Redden, its proprietor and directress, desired to relinquish her charge in favor of the Good Shepherd with whom she had become acquainted on a visit to Hammersmith, London. This request was granted and three religious under the direction of Mother Mary of the Visitation began their work on March 17, the Feast of Ireland's patron saint. Eight months later, on November 21,[11] the foundation at Aix-la-Chapelle was made with Sister Mary of St. Euphrasia Fey, a native of Aachen, as the Superior in charge. This foundation flourished from the beginning, serving as the parent of other foundations throughout the Rhenish Provinces.

And so the year 1848 came to a close, its sorrows outnumbering its joys. But sunlight was gradually beginning to dispel the gloom.

1848-1866

I do not wish it said any longer that I am French. I am Italian, English, German, Spanish, African, American, Indian. I belong to every country where there are souls to save. When we see sheep to be gathered into the fold, we must not fear to go and pitch our tents on the most distant shores. . . . In America, Africa, Asia, Oceania; everywhere must we go in search of our Lord's sheep.

ST. MARY OF ST. EUPHRASIA

THE last twenty years of Mother St. Euphrasia's life were an extension of that which had gone before, bringing to the Good Shepherd invitations to settle in far-distant places. Indeed the list of foundations made from 1848–1868 reads like a Cook's Tour, extending from Glasgow in Scotland to Neudorf in Austria, on across the Atlantic to the North and South American continents, and far beyond to Bangalore, India. Such invitations resulted in 110 establishments during her lifetime, most of them springing from little more than a dream and the hope of its fulfillment.

The growth of the Congregation added to Mother St. Euphrasia's travels and responsibilities. "We need your advice.Will you come to us?" were the only words required to summon her to the house that beckoned. "My daughters need me. I must go to them. Less than that I cannot do."

Once she got to Angoulême, a foundation she knew well, at six o'clock in the morning, having traveled all night. Upon arrival at the Cathedral residence she was hospitably received by the Bishop's cook, an old friend.

"It is surely good to see you again, Reverend Mother. Come rest here in the drawing room until Monseigneur Regnier returns. He left for the Cathedral some time ago."

"Thank you, Mary, but I'd prefer to wait in your warm and cheerful kitchen. That is, if you do not object."

"Object, Mother St. Euphrasia? I shall be honored."

"Not that, Mary. This will be just an informal visit between friends."

Mary's homely face shone radiantly. "Oh, Mother St. Euphrasia, you must have read my thoughts. I said to myself when I built the big fire, 'Now, if the good Mother could only see that! It's a fire fit for a queen and she's a queen, if I ever saw one.'"

"You would spoil me, Mary. But at that I'd like to see what a queen's fire is like."

Soon the other servants crowded into the kitchen to greet the Mother from Angers. For all of them she had a smile and a personal message. And a gift too! From her reticule she drew forth sweetmeats for one, a kerchief for another, and in one instance, a watch. Not an expensive watch, but a durable and efficient one whose size made its new owner cry out: "For me, Mother St. Euphrasia? You brought a watch for me?"

"Why not, Jean-Baptiste? Do you not do many kind things for the Sisters? Through them I heard of your approaching birthday as well as your desire for a watch of your own. I hope you will like it."

"Like it, Mother St. Euphrasia? It is what I have always wanted! I thank you from my heart."

Early in 1849 the second American Foundation was established in St. Louis, Missouri, in response to the invitation of Bishop Peter Kenrick. From the start the work grew like "a tree planted by the waters." At that time St. Louis was a rapidly growing city of thirty thousand. The Sisters came directly from Angers, some of them arriving in January, the others, six months later. The first ones who had suffered the rigors of winter travel thought that their hardships had been extreme, but later agreed that their companions had undergone worse trials. From the accounts sent to Angers of "the violent waterspout in the Gulf of Mexico" it seems that the Sisters must have run head on into a hurricane. At New Orleans they were met by an enervating humidity that pressed relentlessly down upon them; the muddy drinking water added to their discomfort. Then they discovered that a slow and overcrowded packet steamer afforded few conveniences and little privacy. Resigning themselves to the in-numerable inconveniences and delays, they conserved their energies for the tasks ahead.

Shortly after the founding of the Good Shepherd in St. Louis Bishop Francis Patrick Kenrick of Philadelphia asked Mother St. Euphrasia for the third American foundation. Ever since he had entertained the pioneer group of Good Shepherd Sisters bound for Louisville he had hoped to have a House in his diocese, a hope revived through the enthusiasm of his brother, Archbishop Peter Kenrick of St. Louis.

Mother St. Euphrasia wanted to accept this invitation; yet she found herself embarrassingly short of funds and personnel. Learning of her predicament the Society of the Propagation of the Faith allocated 1600 francs to her depleted treasury. Then through a co-operative arrangement Louisville and St. Louis loaned a nucleus of Sisters to Philadelphia, the small group being headed by Mother Mary of the Angels, Foundress of Louisville. Later when Mother St. Euphrasia was able to send additional Sisters, Mother Mary of the Angels and her associates withdrew.

In the beginning the Philadelphia Sisters experienced the poverty of Bethlehem, taking possession of their new home with nothing but their personal belongings. The early annals tell of their being obliged to use a board spread across two barrels for an altar and a spoon hit against a drinking glass in lieu of the bell rung at Mass. But in spite of their hardships the Philadelphia Good Shepherd built for the future. "In May 1850 while the citizenry was looking forward to hearing Jenny Lind for the first time six white-robed Sisters of the Good Shepherd quietly began a zealous quest for the lost sheep of the growing metropolis of Philadelphia." [1]

On July 31, 1851, the General Chapter convened at Angers for the scheduled election of the Superior General, an assembly which occurred every six years. Bishop Angebault's willingness to preside at these ceremonies spoke well for the success of Monseigneur Joubert's services as mediator between the Bishop and the Com-munity. Forty-seven Sisters were present, twenty-four of whom were Superiors or Prioresses of other Convents. Many of them had traveled a great distance at considerable inconvenience.

The Bishop had to admit that the Sisters sitting before him in their white habits made a most impressive sight. He sensed the undercurrent of excitement. Knowing that everyone wanted Mother

St. Euphrasia to continue in office, he actually smiled as he announced her unanimous re-election. Because of that gesture of good
will many found it difficult to reconcile this gracious prelate with
the picture they had hitherto carried in their minds. How wonderful,
they thought, if all discord were now at an end!

Following her re-election Mother St. Euphrasia planned to return
to Munich with Mother St. John of the Cross, visiting Paris, Nancy,
and Strasbourg en route. On September 8 she left Angers with mixed
feelings. She longed to visit the Bavarian House and other Convents,
but she dreaded the trip, knowing the toll that travel always exacted.
The trip to Paris was without incident except for Mother's disappointment at her inability to visit her former Superior at the Tours Refuge.
From Paris the Sisters traveled overnight to Bar-le-Duc in a slow and
uncomfortable train. Upon arrival they learned that their stagecoach
had been delayed and might not come until late afternoon. The
prospect of a second night of travel dismayed them.

"What else can we do?" Mother St. Euphrasia said. "It is better,
I think, to proceed, whatever the circumstances." Perhaps she
regretted her decision when she saw the dilapidated stagecoach.
"Nothing but a box on wheels," one Sister sputtered. "The locks on
the doors are broken and the hinges loose. We'll be chilled to the
bone long before we reach Nancy."

Dusk had already fallen when the weary little party set out. Almost
immediately Mother St. Euphrasia was overcome by violent nausea
brought on by jerking and rolling of the old coach. Not until midnight were the nuns able to leave the bumpy vehicle and seek comfort
at a cheerless inn along the way. There the owner resented having
been awakened at such an unheard-of hour and refused to provide
any food for her late guests. "Make coffee at this time of night?
Couldn't think of it," she grumbled in drowsy disapproval as she
shuffled off to bed. By morning Mother St. Euhprasia's vomiting had
ceased, permitting her and her companions to resume their journey.
They did not reach Nancy until after four o'clock in the afternoon,
their delay having already become a matter of concern to the Sisters
awaiting them.

Within a few hours Mother St. Euphrasia felt better and everything
proceeded as planned. The days spent at Nancy, although demanding,
fortified her for the next lap of the journey. Happily her illness did
not return despite the oversized two-decker contrivance in which she
rode. With surprising agility she climbed a tall ladder to reach her

seat at the second level—and remembered herself as a little girl climbing over the rocky coast of Noirmoutier. That daring child and this dignified Sister possessed many qualities in common, one which was a ready willingness to adjust quickly to new situations.

After three days at Strasbourg Mother and her party left for Munich. Mishaps still pursued them. They lost their tickets and were forced to reroute their journey over a more circuitous route. At last on September 25 they reached their destination and the sight of five hundred children of the Good Shepherd fold lined up at the entrance brought tears of happiness to Mother's eyes. One little girl presented a bouquet of flowers from "all of us, dear Mother." These words were a cue for the children to burst into song, causing Mother St. Euphrasia to respond with warm maternal affection. "O my Munich children—your kindness is almost more than I can bear. Thank you from the bottom of my heart."

The entire city acclaimed her as a distinguished guest. Everyone of importance came to pay his respects, the Cardinal-Archbishop, Monseigneur Raisach, leading the procession. Later she was received at the Royal Palace by Maximilian II, whose father, Louis I, had invited the Sisters to the Bavarian capital eleven years previous.

These experiences prompted her to write to Angers: "What shall I say to you of Munich? It is undoubtedly the most beautiful Community in the Christian universe. Mother St. John of the Cross ought to have forewarned me." [2] The Munich Superior had attempted to prepare her for the beautiful convent and attached church set in the midst of a spacious estate but realizing that only an artist could capture the beauty of the place, she had waited for Mother St. Euphrasia to view the buildings and grounds for herself.

Ten days later Mother St. Euphrasia left Munich, visiting the houses in Münster, Aix-la-Chapelle, Namur, Mons, Lille, Amiens, Saint-Omer, and Rheims, returning to Angers on November 6 weary but jubilant. Winter then descended, enabling her to catch up with her extensive correspondence and to make plans for a new project.

Her new project was the reconversion of a large farm outside the Convent gates into an agricultural colony to which girls from prison could be transferred and retrained. On her recent travels she had been appalled by the unsanitary and immoral conditions of penal institutions where discipline was maintained by threats and corporal punishment and hate ruled, shutting out all hope and love. No wonder that the inmates grew surly and belligerent or morose and apathetic. Why should they strive to improve themselves when society rejected them as outcasts? Most of these young women were ignorant of God and the few who had known Him in the past now scorned a Deity who, they believed, had deserted them. With pressing urgency Mother St. Euphrasia used every means to bring about the development of this agricultural center, which she named Nazareth, for she was convinced that a balanced program of work and play carried on in the open would prove salutary and eventually lead to an interest in things of the spirit. Work, she emphasized, was one of the strongest factors in any re-educational program, providing a lift both to body and soul.

The Prefect of Angers secured full government sanction and co-operation, with the result that in late April [3] seventy-five young prisoners were received from Rennes. In their best dreams these bewildered and suspicious newcomers could never have envisioned such a clean and friendly world. The sight of the smiling "White Sisters" made them forget all about their plan to riot. Instead they relaxed, unafraid, willing to try out this farm idea.

Mother St. Euphrasia was with the Sisters that first night. Upon her return to the Convent she reviewed the previous day's happenings. "At first the children were sad and frightened; but as soon as they were seated by the crackling fire of vine branches which was blazing away on the kitchen hearth, they began to chirp—just like little birds. Soon the hot soup, meat, and wine we gave them melted their poor hearts. It was clear to all of us that they had not had such a feast for a long time.

"This morning we had them exchange their prison dress for the frocks you Sisters had made for them with such eagerness and charity. At first they gazed in open disbelief from one to another. But when we took them out into the garden to show them where they were to work, they began to understand. One of the younger ones asked in a hopeful voice, 'You mean we aren't in prison any more? Can that really be true?'

" 'You are at the Good Shepherd, my children,' I answered. 'You have come here to learn to love the good God and to serve Him. And at the same time you will learn how to work so that you may be able to help yourselves and your families. We think you will be happy at Nazareth.'

"A long silence followed. Then the questioner said rather uncertainly, 'Thank you, Sister.'

" 'You must not talk like that,' one of her older companions protested with a forcible gesture. 'Here, they are Mothers. Just think we are to call them Mothers.'

"The little one caught on at once, saying rather shyly, 'Thank you, Mother.'

"My heart sang at her willingness to address me in that manner. I'd scarcely hoped for that spontaneous recognition. We must be real Mothers and watchful shepherds to these unhappy and mistreated waifs. It will be a hard task to guide this new flock, but the reward will be magnificent. God grant that we will not fail these lambs of our fold." [4]

In the future Nazareth was often to prove a great trial but Mother St. Euphrasia persevered, her joy increasing in proportion to the lasting good accomplished among the young prisoners. This project was followed by similar ones elsewhere, the healing earth proving a lasting curative to those who worked on the land. Just as last year's seeds need time and warmth to become this year's life, so the girls found themselves gradually transformed by the unhurried rhythm of the seasons. They discovered a serenity and peace of heart in the unchanging laws of nature, which the Sisters pointed out were the laws of God. When followed, they brought order and peace; when violated, disorder and conflict.

In 1854 Mother St. Euphrasia sent five Sisters to Bangalore, India. Distance and the ardors of travel receded before the summons from Monseigneur Charbonneau, missionary Bishop of Mysore, who came to Angers for the purpose of interesting Mother St. Euphrasia in the vast mission field in the Orient. "If a soul is worth more than a world, Mother General," he said, "millions of worlds await reclamation in the land from which I come. There hordes of pagans live in complete ignorance of Christ."

Mother St. Euphrasia listened and learned. Finally after hours spent in prayer she knew that she must accept this call. When she made known her decision, many Sisters volunteered for service in India. Her problem was not to find enough Sisters but to find the ones best qualified. Above all she knew that they must be women of vision and courage, possessed of almost superhuman stamina and great spiritual integrity.

In everyone's mind Sister Mary of St. Teresa de Schorlemer was the logical Superior for this new foundation. As a member of a German family distinguished for its loyalty to the faith, she had been designated as the Superior-elect of the Mayence Convent located near her former home. That appointment, however, was now canceled at Sister Teresa's request: "I burn with desire to devote myself to the foreign missions."

Sister St. Teresa's interest was founded on the rock of reality. Her brother, Count de Schorlemer, a prominent statesman, once said: "Every Schorlemer is hardheaded, but my sister Fanny is the strongest *man* of the family when it comes to strength of will." However, on the day of her departure from Angers that strength failed her. Overcome by the thought that she might never again see the Mother House she kissed the walls and the floor of her cell and the chapel in which she had made her profession and clung almost fiercely to the door of the Convent as though she could not tear herself away. Her face grew red and swollen from weeping.

Mother St. Euphrasia accompanied Monseigneur Charbonneau and the Sisters as far as Paimboeuf, their port of embarkation. At Nantes, where they spent the night en route, she found her rest disturbed by the muffled sobs and cries that came from Sister St. Teresa in the adjoining room. Once more the parting from all that Sister knew and loved had overcome her, calling forth whispered protests: "I should not go; I cannot go."

Mother St. Euphrasia longed to join Sister Teresa in her Gethsemane but she waited until morning. At the end of Mass she called Sister aside and told her that she need not proceed to Bangalore. "I shall propose someone else in your place and assign you instead to Germany. Loneliness and homesickness are a disease as great as any you would be called upon to cure. My beloved child, I cannot break your heart."

Sister St. Teresa answered with an earnest passion. "But, Mother St. Euphrasia, I want to go to Bangalore. Since I have been at Communion I feel strong enough to brave fires, flames, everything to save one single soul in India. I shall have crosses but with St. Francis Xavier, my heart cries out, 'More, Lord, yet more.' I go full of joy."

One look at Sister Teresa's radiant face told Mother St. Euphrasia that she had no further reason for concern. Sister's travail had ended, leaving in its place happiness and tranquillity.

Because of bad weather, Mother St. Euphrasia thought it best to leave the Sisters in advance of their sailing. Embracing each one of them and entrusting her to Divine Providence, she turned and walked slowly, almost unsteadily, down the gangway and out of sight. This time her eyes, too, were red and swollen.

On January 28 the Sisters set sail from France, arriving in Pondicherry seven months later. Often en route their vessel had been becalmed indefinitely in equatorial waters. Its snail's pace was exasperatingly tedious, but no word nor act could increase it. By the time the Sisters reached India they had almost forgotten what it was like to be in a hurry. This was well, for their next means of transportation was a primitive two-wheel oxcart, run even slower than the sailing vessel. It was also equally unpleasant, rattling and jolting along with a kind of stoic indifference.

Despite their physical discomforts they were intrigued by the countryside through which their route lay. Evidences of poverty were everywhere but the gentle smiles of the people gathered in curious groups along the road were rich and warm. Women wearing threadbare but delicately colored saris were surrounded always by throngs of shy children. Seldom was a woman to be seen without a baby in her arms.

A fortnight later Mother St. Teresa and her companions reached Bangalore, weary but eager to learn the native language and build a bridge of communication between themselves and the Indian people. Their initial project was a school for the children of the English officers of the Civil Service; the second, an orphanage for Indian children. Slowly but steadily they enlarged their sphere of ministrations until they could also open a class for homeless and unwanted older girls. Not until that was under way did they feel that their work as Good Shepherd Sisters had really been launched. To have felt differently would have been a violation of Mother St. Euphrasia's policy of always giving the preference to the penitents and the Sister Magdalens.

In the meantime Mother St. Euphrasia had grown anxious. Six months and more had gone by without any word from the Sisters. For all she knew they might not have survived the trip. Then a letter arrived, which she hastily shared with the Community: "My dear daughters, I can hardly speak. . . . My emotion must be too evident for you not to have guessed that I have something to tell you. Well, so it is, my children. I have had news from the *Mauritius*. Your dearest Sisters, for whom you felt such great anxiety, are safe." [5]

Following letters told about the origins of the foundation destined to become the most populated house of the entire Congregation. In the beginning poverty pursued it, even though the Sisters set all the children to work at some remunerative task. Soon the sewing and embroidery groups were earning a steady income but that money was insufficient to meet mounting expenses. Then the untimely death of one of the Sisters brought about a series of events that resulted in wide and favorable publicity. With the approval of Bishop Charbonneau the funeral procession was planned in keeping with local practices. At his suggestion the dead Sister's body was placed on a bier and borne through the streets on the shoulders of four stalwart Irish soldiers. The unlined countenance and the beautiful white habit of the deceased nun spoke their own message to the friendly natives. Although few of them had known her when she was alive, they knew that she had left home and country of her own free will for the sake of helping their girls attain a better life. Consequently she became the symbol of unselfish service even unto death, firing the imagination of the spectators as they surged forward to catch a glimpse of this "holy woman." Almost as though a signal had been given some fifteen hundred Christians and non-Christians alike fell reverently into line behind the mourners, led by the Bishop himself, wearing his pontifical vestments. At the cemetery many stepped forward in quiet dignity to cast a handful of earth into the grave of the Sister who had lived such a brief time among them.

In every way the affair was a triumph, for never before had Christian priests in Bangalore walked through the streets chanting prayers for the dead. Their appearance now supported the impression that the one who had died had been especially worthy. At once the Indians began to carry gifts of incense, flowers, and fruits to the burial plot of the honored Raniastri (Virgin). When they were asked to offer their gifts to the living rather than the dead, they consented, transferring them to the convent in memory of the one who had gone. In this way they became acquainted with the other Sisters whose kindness quickly won their hearts.

Mother St. Euphrasia's grief was lessened when she learned how this Sister's influence lived on among the people. More than one correspondent wrote: "Sister will do more for the pagans of Bangalore than she or any other religious could ever hope to do in an entire lifetime. Her death has been a gain, not a loss, for the Good Shepherd in India."

In the years to come these predictions proved true for Bangalore inaugurated a series of diversified services almost unlimited in scope and versatility. Among these services were the founding of the Sisters of St. Ann, a religious Congregation for Indian girls begun in 1859, and St. Martha's Hospital, a charitable institution for the care of men, women, and children. From its inception in 1886 through 1953 this hospital has treated 137,493 in-patients and 2,428,796 out-patients, a continuing tribute to the pioneers and their Mother Foundress.

Before 1854 ended Mother St. Euphrasia purchased the historic Benedictine Abbey of St. Nicholas in Angers, later connecting it with the monastery by a carefully contrived underground tunnel or passageway. The beautiful old building situated on a natural elevation above a lake gave the Community additional quarters for the novices and certain classes of Reformatory children. With the number of young prisoners increasing regularly—already there were three hundred at Nazareth—Mother St. Euphrasia hoped to relieve the congestion. She reasoned that the Abbey, huge and fortresslike, would be a perfect place, scenically and strategically, for young women aspiring to become Sisters and young girls striving to find a new and better kind of life. Future results more than justified her expectations.

Whenever she was asked to name particular periods as being the most significant in the life of the Institute, Mother St. Euphrasia would smile and reply, "All of them." Then her soft brown eyes would grow serious and she would continue, "But some are more important than others. First, my coming to Angers in 1831; then, the establishment of the Sister Magdalens in the same year; after that, the erection of the Generalate in 1835; and now, the division of the Congregation into Provinces. The importance of this present step cannot be underestimated. It is a milestone of import."

That milestone was reached on July 21, 1855, the day on which the decree for the establishment of the Provinces was issued. Several factors had brought about this decree, not least of which was the extraordinary growth of the Congregation. By mid-century it numbered fifty-four Houses, including twenty-four outside France, the latest one to be located in South America at San Felipe in Chili. Mother St. Euphrasia had initiated all of these foundations herself. Obviously the correspondence involved in their formation was tremendous. Criteria needed to be thoroughly understood by the ecclesiastics who wanted the Good Shepherd to settle in their respective countries, and the countries needed to be appraised in the light of the Good Shepherd apostolate of service. When these two factors were clarified, the Sisters had to be informed about the country to which they were to be sent and in so far as possible, instructed in the language and mores of that country.

Media of communication were slow; problems, many. Frequently Mother St. Euphrasia would be away from Angers when an important letter arrived. Sometimes it could be handled by one of her assistants, often it could not. On those occasions a bishop might justifiably grow impatient at what he considered an unreasonable delay. With increasing regularity ecclesiastics asked why postulants had to travel such great distances to make their novitiate at Angers, when there was a Convent of the Good Shepherd nearer home.

Mother St. Euphrasia recognized these problems. At the rate the Institute was growing she readily admitted that the administrative load was increasing beyond the ability of one person to direct. Still delegation of authority, indiscriminately given, might bring about the autonomous government of the respective houses, the very thing that she opposed.

As was her unfailing custom she prayed for wisdom and guidance. "Not what I want, dear Lord, but what is best for the Institute. That alone is my desire." Her prayers were answered by a proposal from the Roman Congregation of Propaganda, recommending that she appoint Vicars over the Convents in mission lands or divide the whole Order into Provinces, naming Provincial Superiors, responsible to her in last appeal. Otherwise each of these Superiors would be independent in her own particular territory for the government of the houses under her jurisdiction.

Mother St. Euphrasia accepted this latter proposal because she believed it would facilitate the government of the houses and increase vocations to the Good Shepherd. At the first opportunity she consulted Monseigneur Angebault. Of late he had been more friendly and she hoped he would continue in his mood of amiability. He heard her through and offered no objection to the reorganization of the Institute on a geographical or provincial basis. In fact he thought the step timely and important. But just as Mother St. Euphrasia was ready to leave he declared that under this new arrangement he expected all the Provincial Superiors to be subject to his authority, since he felt that his position as Ecclesiastical Superior of the Mother House automatically gave him this prerogative.

A look of amazement crossed Mother St. Euphrasia's face, but she closed her lips firmly and waited in silence for the Bishop to amplify. Experience had taught her that he rarely held expression of his point of view to a brief statement. In spite of repeated explanations he continued to believe that his authority extended far beyond Angers. No wonder then that her heart skipped a beat. A less resolute person would have been completely intimidated.

Bishop Angebault took the matter to the Congregation of Bishops and Regulars, but his request was denied. For some reason, however, the Congregation decided to appoint him as Apostolic Visitor to the monastery of Angers, the Prefect, Cardinal Della Genga, forwarding the appointment in the name of the body. Bishop Angebault was far from satisfied with this arrangement. In view of what followed it seems certain that Rome failed to appreciate the nature of Monseigneur Angebault's personal antagonism toward the Good Shepherd.

Almost the first thing that he did was to cross-examine every Sister privately.

"What do you think about the division of the Congregation into Provinces?" he interrogated.

"Whatever Mother St. Euphrasia thinks," one after another answered naïvely.

"Have you no mind of your own?"

"Yes, Your Excellency."

"Use it then. I want to learn what you think about this matter."

Calm women stuttered and lost their poise because they were afraid of their interrogator. More than once they had heard him tongue lash their beloved Mother General. They did not want to arouse his ire; neither did they wish to cause Mother St. Euphrasia further anguish. Their efforts fell far short of their intentions. "Just as I thought," he insisted. "She's told you not to answer my questions forthrightly."

After that he required each Sister to fill out and sign a complex questionnaire. Hands trembled as quill pens scratched across the paper. Unaware that the questions were irrelevant because they had already been settled in Rome, many became hopelessly confused. On the other hand Mother St. Euphrasia knew that the matter had been officially determined.

"Do you advocate the appointment of Vicars, or the division of the Congregation into Provinces?" Monseigneur Angebault asked.

"Our Holy Father has expressed the wish that the Congregation should be divided into Provinces; therefore, I approve and request the division into Provinces," Mother St. Euphrasia answered calmly and unequivocally.

But Monseigneur Angebault was not satisfied. Instead he prepared an involved report to the effect that things at the Mother House were in an irregular state. He affirmed that the Institute was in a state of retrogression and would disintegrate completely under its present head. The finished report was then dispatched to Rome and a duplicate copy sent to Monseigneur Joubert, the Bishop's delegate at the Good Shepherd. Monseigneur Joubert protested, saying that he could not share the Bishop's conclusions.

Usually one weakens his own cause by excesses of word and deed, but for a time the opposite seemed true. Only Bishop Angebault's voice could be heard, Mother St. Euphrasia choosing to remain silent under the barrage of his attacks. Prudence and charity restrained her; yet they could not lessen the intensity of her reactions. Being human she was deeply hurt at the Monseigneur's unfairness and inability to appreciate her problems. Although she could not understand God's purpose in permitting these things she did not doubt the wisdom of His design.

The next move in this drama of complication came from Rome. Cardinal Della Genga, growing restive over an unanswered letter sent Monseigneur Angebault, blamed Mother St. Euphrasia for the delay. Illogical though it was, he assumed that she was unwilling to co-operate with the Congregation of Propaganda Fide on this vital matter. At first the Pope disagreed, saying that he had never known Mother St. Euphrasia to be disobedient or insubordinate. Later he reversed himself. He found it difficult to reconcile his latter and erstwhile opinions but the facts stood. Since a letter of import sent to the Bishop of Angers had not been acknowledged, it appeared that pressure on Mother St. Euphrasia's part had withheld his reply. Had the truth been known, Monseigneur Angebault had purposely chosen not to answer this communication. One can only conjecture about his motives.

Before long Mother St. Euphrasia learned that she was being criticized for the stalemate in the affairs of the Good Shepherd. At first the idea appeared preposterous, but it ceased to be when she was told that the Holy Father himself held her responsible. Overcome by these unhappy misunderstandings she wrote an impassioned letter of defense to the Cardinal Protector. Her greatest desire, she stated, was to serve Rome. Never had she conceived of her Institute apart from it. Good Shepherd Sisters everywhere were the loyal daughters of His Holiness. She had not known about the letter sent to Monseigneur Angebault. How then could she be held accountable for it? She and her Council having ratified the matter of the formation of Provinces had themselves been waiting for a recognition of their action. Would not the Cardinal, she asked, relay the contents of her letter to His Holiness, assuring him of her filial devotion and steadfast allegiance? "Nothing," she concluded, "could ever weaken my attachment to Rome and the Holy Father."

Happily her letter satisfied Cardinal Della Genga and caused Pope Pius IX to say with obvious relief: "That is the Mother St. Euphrasia I have known. She must be kept waiting no longer for the decree authorizing the division of her Congregation into Provinces."

The decree was issued immediately. Among other things it meant that as soon as a given region had three Houses it automatically formed a Province with its own Provincial Superior appointed by the Mother General.[6] It meant too that each Provincial Convent would have its own Novitiate, an arrangement that has proved most satisfactory. From time to time, each Province sends a limited number of postulants to Angers for their novitiate but this is done by the individual Provincial Mother, independent of any directive beyond her jurisdiction. In the beginning there were seven provinces with the Provincial Houses located in Angers, Rome, Turin, Munich, London, Algiers, and Louisville, Kentucky. A century later there would be forty-three, including seven provinces in the United States, an expansion that has exceeded Mother St. Euphrasia's most sanguine expectations.

Even though Monseigneur Angebault's opposition increased the difficulties associated with the organization of the provinces, Mother St. Euphrasia's task was lightened by the co-operation extended by the Bishops in whose dioceses the Provincial Convents were to locate. Moreover, she was sustained by the loyalty of the Sisters.

Among her most loyal supporters was a relative newcomer, Sister Mary of St. Peter, the former Countess Mary Leopoldine de Coudenhove, member of an illustrious Austrian family. Although in her early forties, Sister Mary of St. Peter adjusted herself with speed and ease to her new life. Professed on January 6, 1854, she appreciated fully the conflicts that accompanied the birth of the provinces. She was less demonstrative and affectionate than Mother St. Euphrasia but this tall, dark-haired, gentle aristocrat had the same zeal for the glory of God, the same humility, and the same devoted kindness to the suffering and the abandoned. She possessed, too, the keenness of intellect that identified itself with the trials Mother St. Euphrasia was obliged to endure. She volunteered no suggestions but Mother St. Euphrasia, recognizing her unusual perspicacity, invited them. With increasing frequency she conferred with Sister Mary of St. Peter, deciding rather quickly that this new Sister should be formed to the Superiorate. With that in mind she appointed her the Superior of the Modena House in 1857, promoting her two years later to the position of the Assistant General of the Congregation. Thereafter Mother St. Euphrasia and Mother St. Peter were to be closely associated in personal and communal interests. Not since the death of Sister Teresa de Couespel had Mother St. Euphrasia found such an able and congenial associate.

The year 1857 brought two additional Good Shepherd foundations to the United States. In February the first was begun in Cincinnati at the urgent insistence of Archbishop Purcell, and some months later the second was started in New York with the reluctant permission of Archbishop Hughes. The circumstances surrounding the foundations were quite dissimilar. Archbishop Purcell, knowing first-hand the quality of the work being carried on by the Good Shepherd in the neighboring state of Kentucky, gave Mother St. Euphrasia no rest until she arranged to send five Sisters to his diocese. Archbishop Hughes, on the other hand, demurred, saying that he was already burdened with too many young and struggling schools and charitable groups. Furthermore he asserted frankly that he doubted if the Sisters of the Good Shepherd could ever attain the purpose for which they were founded. "They will swamp us," he said, "and the end will be a failure."

Most interestingly it was Miss Foster, a charitable and far-visioned Protestant, who persuaded Archbishop Hughes to change his point of view. At that time Miss Foster was the matron of the Tombs Prison. There she sorrowed at the appalling increase in the number of crimes among young immigrant women. Most of these women had come to New York full of hope and short of funds, only to get into serious difficulty in the uneven struggle for survival that they had met as strangers in a strange land. A group of Catholic volunteer social workers were moved with compassion for these victims, many of them their co-religionists. As a result of their work under Miss Foster's direction they became fired with the desire to bring the Good Shepherd Sisters to New York. Especially were they needed, they believed, to help the girls after their dismissal from prison for without guidance it was too easy for released prisoners to go back to their former kind of life.

Miss Foster listened to accounts of the work the Good Shepherd Sisters were doing in Philadelphia and when she understood that they served all denominations she became their ardent advocate. She went to Archbishop Hughes. Out of a large well of experience she spoke of the need for such an organization in the city of New York. Archbishop Hughes' defenses fell but he still looked upon the coming of the Good Shepherd Sisters as a doubtful experiment. On the other hand Mother St. Euphrasia was delighted at the prospect, although she was not immediately able to furnish the new foundation with Sisters from the Mother House. Instead she appointed Sisters from the Convent in Philadelphia until later when she could send a permanent staff.

On October 2 the Sisters took up their residence in an unpretentious frame house on 14th Street. The next day in distant Angers Mother St. Euphrasia with face aglow reported this latest American establishment: "I cannot put off telling you, my daughters, of the foundation of a new fold of the Good Shepherd. The mere thought of the many souls to be saved plunges me into an ecstasy of joy.

"At last we are to be established in a certain and very densely peopled city. Can you guess which? Yes, it is New York. . . . You know, my dear daughters, how much we desired to see a house of the Good Shepherd in Jerusalem, how we tried different methods to accomplish this, but were unsuccessful. Providence decided otherwise and has now in New York, the Babylon of the New World, sent us compensation for this disappointment."

Almost from the beginning Archbishop Hughes realized that his qualms about the Good Shepherd had been unfounded. Two years later he gave half of the Jubilee alms to the Sisters, which amount formed the nucleus for the purchase of a larger property needed to accommodate the children already under their care. After an extended search for a new dwelling located farther from the city the Mother Prioress finally decided upon the property of the Prime family situated on the East River some miles from the center of the city. The priest who accompanied her was most discouraging. "Why there are no roads open beyond Fifth Avenue!" he expostulated. True, the Mother agreed, but cities had a way of growing and New York would be no exception. "Till the city grows out to us, we'll manage. You must admit that a more beautiful place would be hard to find. There is nothing to lose and much to gain by coming here."

In this respect the Mother Prioress was a prophet. For many years the Provincial House of the Good Shepherd occupied the block between 89th and 90th Streets, with East River on one side and Avenue A on the other. Today that same property is the site of Gracie Mansion, where the mayor of New York city resides. Later when the city was rapidly encroaching on these premises a beautiful estate overlooking the Hudson was secured. Called Mount St. Florence and located on the outskirts of Peekskill only forty miles from New York, it has proved the ideal spot for the work of the Good Shepherd. At first it was used as a convalescent home and later as a home for three hundred young orphans, or preservates, given into the care of the Sisters by the Hon. Elbridge Gerry, founder and first president of the Society for the Prevention of Cruelty to Children. The success of those ventures subsequently led to the transfer of the Provincial headquarters from the bustling life of a large metropolis to this spacious and secluded acreage, remote yet easily accessible. These developments came after Mother St. Euphrasia's death, but she foresaw a long and auspicious life for this particular foundation. Had she known that it was in time to become the largest of all the American provinces she would probably have said, "I had no doubt that such would be the case."

In other ways 1857 was an important year, for on August 6 Mother St. Euphrasia was re-elected the Superior General for the fifth consecutive time. With a gasp of surprise she acknowledged the tribute that had been proffered her: "You mean that I am again to head this great Congregation of Our Lady of Charity of the Good Shepherd? What a tremendous honor—and grave responsibility!" No one could doubt that her candor was spontaneous and genuine. Even Monseigneur Angebault, who had surprised everyone by his willingness to preside, found himself offering his felicitations before he withdrew. A ripple of hope ran across the room. Could this action mean that the Bishop was extending the olive branch to Mother St. Euphrasia?

For more than a year a semblance of peace existed. Then the old trouble burst into full flame. On August 27, 1858, Father Augustine Joubert died. For thirteen years he had used every opportunity to dispel the misunderstandings directed against Mother St. Euphrasia. "If the Bishop really knew Mother St. Euphrasia," he would say, "he could not entertain such thoughts. She is a good and righteous woman dedicated to the mission of saving souls. Were she to try, she could not act in a petty manner."

In December Abbé Le Boucher was named as Father Joubert's successor. During the intervening months Mother St. Euphrasia had become increasingly fearful that the new Superior might not be sympathetic toward her work. Often her premonitions about the future were correct. In this case, however, they appeared unwarranted. Father Boucher, young and vigorous, seemed the ideal appointee, bringing to Mother St. Euphrasia the same devotion she had found in Father Joubert.

Her letters show that she made the new delegate her confidant. "Our Lord has compassionated my affliction in sending me a visitor who has greatly comforted me, and has restored my peace. That visitor," she wrote, "was yourself, dear Father. The good you do to my soul and to my troubled heart is beyond expression; so too is my gratitude. . . . I own that next to the Sacred Hearts of Jesus and Mary I wish to draw near to your kindly heart, that I may disclose to it my anguish. Come then; that is all I can say, except to assure you of my boundless reliance and respectful attachment." [7]

It was a blow, then, when Father Boucher's youthful zeal overcame his prudence, causing him to assume authority beyond the limits of his appointment, investigating rather than serving; interfering rather than encouraging. His understanding seemed to desert him, leaving in its stead dictatorial proclivity. Under the circumstances Mother St. Euphrasia was relieved when he resigned to enter parish work.

In the autumn of 1863 Monseigneur Angebault named Monseigneur de Las Casas, an older man, as his delegate. On the verge of melancholia from a series of nervous disorders, Father Las Casas proved an unhappy choice. Above all he lacked the spiritual joy so necessary to any priest, but especially to one appointed to a Good Shepherd Convent. Within its walls the priest's influence is not limited to the Sisters but extends to the children, many of whom are burdened with psychological and emotional problems. When they discover that their chaplain is heavy of spirit, they make no effort to climb out of their own slough of despond. The unfortunate influence of Father Las Casas' personality was intensified by his determination to change the Rules and Constitutions of the Order, failing to comprehend that he was not empowered to alter its purpose and program as originated by St. John Eudes. Whatever his reasoning he tenaciously pursued the impossible.

With infinite patience Mother St. Euphrasia attempted to explain the situation; then with gentle firmness she stated that "what has been established and approved by the highest authority must be maintained intact. Only the Holy See has power to act in this matter."

An impasse followed. "What can I do?" the harassed Mother General pondered in desperation. "I cannot permit our Constitutions to be violated. Yet we can make no progress unless our postulants receive the habit and our novices and young professed pledge their vows. I must find a way to ward off such spiritual paralysis."

But she could not appease Father Las Casas. His resignation in June, 1867, revived Monseigneur Angebault's latent hostility. From his standpoint Mother St. Euphrasia was guilty of insubordination. He petitioned Rome to remove her from Angers until he could investigate matters unimpeded by her presence. Cardinal Patrizi defended Mother St. Euphrasia, reminding the Bishop of the settlement of 1855, which defined specifically the exact powers of an Ecclesiastical Superior.

Several months passed before Monseigneur Angebault reluctantly authorized one of his Vicar Generals to examine the candidates for clothing and profession, declaring that everything else was to be taken care of by temporary chaplains. This arrangement remained in effect as long as Mother St. Euphrasia lived.

All these happenings affected Mother's health but she applied herself with greater industry to the growth and development of the Institute. Definitely she was the type who finds relief from grief and frustration in action; also, she no doubt hoped to merit Divine favor through even more dedicated service. Once more she saw the fruit of "faith and good works" asserting itself in the United States. This time Bishop Duggan of Chicago beckoned. In answer to his call Mother St. Euphrasia sent four Sisters from the Provincial House in St. Louis, with young Sister Mary of St. John Baptist (Jackson) as the Superior in charge. The trip was arduous, requiring two days of travel and an overnight stop at Mattoon, Illinois. On May 20, 1859, the little party arrived in Chicago.

For six months they lived in a temporary dwelling on Price Street, supporting themselves and the children by laundry and needlework as was their custom, aided by kindhearted neighbors and friends. In November it became necessary to move to a larger house on Franklin Street. Once again the familiar story of growth and progress was being written. The Sisters of the Good Shepherd were in Chicago to stay.

During the ensuing years more than twenty-five thousand young girls were to enter their portals to a new life beneath the Shepherd's eye.

Mother St. Euphrasia kept in close touch with this western outpost in the United States. She might reside in France, but her spirit and influence knew no territorial limits. "I do not wish it said any longer that I am French. I am Italian, English, German, Spanish, African, American, Indian. I belong to every country where there are souls to save. When we see sheep to be gathered into the fold, we must not fear to go and pitch our tents on the most distant shores. . . . In America, Africa, Asia, Oceania; everywhere must we go in search of our Lord's sheep."

The War between the States was still in progress when Archbishop Martin John Spalding of Baltimore petitioned Mother St. Euphrasia to send the Good Shepherd Sisters to the Primatial See of the United States. Until now he had thought it unwise to make this move, pending the return of peace; unwise in the sense that the pressures of wartime would make any effort to aid the Sisters difficult and uncertain. He discovered, however, that there were a number of interested persons ready and willing to help with this greatly needed venture. Among them were Father Thomas Foley of the Cathedral, subsequently Coadjutor-Bishop of Chicago, and Mrs. Emily McTavish, granddaughter of Charles Carroll of Carrollton.

Through the generosity of Mrs. McTavish the Sisters were given a large, well-built old mansion together with one-half of the lot around it. Beautifully situated in the western suburb of the city, the property overlooked a vast expanse of country. Then Mrs. McTavish assumed the responsibility for all the necessary improvements and in addition gave the greater part of the furniture, old and lovely pieces. Later she purchased the remaining portion of the ground for new buildings and gardens, making possible the beautiful rose gardens that have always been associated with the Baltimore Convent.

In accord with Mother St. Euphrasia's directives Mother Mary of St. Ignatuis Ward, the Provincial Superior of Louisville, with four young Sisters started the work in Baltimore on August 6, 1864. The following day the first child was admitted into the Good Shepherd fold. Seldom had a foundation begun under more propitious circumstances.

In New Orleans, however, the situation was quite different. A foundation had begun there on March 13, 1859, under Archbishop A. Blanc. Until 1864 local opposition and the vicissitudes of the Civil

War proved a constant threat to its survival. Then Mother St. Euphrasia recalled Sister Teresa de Schorlemer from Bangalore and placed her in charge of the New Orleans House, hopeful that she would succeed in stabilizing its affairs. The impoverished and embittered city was barren ground for a work of hope and love but for two years Sister Teresa did her best to overcome indifference on one hand and almost violent opposition on the other. She was a woman of calm energy and resolute will but she often feared that she was inadequate for her gigantic task. She persevered until the sudden outbreak of cholera in August, 1866, when the Sisters left their cloister to tend the sick and dying on the streets. Sister Teresa was among the early victims of the scourge but her selfless service and heroic death did much to advance the cause of the Good Shepherd in the far South.

When Mother St. Euphrasia learned that Sister Teresa had succumbed, she wept bitterly. "It is hard, dear Lord, very hard, but such is ever the Way of the Cross. Thy will be done."

XVI

1867-1868

Who shall find a valiant woman?
Far and from the uttermost coasts
is the price of her.

PROVERBS, 31:10

A S THE months went on it had become evident that Mother St.
Euphrasia was overtired. Finally in May, 1867, a severe bron-
chial infection sent her to bed. She coughed incessantly and her
breathing grew heavy and labored. At the physician's orders the Sister
Infirmarian applied unguents and hot cloths to Mother's chest, but
these measures brought no relief. Suddenly Mother lapsed into a
troubled sleep from which she could not be aroused. In baffling unfinished sentences she kept referring to "crosses and more crosses."
When her illness failed to respond to prescribed medication, the Sisters gave her some water from the spring of Our Lady of La Salette.
Almost immediately they sensed a change for the better. Mother St.
Euphrasia opened her eyes and looked brightly about the room. Then
she smiled and spoke clearly: "I have just had a most interesting
dream. It is so real it seems it must have actually happened. . . .
Greatly worried about the crosses which we are having just now, I saw
the Congregation wrapped as it were in an immense net, the threads
of which were broken at many points. As that made me anxious, the
Blessed Virgin appeared and said: 'If you put your hand to it, I will
leave you. It is I who wish to repair it all.' "

None of the Sisters made any comment but they wondered if this
had been a dream or an experience beyond the bounds of earth reality.

Mother St. Euphrasia's convalesence continued well into the summer. But she was still confined to her bed when Sister Mary of St. Augustine, the Superior of the Santiago Convent, and Sister Mary of the Immaculate Conception, a novice, arrived from Chile. With a start of recognition she greeted them like old friends: "You are just as God showed you to me," she said. Clearly she was awed by what appeared to be a special grace of prescience.

From the beginning she felt an affinity for Sister Mary of St. Augustine, recognizing the talents which were later to make this nun one of the most distinguished members of the entire Congregation. One day as the younger Sister sat beside her bed Mother St. Euphrasia spoke with a kind of impassioned certainty: "I was very seriously ill and about to die. But my life was spared so that I might see you."

A few weeks later Mother St. Euphrasia was able to walk unassisted from her cell to the chapel. Her step was unsteady and her voice less vigorous but otherwise she appeared quite like her normal self. The Sisters would have been seriously disturbed had they known the malignant nature of Mother's illness. However, she had told no one about the growth in her side that pained her constantly. Her reticence can be partially explained by her unwillingness to cast a shadow on the extensive preparations under way for her Golden Jubilee of Profession. Although she would have preferred a quiet observance, she cooperated with all the plans which needed her approval.

Three days were given to the festivities, the first day, September 8, to the observance of the Blessed Virgin's birthday; the second, to the ceremony of profession; and the third, to the Sister Magdalens and the children. From beginning to end, the second day was peculiarly Mother St. Euphrasia's. Like many a jubilarian she found it difficult to realize that fifty years had gone by since her own profession. At Mass she identified herself with the young women accepting with joy "the sweet and light yoke of Jesus Christ." More than once she brushed the tears aside, seeing herself in the midst of this happy group each of whom asked "to dwell in the house of the Lord, and of His Holy Mother, all the days of my life." She recalled every detail of that fall day in 1817 when she had spoken her own final vows, smiling as she thought of her earlier attitude toward the little-known name of Euphrasia. Today it seemed strange to think that she had ever answered to any other.

Following this ceremony she accepted a statue of Our Lady of La

Salette from one of the Community's patrons, after which Mother St. Augustine of Chile presented a statue of the Sacred Heart to the Sisters' Choir. In addition she gave Mother St. Euphrasia a beautifully bound Spanish translation of the Sister Magdalens' Rule, first reading aloud the dedication, ending: "How many stray sheep have you not brought back to the fold? How many among you have you not led along the path of perfection by having instituted the monasteries of the Sisters of St. Magdalen, by having given them a guide to Heaven in the beautiful Rule we offer you today, translated into St. Teresa's mother tongue?"

Those who were present always remembered the almost ethereal smile that lighted Mother St. Euphrasia's face. In silence she placed the gift over her heart, emphasizing her affection for St. Teresa.

Each evening Mother St. Euphrasia sat at an open window and watched the happy celebrants crossing and recrossing the lawn, bearing tapers and singing familiar hymns and French cantiques. She smiled and waved, speaking informally with the groups who stopped before her to recite verses or sing songs they had composed in her honor. The friends, the lights, the music, and the love behind them touched her heart. Naturally she talked about the early days of the Institute. "When I recall how we began this foundation, I say we ought never to be discouraged. It was poverty, the most utter, the most absolute. And the greater the poverty, the crosses, and the humiliations our monasteries meet with, the more sure they will be to receive graces. I love that saying, 'Grace is a fruit of the Cross.'"

Mother St. Euphrasia entered the final day of the festivities, fatigued but happy. Surrounded by the Sister Magdalens she spoke the words they loved most: "You are the joy and the crown of my work. I am truly your Mother Foundress." Finally the children came with their bouquets and handicraft offerings. In the excitement one of the orphans fell face forward upsetting her basket of flowers and soiling her new dress. She tried not to cry but the tears came spilling down her cheeks. "Come here, my child," Mother said, wiping away the hot tears with her own handkerchief. As the child tried to recover her self-control, Mother comforted her, saying that the dress, though wrinkled from her fall, could soon be made good as new. "Now pick up the flowers and bring them here. I'll keep them in fresh water. They are very pretty. Thank you for gathering them for me."

With a smile the little girl bent down to reclaim the strewn flowers for "Our Mother." The Sisters near by smiled too. "It has always been like this. Whether it was a stubbed toe or a broken life, Mother St. Euphrasia has wiped away the tears and bitterness and sent the child off singing. Even our most stubborn culprits have melted under the warmth of her love."

During the succeeding months Mother St. Euphrasia grew noticeably weaker. However, she never referred to her increasing disabilities and the long, sleepless nights that brought her no rest. When urged to lie abed in the morning, she replied: "Would you deprive me of my only consolation? I have so often told you, Holy Communion is my very life. . . . What would have become of me during these last two years without the Bread of the Strong?"

Still she carefully avoided revealing the nature of her illness. She had her own reasons for this guarded silence, unwise though they were. Foremost was a mother's prerogative to spare her children undue concern. She still worked many hours daily, handling her voluminous correspondence; she still could keep ahead of her competent secretaries. Mother St. Peter sometimes protested that she was driving herself too hard but Mother St. Euphrasia begged her not to be concerned. "The time will come soon enough when I shall not be able to take care of these things. Until then I want to remain in close touch with our Houses, particularly our most recent ones in Belfast, West Philadelphia, and Peekskill."

Happily a number of Prioresses from the French Houses were able to return to Angers for Mother St. Euphrasia's Feast Day on March 13. To their relief she consented to use a wheel chair for her traditional visits to the many shrines on the Convent grounds. Twice she left the chair, once at the Chapel of the Immaculate Conception and again at the Shrine of St. Joseph, saying, "I must make these visits on foot." At the conclusion of the Feast the visitors were reluctant to depart, wondering under what circumstances they would next see their beloved Mother General. With a heart full of filial love one of the group whispered hopefully, "You will let me come soon again, will you not, dear Mother?"

Mother's reply misled her. "My child, you will indeed come again soon, but you will need no permission."

The departure ceremony for the Sisters assigned to the new foundation of Altstätten, Switzerland, was set for March 25. According to custom Mother St. Euphrasia was to conduct the Sisters chosen for this House to the altar where they would pledge their fealty to the Institute. At the appointed time she rose in her place and carefully surveyed the distance that lay between her stall and the altar. It was only sixty feet but it looked like six hundred. Suddenly her legs refused to support her and she clung to the edge of her *prie-dieu* to keep from falling. Turning to Mother St. Peter she said softly, "I cannot make it."

"Lean on me and we'll make it together," the Mother Assistant replied. "It is not so far away."

"Not so far, but too far. It is much too far." Then Mother St. Euphrasia spoke to the waiting Sisters. "My dear children, I am sorry that I am unable to lead you in the procession. But you might as well ask me to walk to St. Nicholas, three-fourths of a mile away."

Her statement frightened them. This was the first time they had ever heard their Mother admit that she was not able to discharge her duties. Evidently she must be far more seriously ill than they had supposed. Four days later on Passion Sunday she made the effort to join the Community at midday recreation. Temporarily her presence allayed the Sisters' fears. Yet when they looked closely at her pain-racked person they saw that she was only a wraith of her former vigorous self. Her quick little walk had disappeared, leaving in its place an enfeebled and shuffling gait, and her face, usually so mobile, showed the ravages of prolonged suffering and sleeplessness.

In spite of these physical changes her mental abilities were not impaired. Later that same day, March 29, 1868, she dictated a letter authorizing the Provincial Mother of St. Louis to open two new Convents in the United States to be located respectively in Brooklyn, New York,[1] and St. Paul, Minnesota. From her bed she signed the document that brought the number of Houses of the Good Shepherd in the United States to 14 and the total number in the fold to 110. With a sense of deep satisfaction she lay back on her pillow. She knew that she had just made her last two foundations. In the future someone else would be responsible for the continuing growth of the Congregation.

Two days later Mother St. Euphrasia grew worse. After a cursory examination Dr. Farge, the physician in attendance at the Convent, diagnosed Mother's trouble as possible inflammation and congestion of the liver. Her high fever and aggravated nausea led him to think that she might also be suffering from an organic stomach disorder. Later Dr. Pelletier, Mother's nephew, concurred with Dr. Farge but he, too, was handicapped by his aunt's resistance to a thorough physical examination. Under the circumstances Dr. Farge advised the application of a mustard compress to the liver area, hoping that it might alleviate her suffering.

Mother St. Euphrasia asked to apply the compress unaided. "I can take care of it," she assured the reluctant infirmarian, who later blamed herself for not having insisted on carrying out the doctor's orders. Even then she might not have discovered the cancerous growth Mother sought to conceal had not the mustard compress slipped and fallen over this open wound causing Mother to cry aloud in anguish, "Sister, dear, help me; the pain is intolerable."

For a moment the infirmarian stood horror-struck. Then with almost superhuman effort she pulled the burning plaster away from the infected ulcer which had for so long constituted Mother's Gethsemane.

"Dr. Farge must see this," she insisted.

"No, Sister! No! I do not wish that."

"But I must be shown how to take care of this wound."

"Not by Dr. Farge, Sister," Mother St. Euphrasia protested. "Otherwise, I would have consulted him long ago." Her delicacy in this matter was a surprising revelation. Weak and prone though she was, she refused to undergo the distasteful examination. However, she agreed to a Sister of St. Mary's coming regularly to dress and bandage her side. She knew that the inroads of the disease were too far advanced to respond to any medication but she endured the additional pain and encumbrance of the dressings for the sake of the Sisters. With a heavy heart she realized how much sorrow her extreme modesty was bringing to them.

During Passion Week Mother's suffering grew more intense. Still there were times when she summoned the Council to her bedside and disposed of vitally important matters pertaining to the welfare of the Congregation. One of these matters was the appointing of the Sisters who were to make the new foundation of Aden in Saudi Arabia.

On the Friday of Passion Week she said: "This is a true Passion Week, my dearest Sisters! It is evident that Our Lady wishes me to stand beside her on Calvary. Fiat. . . . It is my desire to die there whenever Our Lord should see fit. It distresses me though to think how you all suffer with me. May God's Will be done!"

After a night and a day of constant nausea Mother St. Euphrasia's spasms ended temporarily. Seizing this respite she asked that the last rites be administered. Father Cellier, the chaplain, came in haste, the sickroom being made ready by many willing hands. Several Sisters knelt at the foot of Mother's bed with other Sisters kneeling just beyond the threshold. Choked with tears their voices were scarcely audible as they answered the prayers for the dying. Mother's voice, though low, was clear and resolute. Some hours later Father Cellier returned with the Blessed Sacrament. He waited at the improvised altar when he saw that the Mother General wished to speak. Faintly but firmly she pledged her vows anew. "I, Sister Mary of St. Euphrasia Pelletier, confirm and renew with my whole heart the Vows which I have made to my God, to serve Him forever in the Congregation of Our Lady of Charity of the Good Shepherd of Angers, by Obedience, Chastity, and Poverty, as well as by the fourth Vow to labor for the Salvation of the Souls of the persons who enter our Houses. . . , in the Name of the Father, of the Son, and of the Holy Ghost, and in honor of the Most Holy Virgin, Mother of the Congregation. Amen."

Mother St. Euphrasia stopped momentarily and then continued: "O my God, I very humbly ask pardon of Thy Divine Majesty for all the sins by which I have offended Thee, by not having served Thee as I ought to have done. Our Sisters, I humbly beg pardon . . . for all the pain or disedification I have ever given, and beg you to pray to Our Divine Lord that He may give me the grace of resignation to His will, and final perseverance. . . . I forgive from my heart all the persons who have caused me sorrow. The Community never has."

Many of the Sisters sobbed aloud at the thought of their unworthiness. Then Mother St. Euphrasia repeated the words made famous by her noted exemplar, St. Teresa of Avila: "I profess that I die a true daughter of the Holy Catholic, Apostolic, Roman Church."

With a nod she indicated that she had finished. Father Cellier then attempted a few words of comfort but broke off suddenly to hide his own mounting emotion, ending with the familiar words of the ritual: "Receive, dear Sister, the Body of Our Lord Jesus Christ as a Viaticum unto life eternal."

Silence held them all. A glass of cold water placed on Mother St. Euphrasia's bedside table remained untouched. After a lengthy interval she opened her eyes and spoke very softly: "I am making my thanksgiving." A little later she was persuaded to take a few sips of water. Then she spoke directly to the Sisters: "I beg you all to be closely united. If you should have any little misunderstanding, forgive one another. Oh, this dear Congregation. Love it always faithfully. Promise me that you will always uphold it."

"We promise," the Sisters pledged in unison.

"Watch over your treasure," Mother St. Euphrasia continued. "This dear Congregation is in the hands of God."

Here Mother Mary of St. Peter (de Coudenhove) spoke for them all: "Mother dear, what will become of us now that you are going to leave us?"

"Do not be disturbed. I shall be able to help you more effectively when I am in the presence of God than I ever could while on earth. But I wish to exhort you to be ever loyal to Rome, to the Holy Father, and to our Cardinal Protector. Do as I have done. It is true that the attachment I have had for Rome has cost me many sorrows, many crosses, and the greatest difficulties. Yet in spite of all I have suffered, I die happy that I have ever been attached to it. Oh, love Rome. There is the light. There is the column of fire which enlightens the world. . . ."

The Sisters knew that Mother should be hoarding her precious energy; yet they sensed the importance of her instructions. Her next words showed that her mother's heart held them in close embrace. "Take care of our dear penitents, of our dear children." Then she murmured: "Those dear Magdalens, I may call myself their Foundress. What a comfort St. Mary Magdalen has always been to me. She is my patroness." This disclosure humbled them all.

After a brief rest Mother said almost matter-of-factly: "It is time to write the foundations."

"We sent them word this morning, dear Mother," Mother St. Peter replied.

" 'Tis well; 'tis well," Mother St. Euphrasia whispered. Then she listed in turn all of the 110 Houses scattered over five continents, stopping occasionally to make some suitable comment. The list concluded, she blessed the Sisters, present and absent. "Tell my beloved daughters that I bless them all and that I embrace them with tenderness. At this supreme moment not one of them has been forgotten."

A sudden attack of vomiting cut short this discourse. All but the nursing Sisters left the room quietly to await the word that would soon recall them. No one believed that Mother could possibly survive the night.

The next morning she had rallied sufficiently to request a branch of blessed palm. This emblem of victory she kept on the table beside her until she died. Then it was planted near the Chapel of the Immaculate Conception where it took root and grew, later providing cuttings for many foundations. As the day progressed Mother improved slightly but she continued to be a very sick person. Once she remarked: "Just last Sunday I was with you all at recreation but it was only love that kept me up."

"Yes," a Sister replied softly. "How many marks of love you have always given us!"

"And you to me, dear children," she responded, her eyes filling with tears. "I feel your love deeply. Excuse this moment of weakness. I weep because I love you so much."

Later that Palm Sunday afternoon a telegram arrived from Cardinal Patrizi, conveying the Apostolic Blessing and personal greetings of the Holy Father together with the Pontiff's prayers and those of the Cardinal.

Stirred by this message from Pius IX, Mother St. Euphrasia made the Sign of the Cross over the greeting and kissed it tenderly. "Please place this beneath my statue of the Holy Family," she requested. "They will guard it well."

Two hours later just as the Angelus bell was ringing, Monseigneur Angebault accompanied by one of his Vicars appeared unheralded at the door of the Mother House. Almost a year had gone by since his last visit. When he had not come at the time of Mother's Golden Jubilee, one of the newly professed religious had remonstrated to her Novice Mistress, saying, "I cannot bear to have our dear Mother hurt by anyone." Moved by this outburst the Novice Mistress told Mother St. Euphrasia of the young Sister's solicitude. Equally moved Mother called for the young nun. "So, my dear child," she said, "you felt for your poor old Mother. I thank you for your thoughtfulness. The Bishop's absence has indeed pained me deeply." This was her only reference to the sorrow she had carried in her heart during the general rejoicing.

In view of the Bishop's known antagonism to Mother St. Euphrasia and the Good Shepherd, one can imagine the drama that ensued at his coming. Remembering Mother's injunction always to treat every guest hospitably, the Sisters received the Bishop as though he had been momentarily expected. And in a sense he had been, for vigil lights burned night and day on the main altar as evidence of the many prayers that were being offered to God for this reconciliation. Every Sister wanted the Bishop to visit Mother St. Euphrasia in her last hours; yet many feared that he might not come and no doubt, some feared that he might. In any case, his presence electrified the entire household.

Only a few moments transpired before he was taken to Mother St. Euphrasia at his own request. With kindly countenance and gracious manner he entered the sickroom on the first floor to which she had been transferred in the early stages of her illness.

"My dear daughter, I have come to bring you my blessing. I have already remembered you in Holy Mass and in my visit to the Blessed Sacrament."

"I am very grateful to you, Monseigneur," she answered with evident pleasure. "It is good of you to come."

The Sisters then withdrew, leaving Mother and the Bishop together. No one can say what words passed between them. Perhaps in that brief and final interview Monseigneur Angebault was given the illuminating grace to see Mother St. Euphrasia as she truly was. In any case, the visit of the Bishop brought Mother St. Euphrasia the kind of happiness she had long been denied in her personal relationships with him.

On Monday Mother St. Euphrasia received the Eucharist, but after that uninterrupted nausea intervened for twelve successive days. She became, as someone has said, "an oblation of pure pain." Evidently she was not given sedatives for there seems to have been no period, however brief, when she was not in possession of her senses. On Thursday of Holy Week she said regretfully: "This is the first time in all my life as a religious that I have not been able to receive Our Blessed Lord on Holy Thursday."

The next morning she approved the construction of a Community Chapel at Loos, Belgium. "It brings me happiness," she said, "to be able to give, on this Good Friday, the permission to erect a new sanctuary in honor of Our Blessed Lord." Except for this one matter of business she spent the rest of the day in close identity with the agony and death of God's beloved Son. On the Feast of the Resurrection she found it especially hard to be denied the Holy Eucharist, but she did not complain. Instead she implored the Sisters: "Do not pray that my life may be prolonged. You will only be retarding my happiness." Through her words they realized afresh that death is a triumph and not a desolation when one truly believes in the Risen Christ.

Two days after Easter Father Roux visited Angers. For six years prior to his recent transfer to Rennes as Superior of the Oblates of Mary Immaculate this priest had been Mother St. Euphrasia's confessor. Upon his arrival she greeted him solicitously. Later after he had heard her confession and made ready to leave the room she turned to the Sisters who had re-entered and said: "He alone has been faithful to me always."

Knowing that the Congregation was soon to be without a Superior General the Council Sisters endeavored to prepare themselves for this eventuality. Hopefully they asked Father Roux if Mother St. Euphrasia had talked to him of her possible successor.

"We spoke of the matter outside of Confession," he replied, "but she prefers not to name anyone. She prefers instead to leave this matter in the hands of God."

That was like her, they agreed. Yet they waited patiently for any sign that might reveal her wishes. Mother St. Euphrasia sensed their anxiety. One day after she and Mother St. Peter had been alone for some time, she said to the Sisters: "Do not worry. . . . Sister Mary of St. Peter has been my support; she will be yours, too."

With increasing frequency Mother St. Euphrasia referred to the life beyond mortal reality. More than once she said: "There is a great hill that I must climb. And I must go across the water . . . afterwards I shall find rest." One day while in a state of semiconsciousness she remarked impressively: "Oh, how beautiful Heaven is! I see Our Lord in the midst of His elect. . . . Oh, if I only had the strength to cross the torrent and to scale the mountain. . . . I feel that Our Blessed Lady is there beside me . . . she tells me that I have only a lake to cross but how many rocks . . . how many rocks! . . . Afterwards I shall be in port. . . . If I can climb as high as Our Lady has shown me, I shall find the Lord of Peace." These revelations in no way lessened Mother's concern for the welfare of others. Repeatedly she begged the Sisters to spare themselves. "What a burden I am to you!" she often said. "You may be sure I shall not forget you after I reach Heaven. Do go and rest a little while now; you can come back to me later."

Thus she neared the end of her earthly pilgrimage. Broken in body but triumphant in spirit she greeted the Superiors in turn as they arrived from their own Convents, giving to each one a special message for her Community and nation. On Monday and Tuesday, preceding her death, she was able once more to communicate; then her infirmities asserted themselves. On the last day of her life she rallied long enough to reach out in her love to the missions in distant lands, bringing them figuratively into her presence. Her mind remained lucid and keen. To one of the Sisters she said: "We name you Superior of Oran. I trust that House to you."

Exhausted she lay back murmuring, "I must rest a few minutes." Some time later she asked for the Superiors whom she had not yet seen. They had scarcely reached her bedside when her tremendous courage failed her. Instead of words of greeting she uttered words of farewell: "Good-by! Good-by, my daughters! Good-by, dear Institute! I commend you all to God!"

She was never to speak again. It was nearing six o'clock on the evening of April 24, 1868, when Mother Mary of St. Euphrasia Pelletier, the wise virgin, went quietly forth to meet her bridegroom, having always remembered to have ready the oil in her vessel with which to light her lamp for his coming.

As she had requested, her mortal remains were buried in the chapel she herself had designed many years previous. "Afterwards," she had said, "afterwards, my dear daughters, I wish you to keep me in the Chapel of the Immaculate Conception. I love that chapel because there I shall be near our works. The Magdalens, the penitents, and the children can come and pray there."

So it shall ever be as long as the Angers Mother House of the Good Shepherd shall exist.

After Mother St. Euphrasia's death, she who had healed many sick persons during her lifetime responded generously to the prayers of sincere supplicants, bringing them peace of heart and in many instances freedom from pain and disability.

One incident is representative of the many cures attributed to her intercession. At the Good Shepherd Convent in St. Louis Mary Ryan committed voluntarily by her parents on the charge of incorrigibility proved a real trial to everyone. Willful and truculent she defied all authority, refusing to listen to reason or admonition. Everything displeased her. Consequently the desire to run away soon became an obsession. Early one morning she arose quietly, dressed, opened the dormitory window and before the Dormitory Mistress and the other children could restrain her, jumped forty feet to the stone pavement below. Her back was broken in the fall. Physicians summoned in haste declared that she was dying.

Meanwhile a wave of prayers to Mother St. Euphrasia had started, begging her to save the child. To the doctors' amazement Mary Ryan was still alive at the end of three months. Her weakness and suffering were extreme, but her attitude was one of confidence. In every way she was a different person, amiable, trustful, and uncomplaining.

"Mother St. Euphrasia has saved my life," she kept repeating. "She will make me well. Wait and see."

In the face of the doctors' insistence that complete recovery was impossible Mary began a novena to Mother St. Euphrasia, begging for a cure. Until the final day of the novena Mary's condition showed no change. Then the impossible happened. Unassisted she arose from her bed, dressed, and walked out of the room. Upon reaching the hall she increased her pace, breaking into a run and calling out joyously: "I am cured! I am cured! Mother St. Euphrasia has cured me!" Numerous examinations over a period of months by many physicians resulted in the unanimous opinion that this patient, contrary to medical prognostication, had been completely cured.

With growing fervor Mother St. Euphrasia was hailed as patroness of vocations and invoked with success against the dread disease of cancer. Quite early, earnest thought was given to the practicality of introducing her cause at Rome but action was deferred for more than twelve years. All knew that the tremendous labor of research involved in the various processes leading to canonization together with the magnificence of the final ceremony entailed formidable and continuing expense.

Then Mother St. Augustine of Santiago received spiritual direction. One day in 1880 as this Chilean Prioress lay ill in bed her thoughts turned affectionately to the late Mother General of the Good Shepherd. Suddenly she felt drawn irresistibly to the church. Making her way there with difficulty she arrived just as the chaplain was elevating the Blessed Sacrament for adoration on the altar. Clearly and distinctly she heard these words coming from the Host: "It is urgent that my faithful spouse be glorified; she who has glorified me so much."

"But, Lord, that will cost a great deal of money," Mother St. Augustine replied.

"The mountains will give gold and silver, if it be necessary," the voice assured her.

As might be expected Mother St. Augustine hurried to communicate with Angers. Duly impressed, Mother Mary of St. Peter (de Coudenhove), the second Superior General, petitioned Pope Leo XIII to appoint a Court to examine into the life and virtues of her noted predecessor. From the beginning His Holiness displayed keen interest.

In 1886 at a tribunal in Rome the Superior from South America

was asked her reasons for desiring the canonization of Mother St.
Euphrasia. She replied: "In order that the Will of God may be accomplished." Because her words differed from the accepted formula
"For the glory of God" she was requested to justify her use of them.
Obviously moved by her explanation Leo XIII agreed to initiate proceedings by appointing the Court of Inquiry at Angers, naming as its
president Monseigneur Freppel, the successor of Monseigneur Ange-
bault.² Ten years later on December 11, 1897, the same Pontiff con-
curring with the opinions of competent officials, Cardinals, and consultors declared Mother Mary of St. Euphrasia Pelletier, Venerable.

Following the introduction of Mother St. Euphrasia's cause the
process continued despite the widespread expulsion of religious orders
from France and the inevitable delays brought about by World
War I. Finally on January 29, 1924, the Sacred Congregation of Rites
proclaimed the heroism of the virtues of Mother Mary of St. Euphrasia Pelletier, the Servant of God. On February 24 Pope Pius XI
listened to the reading of the decree in the Hall of the Consistory.
The Congregation of the Good Shepherd represented at this assembly
by Mother Mary of St. Domitilla Larose, the fourth Mother General,
and fifty-two Sisters then heard the Holy Father speak these portentous words: "It has been duly established, in the case and for the
effect of which there is no question, that the Venerable Servant of
God, Sister Mary of St. Euphrasia Pelletier, did practice to an heroic
degree the theological virtues of faith, hope, and charity toward God
and neighbor, as well as the cardinal virtues of prudence, justice, fortitude, and temperance, and all that they imply." ³

Following this decision Monseigneur Rumeau, the Bishop of
Angers, expressed the filial gratitude of the Sisters of the Good Shepherd at the issuance of this decree and proceeded further to extol the
attributes of their Mother Foundress. His Holiness then responded
to Bishop Rumeau's allocution.⁴

The apostolic Benediction brought to an end the ceremonies that
had advanced the cause of Mother Mary St. Euphrasia Pelletier one
step nearer completion. The remaining steps were reached respectively on Good Shepherd Sunday, April 30, 1933, and on the Feast of
the Ascension, May 2, 1940. On the former date Pius XI acclaimed
Mother St. Euphrasia a *Beata*, and on the latter Pius XII ⁵ raised her
to the honors of the altar, reading the formal canonization decree that
proclaimed her publicly and forever as St. Mary of St. Euphrasia
Pelletier. "To the honor of the Most Holy Trinity and for the exalta-

tion of the Catholic faith and for the increase of the Christian religion, through the authority of our Lord Jesus Christ, of the blessed Apostles Peter and Paul, and through our own authority . . . we decree and define as saint the Blessed Mary of St. Euphrasia and order her name to be written in the book of saints."

Prominent among the throngs that came from all over the world to attend the colorful ceremonies of Beatification and Canonization were delegations of the Congregation of Jesus and Mary, familiarly known as the Eudist Fathers. Also present were representatives of the Sisters of the Refuge whose reconciliation with the Good Shepherd had been effected in 1925 at the time of the canonization of St. John Eudes. On that occasion a Refuge Sister was heard to say: "This day is long overdue. After all Mother St. Euphrasia was our Sister before she was the Good Shepherd Mother." Prior to Mother St. Euphrasia's Beatification the Very Reverend Mathurin Jehanno, Superior General of the Congregation of Jesus and Mary, manifested his good will toward the Good Shepherd by addressing a circular letter to all of its members in which he made known his desire to have the statue of Blessed Mary of St. Euphrasia Pelletier placed alongside that of St. John Eudes "in all our churches and chapels." The Sisters of the Good Shepherd have extended this same courtesy of affection to the Founder of their Institute. It is true that St. Mary of St. Euphrasia Pelletier was the Foundress of the Sisters of the Good Shepherd but her Congregation, she consistently affirmed, was an extension, and not a replacement, of the work of St. John Eudes. As Rome has so aptly said, she was "the ingrafter of a large branch on the Order of Our Lady of Charity."

XVII

Let not folk be too secure in judgment,
as who should count the ears upon the field
ere they be ripe;

for I have seen first of all the winter
through the thorn display itself hard
and forbidding and then upon its summit
bear the rose:

and I have seen ere now a ship fare straight
and swift over the sea through her entire
course, and perish at the last, entering
the harbour mouth.

DANTE, *Il Paradiso*, Canto 13

THE assembled guests waited expectantly until an attractive brunette of seventeen, wearing the regulation school uniform, dark red jumper with white cotton blouse, appeared before the footlights to explain that the skit to be presented had been written and staged by the girls themselves.

"The theme of our program," she said, "is twenty-four hours of sunshine. You'll find that the popular song of that name provides the motif and background music. This project is the result of the fun we've had and the work we've done in our Speech, Music, and Clothing Departments. Each one has made the clothes she wears. Because we wanted to be more than mannequins we have become dramatists and musicians, too. From now on, the play's the thing, and the actresses, the upperclassmen of St. Joseph's Academy."

Then followed a dramatic account of a day's activities at the school. With the ringing of the rising bell, tousle-haired, sleepy-eyed adolescents jumped out of bed and dressed for Mass, breakfast, and household chores; then a dash to personal lockers to change into school uniforms, worn until time for basketball, softball, and tennis. In the Clothing Class twelve girls were putting finishing touches to pastel formals to be worn first in the May-day Procession and later at the Junior-Senior Banquet.

"Isn't it fun?" one girl asked another.

"It's twenty-four hours of sunshine," came the tuneful reply as the girls pushed brooms, made beds, mixed cakes, and clicked typewriters. One girl quipped, "Home was never like this." At that remark many of the audience, largely composed of probation officers, social case workers, and representatives of the juvenile courts, nodded agreement. The play came to an end with the big clock in the background striking the bedtime hour, as young voices muted the theme song and the girls joined in night prayers before getting into bed. Twenty-four hours of sunshine!

Three weeks later and several hundred miles distant another audience gathered to attend the joint Commencement Exercises of the secondary and elementary divisions of Mt. St. Mary's School. As the organ broke into a familiar processional, sixteen happy seniors wearing white academic robes and white mortarboards with blue tassels entered the chapel and took their assigned places. Behind them were ten eighth graders in bright summer dresses. Audience reactions were varied. "It's magic, sheer magic." "Unless one sees this transformation one simply wouldn't believe it was possible." The Bishop bestowed the diplomas and certificates, a fact which gave the event a special decor.

Ceremonies concluded, families and friends joined the graduates at an informal reception. As on Visitors' Day, diversities of heritage and environment were apparent. A poorly-dressed middle-aged woman drew her motherless niece to her in warm embrace; a laughing Italian family of five posed for pictures with their Maria; and a proud group of Negroes waited their turn to felicitate Jean, today's valedictorian. "We wouldn't have missed this for anything."

Unfortunately Emily overheard the remark. So far her Dad had not arrived. As her eyes again searched the door, Miss Bates, the friendly social worker who had first brought Emily to the Home, spoke to her: "Congratulations, Emily! I'm terribly thirsty, aren't you?" When Emily admitted that she was, Miss Bates took charge. "I'll serve you, for this is your day." Over their lemonade the girl told Miss Bates of her disappointment. "It's too late now, but maybe he'll come tomorrow," she said hesitantly. "I don't think he'll overlook my graduation entirely."

"But if he should?" Miss Bates queried.

For a few seconds Emily said nothing. Then she smiled, "I'll not mind too much. You see, Miss Bates, I'm going to become a Sister Magdalen."

"Well, that is news, Emily."

"You're the first person I've told. I'm leaving here on Monday to work in a department store until the end of the summer. Mother Raphael says I must put my decision to a test out in the world, but in September I'll return to spend another year in the Class and help Mother Raphael with the new girls. When I first came here, Sister Magdalen of St. Eugene was still a member of the Class. If it hadn't been for her, I'm sure I'd have run away. Will you ever forget how scared and unhappy I was?"

"No, I'll never forget," Miss Bates answered with deliberation. How could she forget the pitiful, bald-headed child she'd brought here nearly three years previous? Mistreated by her waspish stepmother she had become the frightened and nervous target of the woman's barbed tongue. When Emily began to lose her hair, her stepmother made fun of her until Emily finally broke into a beauty shop intent on procuring a substitute for her lost tresses. Caught by the police she was later placed on probation and returned home; then goaded almost to the point of frenzy she took revenge one night by cutting off her sleeping stepmother's heavy braids. A crisis resulted in the child's being committed to the Home of the Good Shepherd. Miss Bates had brought many girls to the Sisters but none had ever been so odd-appearing and so thoroughly miserable as poor hairless Emily. Looking now at the girl's lovely shoulder length hair she felt a keen satisfaction.

Not all of the girls come to their graduation serenely, uneventfully. Sometimes girls are removed from the Home by a parent who appears able to offer a stable environment, only to fall into circumstances too disintegrating for them to carry their schoolwork or maintain the equilibrium they had found in the Home. Then they may be returned and in a second attempt achieve vocational training and their high school diploma.

Alva Johnson, a Negro girl, was one who might have left the Home earlier than she did had she not put her graduation ahead of her so-called freedom. She was seventeen when she came before the judge with her unusual request. She was a fine-looking girl, tall, slender, with clear-cut features and straight black hair that shone almost blue in the winter sunlight.

"Please let me stay, Judge. I only have six more months in high school and I do want my diploma before I leave."

The record showed that Alva's father had divorced her mother three years previous and had married almost immediately. Torn between the two parents, the girl went to live with her paternal grandmother, but the grandmother's work as attendant in a powder room kept her from home six days a week so that Alva was soon cutting school. Suspended, reinstated, suspended again, she was finally placed in the Home of the Good Shepherd by her grandmother. Now the grandmother had died suddenly and Alva's good record permitted her to go to Alabama with her father for the funeral and to remain there, if she wished. She did not wish.

"I want to go but I can't afford to miss the ten days of school. In six months I'll graduate. I'm asking you to grant me an extension."

Although admittance, graduation, dismissal appear to be routine matters following a certain pattern, still each girl is an individual person, and not a case, throughout her stay. In admittance there are certain matters to be clarified. The Sisters have to decide whether to admit a girl whose record indicates that she will probably be difficult. Sometimes a girl has deliberately broken parole or failed to co-operate with those responsible for her in a boarding home or county home school. Sometimes newspaper publicity has added a hazard. But ordinarily only two types of deliquent or predelinquent girls of normal intelligence are excluded from admission—the common streetwalker and the sexual deviate. Some Homes do not accept an expectant mother, quietly transferring any recent entrant found to be pregnant to a qualified maternity home. On the other hand, an unmarried mother whose child has died or been legally relinquished is eligible.

Girls are expected to be of normal mental ability. Despite that policy people sometimes ask, "But aren't the girls at the Homes of the Good Shepherd mentally retarded?" Formerly the public assumed that institutionalized delinquents were recruited from the ranks of the feeble-minded, but reliable mental testing programs now used by all first-rate rehabilitative training institutions have proved this assumption false. Studies of the intellectual capacities of the girls in the Homes of the Good Shepherd show that the majority are of normal intelligence and that the total number in residence at any one time offers a fairly typical cross section of the adolescent population of the country. Naturally there are a few of limited intelligence but their number is balanced by a group of the intellectually precocious. Girls with low intelligence fit easily into a pattern of constructive training, while problems of physical and emotional adjustment are increased by the precocity of adolescents of superior endowments.

A Home of the Good Shepherd is first of all a home, a place where love dwells, where a child may feel secure in affection, disciplined in habits, happy in play, eager in friendly relationships. Sometimes outsiders think that the Homes look forbidding because they are often large and walled in. Occasionally ridiculous statements get into circulation. "They have the girls behind barbed wire fences." "Did you ever see a Home without a high wall? That way, no one knows what goes on behind the walls." "They read every letter a girl gets." "They make the girls work like slaves."

Actually the high fences, often with barbed wire atop, keep out prowlers, and give the girls privacy in their recreation, especially when a Home is situated in the heart of a crowded city. The Sisters do read the incoming mail for the obvious reason that many girls are tangled in outside problems from which it has seemed best to remove them.

As for the work required of the girls, each Home of the Good Shepherd is also a school. The work done by the children must be on a par with that done in accredited private and public schools. In this way a girl's standing is maintained upon her transfer to an outside school. To be less than standard would be to defeat the purposes of the Home, one of whose goals is reclaimed personalities, made adequate through training and love to meet the demands and opportunities of a long and happy life. Quite clearly grade and high school faculties must satisfy all the standards of the state in which the school is located.

Extracurricular activities are abundant. Using play as a starting point, the Sisters employ a well-balanced program to teach the essentials of good citizenship. Playgrounds have modern gymnastic and recreational facilities—tennis, volleyball, basketball, ice and roller skating, square-dancing platforms, sometimes swimming pools and picnic grounds with open fireplaces. Indoors there are dramatics, choral work, debating, editing of a school paper—all sorts of school organizations.

Most Homes operate school banks and school stores in which the girls may deposit their allowances and the money they may earn by doing household chores, sewing, laundry work, and the like. The form and size of each girl's allowance varies according to the policy of the individual school. Most schools also have a system of merits and demerits worked out by the girls themselves. At one Home, for example, where the girls receive $3.50 a month and an additional credit allowance of $1.50 at the school store, each demerit carries with it a twenty-five cent reduction.

Most of the schools have some sort of industry through which the school earns part of its support. Some schools run a laundry, some a bakery, some specialize in practical sewing, et cetera. Often the girls are given their vocational training in the industry upon which the school specializes, but training in other vocations is always available. Only girls sixteen years of age or older work in these industries; no girl works more than four hours a day and her job is changed each hour. As might be expected the industries of the locality often affect the offerings of a particular school. For example, a few schools give their girls training in the use and operation of power sewing machines. The presence or absence of factories in the immediate vicinity determines the need of this type of instruction. Many a factory supervisor or department manager admits with pride that she received her basic training in the Home of the Good Shepherd.

Whether or not a Home has a specialized industry, every Home offers vocational training so that upon graduation a girl is able to support herself. Typing, shorthand, and secretarial subjects are always popular. Today most of the Homes offer courses in cosmetology under the direction of certified instructors. Credits earned as a member of these classes can be transferred to any other cosmetology school, thus enabling a girl to qualify as a licensed beauty operator within a relatively short time after her release if her term of residence is not sufficiently long to permit finishing the entire course before graduation. These courses prove highly satisfactory as therapeutic devices. Girls with unkempt coiffures find it difficult to resist the social pressures of their associates. "What excuse do you have for not looking your best here?" they are asked repeatedly by girls expertly trained to give shampoos, scalp treatments, finger waves, and permanents. "Come over to the shop and we'll make a new Jill out of you."

Making use of the LEARNING BUSINESS BY DOING BUSINESS program of free enterprise a number of the schools within the Good Shepherd Homes support thriving Junior Achievement projects. These projects permit the girls to earn as they learn the fundamentals of a practical business within and without the Home while constantly associating with their sponsors, advisers, consultants, and clientele on an adult basis. These contacts, however, are not confined to adults. At regular intervals meetings are held in which student representatives from all local Junior Achievement groups exchange ideas in informal seminar fashion. Furthermore, delegates from the various Junior Achievement Companies are chosen to attend the National Association Junior Achievement Conferences—popularly referred to as NAJAC—held each summer in different cities throughout the nation. At these conferences the Good Shepherd girls participate with grace and confidence.

Among the Good Shepherd Junior Achievement Programs the Milwaukee or Wauwatosa Center maintains its own headquarters and encourages the girls to affiliate with at least one of the several miniature companies in operation. Annually since its inception in 1949 one or more of its areas have received national awards in such activities as silk-screening, choral work, plastics, ceramics, and leather-craft. The Sisters in charge believe that this program enables its participants to achieve a high degree of efficiency in personal and public relations, and at the same time to acquire types of specialized vocational and commercial training that can be used advantageously in the future.

Frequently the term "Girls' Town" is used in connection with some particular school conducted by the Sisters of the Good Shepherd. However, the school in Carthage, Ohio, a suburb of Cincinnati, lays claim to the official title of "Girls' Town of America." In 1947 the late Father Flanagan, a warm friend of the Good Shepherd, visited Our Lady of the Woods School in Carthage. When told that the school had been in operation for nearly nine decades, he declared: "Why, then, this is the original Girls' Town of our nation!" His spontaneous remark led before long to an official christening ceremony presided over by the Mayor of Cincinnati. Under its new name the school has grown in favor and stature.

Cost of maintaining a Home is underwritten by various means in addition to any specialized services offered the public. In some instances part of its cost of operation is met from funds furnished either by the state, the county, or both. Frequently a Home is a Red Feather Agency of the local community chest, usually operating as a unit of the Catholic Charities Group. However, since such funds can seldom be used for buildings or plant improvement, a Home must also depend upon voluntary contributions and money-raising projects. To a large degree the size and nature of these contributions determine the kinds of additional services made available to the girls.

The religious emphasis of the Homes is, of course, Catholic. Girls who are Catholics by birth and baptism, if not by training, are usually in the majority but in certain Homes, particularly in the South and Far West, non-Catholic girls may outnumber Catholic girls. The pattern of religious affiliation tends to follow the total population pattern. In one Home a recent survey showed that only seven out of fifty girls were Catholic; in another, seventy-five out of two hundred; in a third, the number was about evenly divided.[1]

This study, and similar ones, make clear that allowance is made for religious convictions, other than Catholic. Non-Catholic girls are required to attend Chapel services but are not asked to participate. If a girl of Protestant background wishes to become a Catholic, she is usually persuaded to wait until she has left the Home. Better for all, girl, church, and public, that she be perfectly sure of her conviction and not change her mind later. Girls with no religious background are encouraged to become Catholics. The Sisters maintain these Homes in order to show compassion to misguided children and to save their souls. Naturally Catholicism is woven into the fabric of daily life. Girls frequently respond sympathetically to this belief; they become accustomed to attendance at Mass and the celebration of Holy Days; they learn to know well the patron saints of their friends and teachers. A Catholic can feel pride and assurance in the fact that girls so surrounded by Catholic custom and exposed to a sound Catholic point of view are more than likely to lean in the direction of the Church. Likewise, a non-Catholic may be assured that non-Catholic children are treated with respect and impartial love. The question of pressure seldom arises, for people of all faiths are inclined to turn with gratitude toward the care provided in the Good Shepherd Homes.

The Good Shepherd Sisters believe in the therapy of religion. After all, when a girl knows a God who loves her, who cares for her problems, and aids her efforts to be her best and most real self, she has a tremendous asset. She is never dependent on her own meager resources, a condition with which most of these girls have had all too much experience. Just as the girls are vocationally trained in the Homes, so are they spiritually fortified for the purpose of making them better able to meet the vicissitudes and opportunities of every-day living.

Teachers and leaders though the Sisters are, they are also cloistered religious, whose Order is partly active and partly con-templative. Long ago the Sisters in the United States dispensed with the lattice grille, retaining it only for safety and convenience of the portress or for the artistic beauty of its intricate craftsmanship in certain chapels. Despite these adjustments the Sisters of the Good Shepherd rarely leave their Convents, their travels outside the enclosure being prompted only by such urgencies as travel from one center to another, specialized medical treatment or hospitalization, attendance at important social-service or charitable conferences, and in the case of the younger Sisters, enrollment at higher institutions of learning for the purpose of finishing undergraduate studies or acquiring advanced degrees.[2] In 1948 the General Chapter voted to discontinue the services of the *touriere* Sisters. Since then all of the Good Shepherd Nuns engage in the same work, the contacts with the general public being made for them by qualified lay persons. Today the staffs of most Homes include one or more full-time social workers and psychologists, to whose services are added those of the probation officers and case workers associated with the courts and charitable bureaus or agencies. In every community the Mother Directress is as well known to the judge of the juvenile court as though she sat daily in his chambers or met with him at the con-ference table.

Through the years the story of the services of the Good Shepherd has steadily been one of adaptation to differing needs. Methods may change with the times but the reason for being and the goal of accomplishment have always been zeal for the salvation of souls. The responsibility of each Sister of the Good Shepherd as conceived by St. Mary Euphrasia holds elements in common with that of St. Michael, the Archangel. Like him she, too, is a guardian of souls, striving to wrest them from the forces of evil. It is no accident that in every Home the statue of the conqueror of the rebel angels stands guard at the threshold, reminding those who enter that the chief of the heavenly hosts is also their champion and defender.

The Congregation of the Good Shepherd is divided into Provinces, seven of which are located in the United States. Los Angeles, the most recent, was formed in October, 1945, as a center for the mission work done in the Philippines and Hong Kong. While each Provincial

Head is in close communication with the other Provincial Mothers, she is an independent agent, subject only to the Superior General in Angers, France. Under these circumstances the specifics of the Good Shepherd program can naturally be expected to vary somewhat from province to province.

For instance, the Peekskill Province serving the metropolitan area of greater New York accepts pregnant girls in most of its Homes, feeling that the care of these disturbed young people is in keeping with the spirit of the Good Shepherd. Elsewhere, however, expectant mothers are usually referred to other institutions, the Sisters reasoning that their facilities make it impractical to merge pregnant and nonpregnant adolescents.

Likewise the population of a community reflects itself in the student pattern of a particular Home. In Peekskill the number of Puerto Rican girls has increased 30 per cent or more within the last three years, the increase caused by the unprecedented Puerto Rican influx in near-by New York. The rosters of the Homes in the Southwest reveal a predominantly large number of Spanish-speaking children; in Los Angeles one-third of the girls are of Spanish and Mexican lineage. Obviously the problems brought by urban children coming from overcrowded home conditions are not the same as the problems of children of migrant workers accustomed to sleeping in the open or in improvised camps adjacent to the crops which provide their livelihood.

Some people associate the Sisters of the Good Shepherd with the work being done in conjunction with the A.A. for women alcoholics,[3] or with the care and comfort of aged and homeless women.[4] Others identify them with the lay retreat [5] movement. Whatever projects they engage in, however, are directly related to the ministry of reconciliation to which they are pledged. Under no circumstances do the Good Shepherd Sisters depart even temporarily from their primary apostolate until they have first made certain that the needs of "the children" and the Sister Magdalens are being met properly. Such is in keeping with Mother St. Euphrasia's instructions that these two groups always be given preferential consideration.

A special kind of preferential consideration is provided at the Homes in New Orleans and in New York City, where girls may be brought by the proper authorities at any time of the day or night to be cared for until they are to appear in juvenile court. Usually a girl's immediate need is physical rest. Often in her fear at being apprehended by the law she has done foolish and even dangerous things but whatever her misconduct she has gone too long with an insufficient amount of sleep. When she finds herself in a clean and attractive place, she relaxes, suddenly to discover how very weary she is. Upon her entrance many a girl sleeps the clock around. Following this initial rest her daily calendar is built with care.

In New Orleans this precourt service supplements the regular program of re-education one normally associates with a Good Shepherd Home. In New York City, however, the Euphrasian Residence on East 17th Street is solely a detention center, specializing in the treatment of the problems that harass adolescent girls pending their appearance in court. There the mornings are ordinarily given over to visits to medical centers, psychiatric clinics, and juvenile court, and the afternoons to naps for the pregnant girls and handicraft activities for the others. In the afternoons, too, personal laundry and grooming are taken care of with the most up-to-date and efficient equipment being placed at the girls' disposal. These girls often declare that it is like heaven to have a chance to stay clean. "When you're broke," one girl was overheard to say, "you learn that cleanliness is one of the most expensive things in the world."

Each day's activities provide for choir practice, religious instruction for the "ought-to-be" Catholics, and recreation for all, starting with a Sister's playing the piano and the girls' singing a wide range of their favorite songs. Group singing is augmented by good movies, TV programs, and dancing—social, square, and even ballet dancing—but always dancing. Before too long the quiet and peace of this ordered environment release tensions and make little girls out of pseudo-sophisticates, many of them sobbing with genuine relief as they join voluntarily in night prayers. More than one girl has said as she left the Euphrasian Residence, "I surely hope I'll be sent to a Good Shepherd Home."

In every nation the names of certain Good Shepherd Sisters are known far beyond the confines of any one Province. This is peculiarly true of Mother Mary of St. Francis Xavier Hickey, and Mother Mary of St. Ursula Jung.

First, as Visitor General to the American Convents (1920–1933) and later as Head of the St. Paul Province (1933–1953), Mother Mary of St. Francis Xavier has performed a brilliant and continuing service for the Good Shepherd. Convinced that light and attractive surroundings and an enriched curriculum providing for both vocational and academic training were indispensable for morale, she advocated the modernization of the Homes in the United States architecturally and educationally. Under her direction high school courses were introduced and classes in home economics, arts and crafts, music, and commercial subjects added to the elementary grades that had formerly comprised the general school program. Her approach was motivated by the circumstances the girls would meet upon their return to society. "If a woman can cook and sew and live within her husband's means," she said, "the chances are great that she will make a success of her marriage. We should endeavor not only to build a home within a Home for our girls, but to prepare them to become good homemakers themselves. This we can do more efficiently by training them in the fundamentals of homemaking."

For more than a decade Mother St. Francis Xavier made extended and repeated visits to all the Convents in the United States, familiarizing herself with the problems indigenous to each separate one. She was particularly interested in the establishment of needed medical and dental clinics, refusing to be defeated, using objections as a springboard to her projects. Today the success of these clinics stands as a witness to her progressive leadership. Invariably her fight against the evils of juvenile delinquency resulted in the improvement of the moral and civic tone of the localities in which the Homes of the Good Shepherd function.

The name of Mother Mary of St. Ursula Jung of Angers, France, also evokes widespread recognition and esteem. Since her election as Superior General of the Congregation on May 15, 1940, she has visited Good Shepherd Convents throughout the entire world, becoming acquainted directly with their personnel and problems. As linguist, organizer, administrator, and spiritual head she continually stresses the tremendous importance of professional techniques in the process of re-education. At the same time she has re-emphasized the value of religion in the training of the girls entrusted to the Good Shepherd. "We are responsible for the moral value of the members we give to society. The more conscientiously we have equipped them, the better citizens they will be."

On May 20, 1954, at the Mother House in Angers, Mother Mary of St. Ursula received the Cross of the Legion of Honor from the French Government. In conferring this high distinction M. Paul Tibeyre, Minister of Justice, said: "All the qualities and virtues which make for the wide extent and nobility of the Congregation of the

Good Shepherd—faith; optimism in the future; tenacious, patient will; untiring devotion; laborious organization—all of these you possess in the highest degree."

He then reviewed the salient points of her administration begun during the days when the Mother House was cut off from all the other Houses in France by the Nazi occupation forces, pointing out that the Good Shepherd Mother General has preserved and extended her precious heritage from St. Mary Euphrasia, adapting its methods and procedures to the problems of today's disorganized and unsettled children. In particular, he referred to the diagnostic study centers and transitional homes that Mother St. Ursula has instituted.

As a rule the diagnostic study centers are a part of the Home itself but the transitional program is best set up in a separate building situated some distance away. Its purpose is to enable a small group of girls to live for some months in semiliberty prior to their release. Under supervision but with widening personal freedom they go out daily to full- or part-time jobs, returning to help communally with the running of the house. In many ways the Transition Home is a testing and adjustment center where the girls practice the theories of faith and conduct the Sisters have taught them.

Ask any Sister about the effectiveness of these Homes and she will tell you that they are a matter of utmost urgency. "It is too bad that our finances and limited staff are delaying this project," one Superior said, "but we believe in it thoroughly and are working toward it." With face aglow another Superior answered: "Like Columbus the girls at our Transition Home are constantly making worth-while discoveries. Only the other evening one of them said: 'Sister, I used to think that discipline simply meant do's and don't's. But I've just found out that the word in Latin is "*discipulus*" and that its real meaning is "to learn training in self-control." That suddenly made all the pieces fit together. Why, I know I couldn't carry on, if I hadn't had the opportunity to live in a disciplined environment. One thing sure, it's given me a confidence I didn't have when I first came over here.' "

Such experiences compensate the Sisters for the girls who do not respond to their training. For naturally their efforts are not always successful. Sometimes they are sent children on the verge of emotional and physical anarchy. Others come so full of hate for everyone and everybody that they suspect love in any guise. Some girls with frustrated swains waiting on the outside permit their romantic interest to overshadow everything else. This type of girl is determined to run away at her earliest opportunity, and occasionally she succeeds. Some children are left with the Sisters too briefly for any kind of lasting therapy; others are mentally ill and need prolonged and specialized care elsewhere.

Notwithstanding these exceptions scientific studies and informal observations overwhelmingly acclaim the success of the work done by the Sisters among underprivileged and maladjusted girls. In every Directress' files there are heartening letters from her children, some of whom she has not seen for years.

Zora's gratitude is far from unique. When she first came to the Home dressed in torn jeans and a man's dirty hunting shirt, this frowzy-haired youngster shook her head defiantly. She was mad through and through. She hadn't wanted to come to this place and she wanted it understood right from the start that she didn't intend to stay. For a thirteen-year-old she seemed extraordinarily mature, as she laid it on the line in no uncertain terms. "No one has ever held a Thompson," she screamed, "and no one ever will. They don't make strong enough locks to keep us where we don't aim to be. 'Taint fair sending me here for stealing the coins from the corner news dealer. He was fat and lazy, sleeping on his stool in broad daylight, and I hadn't et in ever so long."

"Did you bring any other clothes with you, dear?" Sister Francis asked.

"No, why should I? I'm covered. Ain't that enough?"

Sister nodded her head, adding, "Come with me and have a good, hot bath. After that I think you'll feel better."

"A bath, what for? Didn't you hear me say I ain't staying? Thompsons have ways of getting out of places like this."

"Oh!" the Sister said with feigned surprise. "I hadn't known you'd been at a Good Shepherd Home before."

"Haven't, but these places that want to keep you are all the same. I tell you, ma'am, I've no use for them."

Sister waited until the child had exhausted herself. Then she mentioned the bath again, this time handing fresh towels and soap to the weary little fighter. After that she had no trouble in persuading Zora to take a bath.

When the water had been run and tempered, Zora took off her filthy clothes and stepped gingerly into the tub. For a long time she just sat, making no effort to lave herself. Then she washed herself timorously; then vigorously, consenting rather amiably to a back scrub. "That sure feels good," she said. "You know, Sister, this is the first tub bath I've ever had. Can't remember anything I've enjoyed as much."

With disdain she looked at her clothes lying in an untidy heap on the white-tiled floor. "Sister," she implored, "do I have to put those dirty old things back on?"

Zora Thompson didn't run away from the Home of the Good Shepherd. In fact, she never tried to. She was kept far too busy learning about personal sanitation and grooming, and also about grammar and God. In every way her response to the Good Shepherd training was unusually satisfying. Today at twenty-five, she is an attractive and well-disciplined young woman with a devoted husband and three stirring but well-behaved children. Regularly this little family visits Zora's "Alma Mater" where her husband invariably tells the Sisters with undisguised pride, "I do wish you could visit us and see the kind of housekeeper my wife is. She's the best. Absolutely the best."

At this Zora exchanges a smile with Sister Francis.

Not too long ago in one of the larger Homes Mother Teresa, the Directress of the Girls, sat down to read her mail. Conspicuous among the letters was an envelope postmarked in a city halfway across the nation. Even without a return address in the upper left-hand corner she recognized the writing as Leone Starr's, vigorous and full of personality like Leone herself.

With a smile Mother Teresa broke open the letter. Immediately it brought tears of joy. "Mother, dear," she read, "Jim and I are sending you this enclosed check for fifty dollars as a Christmas gift for the girls. If we weren't having a baby, we'd have made it more. I used to wonder when I was at Holy Trinity School how you managed to make Christmas such a wonderful day for all of us. Sometimes, I'd try to figure out where you found the money for the special gifts and treats you gave to girls like me who had no folks, or to girls whose folks didn't care about them. Both Jim and I say this money is a payment on our debt of gratitude to you and all the other Good Shepherd Sisters. Without your love and guidance, I'd have been a nobody. I was a rascal, wasn't I?"

Now the tears were falling fast, but Mother Teresa made no effort to reach for her handkerchief. Instead she saw a tough, little red-haired fourteen-year-old who had been transferred from a Home in another state. Already at that age Leone had had a run-in with the police for acting as an accomplice in a gas-station hold-up. The Sisters had written that they felt Leone's chance for rehabilitation depended upon her getting far away from her former environment. "She's not trying here," they wrote, "knowing that when she is released, she'll be recognized by the local police."

"Don't know where my mother and sister are. Don't know who my dad is. Don't care either." These had been Leone's first words to Mother Teresa. Then she'd added quickly, "I'm a mean one, and I don't figure to change. What's the use?"

"Yes, she was a mean one," Mother Teresa recalled. "Sly, untruthful, and almost pathologically jealous of the other girls. But she was musically talented. It was through her love of music that I finally got through to her hidden self, even if it did take a major crisis to do that."

The crisis had come on the Feast of the Mother Superior. Leone, who had learned to play the organ, was charged with the responsibility for the music, but she "blew her top," as she later said, and burned the music for the Mass the girls were prepared to sing. In addition, she threw away the key to the music press, her act making it necessary for Mother Teresa to break the lock. Otherwise, there would have been no formal music of any kind for the Feast.

For the next month Mother Teresa herself played the chapel organ, turning a deaf ear to Leone's pleas and promises. Then she gave Leone another trial, making it clear that this was a trust to be guarded, for there would be no second chance.

Leona did not betray that trust. Chastened and contrite, she frequented the Sacraments, applied herself to her commercial studies, and made good in the business appointment Mother Teresa and the social worker secured for her. Then came the day when Leone telephoned: "I have a boy friend, Mother. He's a dental student at the University. May we come out Sunday?"

As so many of the girls do, Leone brought her date out to meet the Mothers. Regularly, thereafter, she and Jim called. Today, married and happy in their shared faith, this young couple had sent the Good Shepherd a payment on "our debt of gratitude."

"What more is necessary," Mother Teresa thought, "to point out the efficacy of our training? Why, it's six years since I've seen Leone, and yet she writes a letter like this. It gives me courage for my work with the newcomers, some of whom are just as confused as Leone ever was. But like her they are souls to be saved and not just girls to be disciplined."

Mother Teresa's words summarize the apostolate of the Sisters of the Good Shepherd which knows no limits of creed, class, color, or ancestry in ministering to every form of human misery. Truly the Sisters are all keepers of the shepherd's gate, opening it inward to receive desolate and maladjusted girls to a new life; or swinging it outward to send happy and eager young women into a new world.

Notes

The following references have been used in the notes:

Pasquier, Vols. I and II: *Life of Mother Mary of St. Euphrasia Pelletier, Translated from the French of the Right Rev. Monseigneur H. Pasquier.* London: Burns, Oates, & Washbourne, Ltd., 1893.

R.G.S.: *Blessed Mary of St. Euphrasia Pelletier, By a Religious of the Congregation.* London: Burns, Oates, & Washbourne, Ltd., 1933.

Powers: *Redemption, The Life of Saint Mary Euphrasia Pelletier.* Manila: 1940. Good Shepherd Press.

Saudreau: *The Secret of the Sanctity of Saint Mary Euphrasia Pelletier, Foundress of the Congregation of Our Lady of Charity of the Good Shepherd of Angers.* A translation and adaptation of *Graces et Fidelites* by Monsignor August Saudreau. (Mimeographed and distributed shortly after canonization. Not copyright.)

Conferences and Instructions: Conferences and Instructions of Saint Mary Euphrasia Pelletier, Foundress of the Generalate of the Congregation of Our Lady of Charity of the Good Shepherd of Angers. Westminster, Md.: The Newman Bookshop, 1943. Likewise editions by other publishers.

CHAPTER II

[1] Son of Joseph Pelletier, Sieur de la Garconnier from the name of his estate in Touvois. Notary and *procureur.*

[2] Nee Anne Aimée Mourain of Soullans.

CHAPTER III

[1] Pasquier, Vol. I, p. 20.

[2] The word "religious" comes from the Latin verb "religare," to bind or to tie down. Often priests, monks, or nuns are referred to as "religious." The use of this term does not necessarily mean that they are excessively holy people—though usually they are. It does mean, however, that they are bound by vows of promise and conduct.

[3] *American College Dictionary*, Text Edition (New York: Harper & Brothers, 1948)— Monseigneur: (1) a French title of honor given to princes, bishops, and other persons of eminence. (2) a person bearing this title. Monsignor: Roman

Catholic Church. (1) a title conferred upon certain dignitaries. (2) a person bearing this title.

4 Saudreau, p. 3.

5 Father John Eudes (1601–1680) was beatified in 1909 and canonized by Pius XI on May 31, 1925. Hereafter he will be referred to as St. John Eudes.

6 Powers, p. 74.

CHAPTER IV

1 Known in religion as Sister Mary of St. Stanislaus Bedouet.

2 Every Sister of the Refuge as well as every Good Shepherd Sister receives Mary as her first name.

3 Pasquier, Vol. I, p. 41.

4 Not then printed.

5 Pasquier, Vol. II, p. 42.

6 St. Dositheus died about 530 in Gaza.

7 R.G.S., p. 55.

8 Pasquier, Vol. I, p. 43.

9 Saudreau, p. 7.

10 Sister Mary of St. Euphrasia wore the silver heart hidden under her habit for a year before she wore it openly as the professed Sisters do.

11 Powers, p. 88.

12 Saudreau, p. 9.

13 The word "evil," somewhat archaic today, was commonly used in the nineteenth century.

14 *Conferences and Instructions*, pp. 12–13.

15 Powers, p. 103.

16 During the octave of the Assumption.

17 Part of the legacy given the Sisters by St. John Eudes.

CHAPTER V

1 The poem "St. Mary Magdalen" is used with the kind permission of the author.

2 Statutes for the Sister Magdalens, Chap. 3, p. 9, sec. 11.

3 The verses of "Song of the Host Maker" first appeared in the mid-twenties in the *Sentinel of the Blessed Sacrament*, published by the Fathers at St. Jean Baptiste in New York. At that time Father Peter J. Dolin, S.J., made certain changes in the wording of some of the lines, having been given permission to do this by the editor and his own Father Provincial. Father Dolin, however, humbly disclaims any credit for this beautiful poem, saying instead: "I have always referred to the 'Song of the Host Maker' as having been 'adapted from the *Sentinel*.' "

4 In 1947 at the General Chapter of the Good Shepherd in Angers the Community of the Sister Magdalens was given the status of the "Auxiliary Contemplative Branch of the Congregation of Our Lady of Charity of the Good Shepherd of Angers." In addition the Sisters were granted the permission to take a fourth vow, i.e., "to pray for the salvation of souls, particularly for all the works of the Good Shepherd," pending recognizance from Rome. That official action came in 1950. Since then the Sister Magdalens have added this fourth vow to their regular vows of Poverty, Chastity, and Obedience.

Chapter VI

[1] Powers, p. 127.
[2] Pasquier, Vol. II, p. 80.
[3] *Ibid.*, Vol. I, p. 85.
[4] *Ibid.*, Vol. I, p. 85.
[5] *Ibid.*, Vol. I, pp. 86–87.
[6] *Ibid.*, Vol. I, p. 92.
[7] Powers, p. 137.
[8] *Ibid.*, p. 137.

Chapter VII

[1] Saudreau, pp. 21–22.
[2] Powers, p. 140.
[3] Saudreau, p. 22.
[4] R.G.S., p. 99.
[5] Saudreau, p. 22.
[6] *Ibid.*, p. 23; Powers, p. 143.
[7] Evidently Sunday, May 21.
[8] Pasquier, Vol. I, p. 21.
[9] *Ibid.*, Vol. I, p. 105.

Chapter VIII

[1] The Count's full name was Count Augustine le Roy de la Potherie de Neuville.
[2] R.G.S., p. 103.
[3] Pasquier, Vol. I, p. 107.
[4] Saudreau, p. 25. (Since 1246 the Feast of the Corpus Christi in honor of the Holy Eucharist has been celebrated on the first free Thursday after the octave of the Pentecost. As a rule it falls about mid-June.)
[5] *The Social Work of the Sisters of the Good Shepherd* by Sister Mary of St. Teresita, R.G.S., M.A. Cleveland: Cadillac Press, 1938.
[6] Pasquier, Vol. I, p. 119.
[7] *Ibid.*, Vol. I, p. 109.
[8] Sister Mary of the Angels Porchér.
[9] Mother Euphrasia's own words. Entry for August 3.

Chapter IX

[1] Most Reverend Monseigneur Philip-Mary-Theresa-Guy Carron.
[2] Sister Mary of St. Seraphine Houdin was the first Mother Superior of the Le Mans foundation.
[3] *Juxta Crucem*, Life of Basil Anthony Moreau, C.S.C., by Gerald M. C. Fitzgerald, C.S.C. New York: P. J. Kenedy and Sons, 1937, pp. 47, 48.
[4] Le Mans was the capital of this geographical area.
[5] Preservates.
[6] See Fitzgerald, p. 50.
[7] Monseigneur Carron died on August 27, 1833.
[8] Pasquier, Vol. I, p. 134.
[9] R.G.S., p. 131.
[10] Fitzgerald, p. 51.

¹¹ Le Mans separated from Angers in July, 1834.

¹² Originally Monseigneur Fustier had read the *Exeat* aloud to the Tours Chapter in Mother's presence. His death in May, 1834, robbed Mother St. Euphrasia of a loyal friend.

¹³ R.G.S., p. 135.

¹⁴ This building had been occupied only a short time before by St. Madeleine Sophie Barat, the Foundress of the Sisters of the Sacred Heart.

¹⁵ Pasquier, Vol. I, p. 160.

¹⁶ Letter written by Mother St. Euphrasia on December 25, 1833.

¹⁷ Powers, p. 180.

¹⁸ Pasquier, Vol. I, p. 172.

¹⁹ Pasquier, Vol. I, p. 175.

²⁰ *The Social Work of the Sisters of the Good Shepherd*, p. 94.

²¹ With Sister Mary of St. Sophia Lavoye in charge.

²² R.G.S., p. 138.

²³ Pasquier, Vol. I, p. 180; *Instructions*, Jan. 23, 1858.

²⁴ R.G.S., p. 139.

²⁵ Powers, p. 204.

²⁶ Powers, p. 206. Generally speaking, such affairs usually required two years or longer for settlement.

²⁷ The Brief, or Apostolic Letter, sent in the name and under the sacred authority of the Sovereign Pontiff, quotes textually the Decree issued. The various points automatically become law. At the same time it proves that the Institute has been found acceptable and that the Church recognizes it unequivocally.

1. The House of Angers and all the Houses founded by it will observe the Rules established by Father Eudes and approved by the Holy Apostolic See.

2. The Superior of the House of Angers, besides the government of her own Monastery, will have that of all the Houses founded by it or to be founded in the future.

3. The attributes of this Superior General shall be: to found new Houses with the consent of the diocesan Bishop; to visit those which have been founded; to watch with care that the Rules should be observed and order maintained in all things. She can also admit novices into the Congregation by herself or by the Superiors of the other houses, distribute her daughters among the various houses and transfer them from one to the other. But let her not do anything of importance without the counsel of her assistants, and let every house remain under the jurisdiction of the diocesan Bishop according to the decrees of the holy Council of Trent and the Apostolic Constitutions relative to Congregations of this kind.

4. Every six years a new Superior General shall be elected; however, the outgoing Superior may, after having fulfilled her duties for six years, be elected a second time, or even indefinitely, as long as it shall please the electors to name her.

5. The election shall be made according to the ancient usage. Each house shall appoint two voting Sisters, who will go to the house where the election is to be made, or else they will send their votes in writing under a seal. The election is to be presided over by the Bishop of the place in which it is held.

6. The Superior of each house shall be chosen by the Superior General assisted by her Council.

7. The Congregation of Angers will preserve as heretofore the habit which is proper to it as it is to the ancient Monasteries called of the Refuge; but it shall wear, instead of the white cincture, a blue cord, and an image of the Good Shepherd engraved upon the silver heart which it is in the habit of wearing.

8. The Congregation of Angers will continue to enjoy all the privileges and all the graces granted by the Holy Apostolic See to the ancient Monasteries called of the Refuge.

CHAPTER X

[1] Pasquier, Vol. I, p. 370.
[2] *Ibid.*, Vol. I, p. 382.
[3] Powers, p. 212.
[4] Pasquier, Vol. I, p. 383.
[5] March 10, 1836.
[6] Pasquier, Vol. I, p. 385.
[7] Bourg, 1838: Macon, June 21, 1839.
[8] Powers, p. 257.
[9] April 30, 1933.
[10] Powers, p. 200.
[11] Pasquier, Vol. I, p. 401.
[12] Powers, p. 263.
[13] *Conferences and Instructions*, pp. 19–20.
[14] *Practical Rules*, "Charity toward the Children," pp. 100–101.
[15] R.G.S., pp. 175–76.
[16] Pasquier, Vol. I, p. 416.

CHAPTER XI

[1] Pasquier, Vol. II, p. 31.
[2] R.G.S., p. 201.
[3] Powers, p. 301.
[4] Mother Teresa of Jesus de Couespel had until recently been the Superior at Nice, having founded that Convent upon the completion of her work at Santa Croce in Rome.
[5] Bishop Flaget did not know that English was already being taught at Angers.
[6] Pasquier, Vol. II, p. 49.
[7] Powers, p. 305.

CHAPTER XII

[1] The work in Germantown, Pa., inaugurated for colored girls by Mother Katharine Drexel, Foundress of the Sisters of the Blessed Sacrament, has always been perpetuated by the Sisters of the Good Shepherd.
[2] Pasquier, Vol. II, p. 80.
[3] Mother Mary des Anges Porcher, Angers, France; Sister Mary of St. Louis Gonzaga Baligand, Ratisbon, Bavaria; Sister Mary of St. Joseph Looney, Cashel, County Tipperary, Ireland; Sister Mary of St. Reparata Deleuse, Nice, Piedmont; Sister Mary of St. Marcella Richards, Switzerland.
[4] R.G.S., pp. 265–66.
[5] Pasquier, Vol. II, p. 86.

[6] The terms "monastery" and "convent" are often used interchangeably.

[7] Gallicanism did not disappear completely until after the action of the Vatican Council in 1870.

[8] Among the Congregations that Monseigneur Angebault had directed were La Retraite, St. Charles la Foret, St. Gildas, and Torfou.

[9] Author of *Graces and Fidelites*, later translated and adapted under the title *The Secret of the Sanctity of St. Mary of Euphrasia Pelletier*.

[10] *La Servante de Dieu Marie de Sainte-Euphrasie Pelletier* by Canon Portais, two volumes. Paris: Delhomme and Briguet, 1893.

Chapter XIII

[1] Pasquier, Vol. II, p. 177.

[2] Powers, p. 332.

[3] Pasquier, Vol. II, p. 224.

[4] *Ibid.*, Vol. II, pp. 217–8.

[5] *Ibid.*, Vol. II, p. 247.

[6] This doctrine holds that Mary in the first instant of her conception in her mother's womb was preserved exempt from all stain of original sin. To Catholics it seems reasonable and realistic that the Mother of Jesus Christ, the Saviour of the human race, should have always been free even from imperfection. The doctrine of the Immaculate Conception has nothing to do with the virgin birth of Christ; nor does it involve a virgin birth of Mary.

[7] This Chapel was completed in May, 1833. As shown by its name, Mother Euphrasia's confidence in the Immaculate Conception of Mary preceded the official pronouncement of the dogma by twenty-one years.

[8] A similar engagement had also been promised and recorded in the name of Count de Neuville.

Chapter XIV

[1] Mother Madeleine Sophie Barat (1779–1865) is now a canonized Saint of the Church, her Feast being celebrated on May 25.

[2] Mme. Perdreau.

[3] Pasquier, Vol. II, p. 285.

[4] Blessed Germaine Cousin's canonization on June 29, 1867, brought Mother St. Euphrasia much joy, causing her to have a procession made by the community in honor of the Saint.

[5] Pasquier, Vol. II, p. 303.

[6] *Ibid.*, Vol. II, p. 302.

[7] Powers, p. 378.

[8] The Sisters always referred endearingly to Angers as their Sion.

[9] R.G.S., p. 314.

[10] Pasquier, Vol. II, p. 312.

[11] November 21 is the Feast of the Presentation of Our Lady in the Temple. It is on this day that the Sisters of the Good Shepherd annually renew their vows.

Chapter XV

[1] Centenary, Philadelphia: Sisters of the Good Shepherd, 1950.

[2] Pasquier, Vol. II, p. 354.

Notes

³ Pasquier and Powers offer different dates for the reception of the prisoners at Nazareth. Pasquier uses April 21; Powers, June 26.

⁴ Pasquier, Vol. II, p. 377.

⁵ *Ibid.*, Vol. II, p. 400.

⁶ Before the General Chapter of 1953 a Provincial Mother could be re-elected every six years for an indefinite time. Since 1953, however, the incumbent is limited to two terms of six years each. This change in the tenure of the office does not necessarily mean that each Provincial Mother will automatically succeed herself.

⁷ Pasquier, Vol. II, pp. 526–28.

CHAPTER XVI

¹ From the beginning Brooklyn has been a part of the New York Province, the St. Louis Province immediately transferring the authorization for this particular foundation to the New York Provincial.

² Monseigneur Angebault died in 1869.

³ The decree attesting the heroicity of Mother St. Euphrasia's virtues was promulgated and entered officially in the Acts of the Sacred Congregation of Rites on March 6, 1924.

⁴ Excerpts from the discourse of Pius XI on February 24, 1924:

"We congratulate you on your work which like the light of the stars, shines over all parts of the world and produces everywhere precious fruits of redemption and regeneration. . . . Here we have a magnificent example of . . . poetry of numbers. . . . In less than a century, we can count 282 Houses, truly worthy of the name, and in these Houses over 9,000 religious, over 9,000 great souls, noble with the highest nobility, that of Christ, who work at the very work of Jesus, King of Charity, of Jesus, Shepherd of Souls. . . .

"You have wisely indicated, Your Excellency, the deep root of all this abundance of fruit and spiritual riches. . . . With a happy timeliness you have signaled out those virtues which were particularly characteristic, and you finished by emphasizing . . . her heroic attachment to the Holy See, to Holy Mother the Church, to the person and to the direction of the Sovereign Pontiff, a virtue which was all the more remarkable because in those days Gallicanism still survived with its tendencies, its habits so different from those which the heart of God desired.

". . . We are thinking too, of that anomalous position in which she found herself all her life long, brought as she was face to face with opponents whose holiness and venerable authority she never ceased to revere, but who were, nevertheless, even if only in appearance, in opposition to her. She was obliged to obey and resist; to resist and obey. . . . In that struggle, in that anguish which mounts to heights difficult to attain, she not only constantly maintained her serenity of spirit, but also a clear perception of the cause of her affliction. She perceived always clearly, and with great surety of intuition all that was capable of leading her with security. . . . Hers was a perfection which seemed to surpass all earthly and human capacity."

⁵ Singularly Mother St. Euphrasia's canonization was the first to occur in the pontificate of Pius XII (1940–   ). Prior to his election as Supreme Pontiff he had served as the Cardinal Protector of the Good Shepherd Congregation. Subsequently at his own request he has retained this position.

CHAPTER XVII

1 October 1, 1952, Spokane, Wash. *A Study of the Program of the Good Shepherd Home, Spokane, Washington*, by Mary Campbell McManus. A.B. Thesis, presented to the Faculty of the Graduate School of St. Louis University in partial fulfillment of the requirements for the Degree of Master in Social Work, 1952.

2 In 1944 Mother St. Francis Xavier Hickey, Provincial of St. Paul, inaugurated the Good Shepherd College within the Provincial Home. This college is qualified to offer collegiate instruction and grant the baccalaureate degree to the Sisters in residence.

3 Columbus, Ohio.

4 Normandy, Mo.

5 Indianapolis, Ind.

Bibliography

Blessed Mary of Saint Euphrasia Pelletier. By a Religious of the Congregation. London: Burns, Oates & Washbourne, Ltd., 1933.

BRADBY, E. D. *A Short History of the French Revolution, 1789–1795.* London: Oxford University Press, 1926. Reprinted 1932.

BRUELY, M. EDOUARD. *The Good Shepherd of Angers.* Translated from the French. Angers: Monastery General of the Good Shepherd, 1936.

BURY, J. P. T. *France: 1814–1940.* Philadelphia: University of Pennsylvania Press, 1949.

CHASLE, ABBÉ LOUIS. *Sister Mary of the Divine Heart.* London: Burns, Oates & Washbourne, Ltd., 1924.

CONWAY, KATHERINE E. *In the Footprints of the Good Shepherd: New York, 1857–1907.* New York: Convent of the Good Shepherd, 1910.

COUGHLIN, MARY FOOTE. *A New Commandment.* A Little Memoir of the Good Shepherd Nuns in Chicago (1859–1909). Chicago, 1909.

ELLINGSTON, JOHN R. *Protecting Our Children from Criminal Careers.* New York: Prentice-Hall, 1948.

Fénelon's Education of Girls. Translated from the French by Kate Lupton. Boston: Ginn & Co., 1891.

FITZGERALD, GERALD M. C., c.s.c. *Juxta Crucem.* The Life of Basil Anthony Moreau (1799–1873). New York: P. J. Kenedy and Sons, 1937.

GIBBONS, MARGARET. *Little Nellie of Holy God.* Westminster, Md.: The Newman Press, 1951.

GOTTSCHALK, LOUIS R. *The Era of the French Revolution, 1715–1815.* Boston: Houghton, Mifflin Co., 1929.

KONOPKA, GISELA. *Group Work in the Institution.* New York: Whiteside, Inc., and William Morrow and Company, 1954.

The Little Alpine Flower: Mother Mary of Saint Hyacinth Gonnet. By several Fathers of the Society of Foreign Missions of Paris. Translated from the French. Angers, 1939.

The Little White Shepherdess. By Sister Mary of Our Lady of the Angels, R.G.S. Milwaukee: The Tower Press, 1950; rev. ed. 1952.

MARTINDALE, CYRIL C., S.J. *The Life of St. Anne-Marie Javouhey.* New York: Longmans, Green and Co., 1953.

MAUROIS, ANDRÉ. *A History of France.* Translated by Henry L. Binsse. London: Jonathan Cape, 1949.

MAY, J. LEWIS. *Fénelon, a Study.* London: Burns, Oates & Washbourne, Ltd., 1938.

McMANUS, MARY CAMPBELL. *A Study of the Program of the Good Shepherd Home, Spokane, Washington.* Thesis presented to the Faculty of the Graduate School of St. Louis University in partial fulfillment of the requirements for the Degree of Master in Social Work, 1952.

MIHANOVICH, CLEMENT S. *Principles of Juvenile Delinquency.* Milwaukee: Bruce Publishing Co., 1950.

Mirror of the Virtues of Mother Mary of St. Euphrasia Pelletier, 1888. London: Burns, Oates & Washbourne, Ltd., n.d.

Mother Mary of St. Peter Coudenhove, Second Superior General of the Good Shepherd. Two vols. Angers: Monastery General of the Good Shepherd, 1926.

PASQUIER, R. REV. MSGR. H. *Life of Mother Mary of St. Euphrasia Pelletier.* Two vols. Translated from the French. London: Burns, Oates & Washbourne, 1893.

PELLETIER, ST. MARY EUPHRASIA. *Conferences and Instructions.* Westminster, Md.: Newman Bookshop, 1943.

POWERS, GABRIEL FRANCIS. *Redemption. The Life of Saint Mary Euphrasia Pelletier.* Manila: Good Shepherd Press, 1940.

Practical Rules for the Use of the Religious of the Good Shepherd for the Direction of the Classes. Printed for the Convent of the Good Shepherd, St. Paul, Minn. Westminster, Md.: Newman Bookshop, 1943.

RAYMOND, REV. M., O.C.S.O. God Goes to Murderer's Row. Milwaukee: Bruce Publishing Co., 1951.

ROBINSON, LEO J., S.J., AND CHRISTOPH, VAN FRANCIS, S.J. Introductory Sociology. Chicago: Loyola University Press, 1943.

ST. AMAND, IMBERT DE. Revolution of 1848. Translated by Elizabeth Gilbert Martin. New York: Charles Scribner's Sons, 1895.

SARGENT, DANIEL. Their Hearts Be Praised. Life of St. John Eudes, 1601–1680. New York: P. J. Kenedy and Sons, 1949.

SAUDREAU, MSGR. AUGUST. The Secret of the Sanctity of Saint Mary Euphrasia Pelletier. A translation and adaptation of Graces et Fidelites, mimeographed and distributed in 1940.

SCHAUINGER, J. HERMAN. Cathedrals in the Wilderness. Milwaukee: Bruce Publishing Co., 1952.

SEDILLOT, RENÉ. An Outline of French History. Translated from the French by Gerard Hopkins. New York: Alfred A. Knopf, 1953.

The Social Work of the Sisters of the Good Shepherd. By Sister Mary of St. Teresita, R.G.S., M.A. Cleveland: Cadillac Press, 1938.

Statutes for the Sisters Magdalens, Angers. Montreal: De-La-Salle Printing, 1950.

The Venerable Mother Mary of St. Euphrasia Pelletier. Angers: Mother House of Our Lady of Charity of the Good Shepherd, 1925.

WULF, JOHN B. France: 1815 to the Present. New York: Prentice-Hall, 1940.

Brochures

Annals of the Provincial Convent of St. Paul, Minnesota.

COLLINS, REV. JOSEPH M. Sainte Marie Euphrasia Pelletier, A Saint of Sociology. Brooklyn, N.Y.: Convent of the Good Shepherd, 1940.

EATON, REV. ROBERT. St. Mary Euphrasia Pelletier. London: Catholic Truth Society, 1940.

The Good Shepherd and Its Work. Documentary Review (quarterly), Angers, over a period of several years.

SARGENT, DANIEL. *Saint John Eudes.* Hyattsville, Md.: Eudist Fathers, 1951.

SCOTT, MARTIN J., S.J. *The Life Work of the Nuns of the Good Shepherd.* Columbia, Ohio: Columbian Press, n.d.

The publications of the different Provincial Convents and individual Houses have also been studied. These include Centenary and Jubilee periodicals, vocational brochures and pamphlets and annual letters to the Mother General, summarizing the preceding year's work.

All Biblical references are from the Douay Version of the Holy Bible. New York: Benziger Brothers, 1950.

Miracles Accepted for the Beatification

of

Venerable Mary of St. Euphrasia Pelletier

Mary Magdalen, Memphis:

Mary Magdalen Hodges, a consecrate in the Convent of the Good Shepherd, Memphis, Tennessee, was miraculously cured of inoperable cancer of the stomach midway of a novena of intercession to Venerable Mary of St. Euphrasia. The time was August, 1913. The Jewish doctor in charge affirmed under oath that his patient had been incurably ill, her condition far advanced in the stages of malignancy. Furthermore he attested in writing the nature of the illness and its extraordinary cure.

Mary Olive:

This inquest was made in the See of Arras, France, on the cure of Mary Olive, one of the children in the Good Shepherd Convent there. Mary Olive suffered with a painful and disfiguring malignant ulcer of the face. This lupus covered her nose and part of her forehead. It resisted all medical treatment, steadily growing larger and more painful. Finally the patient and the Sisters invoked the aid of Venerable Mary of St. Euphrasia, placing one of her relics on Mary Olive's tormented face and beseeching Mother St. Euphrasia for a cure. They sincerely believed that Our Blessed Lord would not refuse His beloved daughter's request for one of her suffering children. In the early evening of April 11, 1925, Mary Olive had a hemorrhage from the wound. Three hours later she fell into a restful sleep to be awakened toward dawn by a tingling and prickling of her face. Startled, she put her hands to her face and then called for a mirror. The unsightly ulcer had completely disappeared. Upon the doctor's arrival he declared that such a cure could never have been effected instanteously except by miraculous means. Other physicians were then called in and an exhaustive study of the nature and cure of Mary Olive's disability was made prior to the unanimous assertion that this cure could not be attributed to any sort of physical treatment or medication.

Before the above cures were officially accepted they were subjected to prolonged and merciless study by innumerable medical experts, the majority of whom were not Catholics. Not until November 8, 1927, and November 19, 1930, was the validity of these processes formally decreed.

Miracles Accepted for the Canonization

of

Blessed Mary of St. Euphrasia Pelletier

Mary Louise:

In 1928 Mary Louise, one of Mother St. Euphrasia's girls, began to suffer from tubercular arthritis in her left knee. Over the course of two years this disease spread throughout her body, affecting her other knee and settling in the glands of her neck. An earlier operation for appendicitis had revealed the inroads made by tuberculosis on Mary Louise's entire system. Came the day when the attending physicians said that nothing more could be done for this child. Her death was imminent. Any kind of cure was beyond the realm of possibility.

The Sisters were unwilling to accept the verdict until they had consulted Mother St. Euphrasia. She would, they knew, be permitted to work a miracle, if it were for the good of the afflicted girl. On December 30, 1933, after five years of incredible suffering Mary Louise was instantly cured. Her legs were made straight and she could walk around the house and climb the stairs without any torturous effort or ill effects. The glands in her neck were no longer swollen. X-ray tests revealed no trace of tuberculosis in any of her joints or organs.

The usual exhaustive medical inquiry followed. Meanwhile Mary Louise ran and played, knelt and prayed like the other girls. In time her case was justifiably acclaimed as "another of Blessed Mary of St. Euphrasia's miracles."

This cure occurred in the Good Shepherd Convent of Charenton, Paris.

Honorine:

Honorine was another Good Shepherd girl. She was suffering from tubercular peritonitis. Blood poisoning had taken over, bringing with it fearful swelling and inflammation. On April 28, 1935, the doctor in charge abandoned all hope of saving her life. The following morning Honorine received the Sacrament of Extreme Unction, administered only in danger of death. For hours thereafter the sick girl held on to life by a thread, wavering uncertainly on the brink of eternity. Like the physician the Sisters at the Convent were tempted to give up hope. However, they resisted the temptation, knowing that this was the ninth day of their novena to Blessed Mary of St. Euphrasia in Honorine's behalf. The day was not over and Honorine still lived. Perhaps before its close Mother St. Euphrasia would aid this stricken child.

Exactly at one o'clock in the afternoon Honorine grew suddenly better. The swelling abated and her temperature returned to normal. All previous symptoms were gone. Honorine asked to be permitted to get up and walk around the room. Later in the afternoon the physician called to be met by a grateful and happy patient, who demonstrated her return to health to his satisfaction.

However, the matter did not end there. Like any other alleged cure it was studied with minute and scientific care before it was acclaimed locally as a nonordinary incident. Upon its later submission as a first-class miracle for consideration in connection with the canonization of Blessed Mary of St. Euphrasia, it was subjected to further scrutiny, two additional medical experts judging the diagnosis and cure of the malady in question. When these men attested that Honorine's cure existed and that it could not be explained by the laws of nature, it was deemed worthy of inclusion as supporting evidence. This miracle occurred at the Good Shepherd Convent in Cannes, France.

It is interesting to note that the miracles accepted for the Beatification and Canonization of Mother St. Euphrasia all occurred among the Good Shepherd children. Although there were other miracles of indubitable merit it seemed especially appropriate to extend to her children the honor and recognition of participation in the steps leading to her being raised by the Church to the status of a canonized Saint.

The Apostolic Letter by Which the Venerable Handmaid of God, Mary of St. Euphrasia Pelletier, Professed Nun of the Order of Our Lady of Charity, Foundress of the Institute of the Sisters of the Good Shepherd, was Declared Blessed

PIUS XI, POPE

For a perpetual remembrance of the matter

The Good Shepherd, Our Lord and Redeemer Jesus Christ, Who gave His life for His sheep and Who deigned to die for His flock, moved by His mercy toward us who live in misery and amidst the defilements of indecency and sin, raises pious followers in His Church (to work) for the necessities of temporal affairs, and calls the aforesaid as ministers of Divine grace and mercy for the exercise of a special function of the Apostolate among sinners who strive especially to return to the fold of salvation. However, The Church, faithful Spouse of the Good Shepherd, successfully and uninterruptedly cherishes and cultivates institutions which with charity and with mercy see to it first of all that the erring sheep return to the safe fold of Jesus Christ and that they be aided as much as possible. Undoubtedly, among these pitiable sheep many women and girls are to be numbered who have fallen either because of a wayward life or some misfortune. Because of civil laws and social customs, We regret to say, it looks frequently as though accessibility to redemption for these unfortunates were ruled out. But in order that wayward and endangered women of this kind might be brought back to the fold of the Good Shepherd, that they might be strengthened in the steadfastness of their resolutions, that they might be prudently and fittingly protected against the snares of the world, about a hundred years ago the Venerable Handmaid of God, Mary of St. Euphrasia, bearing within herself the image of the Merciful Jesus Christ, founded the very fruitful Institute now known by all as the "Order of the Sisters of the Good Shepherd." The Venerable servant of God was born within the territory of the diocese of Luçon in the parish of St. Philibertus of Noirmoutier of the pious and upright parents, Julian Pelletier and Anne Mourain, on the 31st day of July, 1796. Because of the turbulent and calamitous storms of the French Revolution she was baptized at home and was given the name of Rose-Virginie. Endowed with an ardent but good temperament, already from her earliest childhood she was marked with a spirit of piety and the other Christian virtues, especially with mercy toward the poor and needy, therein imitating the excellent example of her parents. However, orphaned by the all too early death of her father, she soon entered a college for girls in the city of Tours, and there she proved herself most conscientious in a life of purity and discipline, immune to the attractions of the world and ever solicitous for the daily and regulated exercise of virtues. When she was seventeen years old, after the death of her beloved mother, desirous of serving God, and having experienced the call to some religious community, she determined as soon as possible to enter the Order of Our Lady of Charity of the Refuge at Tours. St. John Eudes had founded the Order of Nuns under the patronage of Blessed Mary of Charity, under the Rule of St. Augustine, in the town of Caen in the diocese of Bayeux. Afterwards this Order spread through many sees in France and was duly approved by the Roman Pontiffs. The purpose of the Order was that its convents were to receive and shield from vice wayward girls or girls in moral danger. Houses of this salutary Institute were called "Refuges" because against the allurements of the world they were like hiding places offered to penitent women by the great mercy of God. The Apostolic Way of Life and works of charity, to which the nuns bound themselves by a special vow of the Order, corresponded precisely to the burning desire with which the Servant of God was aflame, namely of gaining souls for her Lord Jesus in even greater numbers. After she finally conquered the obstacles which her guardian laid in her way, she entered the House of the Refuge at Tours, and the Handmaid of God received the religious habit and the name of "Mary of St. Euphrasia" in the year 1815. After she completed her two years of novitiate and pronounced her vows, she was appraised by the superior of the house to be worthy to be entrusted with the care and direction of the penitent women who had been assigned to the nuns of that house. In spite of her youth, she performed this very difficult task with outstanding charity and admirable diligence.

Then, when she was not yet thirty years old, by the unanimous request of the sisters she was named superior of this same convent at Tours. She ruled the nuns in a reasonable way and with a spirit of kindness, and she deemed nothing so pleasing as to increase the number of the postulants or of the penitents and she considered nothing so precious as to work with all her might for the spiritual progress of all. But when not long after, there was question of erecting a house in the city of Angers in which, according to the Constitutions of St. John Eudes, wayward girls or girls in moral danger were to be received and brought back to God, the Venerable Servant of God, Mary of St. Euphrasia, was called to found the new institution. It was from this convent at Angers, now enlarged and improved, that the highly esteemed Congregation of the Sisters of the Good Shepherd took its origin, which thereafter spread to such an extent that more than three hundred well-equipped houses are in existence all over the world in which over nine thousand daughters of the Venerable Handmaid of God most diligently lend their energy to the fulfillment of the work of Jesus Christ, the Good Shepherd of souls. But the beginnings of the work were weighted down by difficulties of every kind which proceeded either from men or from the lack of food and of the other necessities of life. Mary of St. Euphrasia, however, daily showing herself an exemplar of virtues, and perpetually on the alert to overcome all obstacles with a ready trust in God, saw to it that her new congregation was strengthened and in fact undauntedly expressed a desire for an increase of her congregation so that the good of souls might be nurtured more and more. Therefore, already in 1835, scarcely four years after its foundation, the convent of the Good Shepherd at Angers flourished with a conspicuous number of sisters as well as novices and penitents. But when at that time in other dioceses of Gaul, convents similar to the one at Angers sprang into existence, convents which the Venerable Servant of God had founded, Pope Gregory XVI, Our Predecessor, in an Apostolic Letter given under the signet ring on the 3rd day of April, 1835, named the superior of the convent at Angers the superior of the entire new Congregation of the Daughters of the Blessed Virgin Mary of Charity of the Good Shepherd. At the same time, of course, the house at Angers was appointed the principal house and general seat of the novitiate. Although the foundress herself was very often not in the best of health, broken neither by her labors nor by adversities, until her death, day after day she supervised the Institute of the Good Shepherd with unswerving diligence. Ever was she strong with the fortitude which is of God, in hardships, in great difficulties and in the untoward incidents of life to an extent that nothing was able to disturb her tranquility of soul. But in fulfilling the burdensome office of Superior General, she conducted herself with gentleness and prudence; most obedient to the Roman Pontiff and the Holy See, she wanted the Institute to be especially devoted to them. In charity toward her neighbor which her works prove in so eminent a degree, she was a gleaming example, and she frequently urged the sisters that they should send no one away who was willing to return to a penitential life even though a scarcity of worldly goods and a lack of room should dictate otherwise. She put no task so constantly before her eyes as fostering as much as possible the salvation of souls and the glory of God. Finally, when she had scarcely reached her seventy-first year, the Venerable Handmaid of God began to fail during a fatal and very severe illness which lasted for several months. After having been fortified by the Sacraments of the Church, she peacefully fell asleep in the Lord during the evening hours of the 24th day of April, 1868. Because of the reputation for virtue with which the Servant of God had adorned her mortal life and also because of heavenly prodigies with which God was reputed to have confirmed the sanctity of His Handmaid after her death and funeral, in order to make a judgment about the honors of the Blessed in Heaven in favor of the Handmaid of God herself, the Cause began to be discussed in the Congregation of Sacred Rites and through a decree released on the 11th day of December, 1897, Pope Leo XIII, Our Predecessor of recent memory, signed the document for the Introduction of the Cause. When the same was introduced and after certain trifling objections were dismissed, it made such progress that soon discussions were begun on the virtues of the Venerable Servant of God, Mary of St. Euphrasia. We Ourselves in the year 1924 on the sixth day before the Kalends of March solemnly approved and declared these virtues endowed and adorned with so heroic a quality. Thereafter, when the question of the two miracles which were said to have been worked by God through the intercession of Venerable Mary of St. Euphrasia had been discussed, and after the twofold session, namely, the so-called ante-preparatory and the preparatory, as well as the general session which was conducted in Our presence on the 20th day of December of last year, where all points were investigated with keenest scrutiny, We Ourselves on the 8th day of the month of January of this year solemnly declared that the miracles presented are certain and that further steps in the Cause may be taken. Therefore, since a decision was pronounced concerning heroic virtues and miracles, according to the rules of the sacred court, that point is beyond discussion, namely, whether the Venerable Handmaid of God should safely be considered among the Blessed of Heaven. This question was presented to Our beloved Son, Cajetan Cardinal-Priest Bisleti, whose Titular Church is St. Agatha of the Goths, Cardinal Relatos of the Cause, in the general sessions held in Our Presence in Vatican Palace on the 31st day of January of last year. All who were present, the Cardinals as well as the Consultors of the Congregation of Rites, answered affirmatively by unanimous consent. We, however, in a matter of such importance postponed manifesting Our mind until We begged help from the Father of Light by strenuous prayers. But when We had performed this urgent task, We at last on the 5th day of February of this year, namely, on the Fifth Sunday after Epiphany, after the celebration of Mass, in the presence of Our beloved Sons, Camillus Cardinal Laurenti, Prefect of the Sacred Congregation of Rites and Cajetan Cardinal Bisleti, Advocate of the Cause, and also Our beloved sons, the Secretary of the Congregation of Rites and the Promoter General of the Faith, by Our supreme authority pronounced that they could *safely* proceed toward the solemn beatification of the Venerable Handmaid of God, Mary of St. Euphrasia. This being the case, We, acceding to the wishes of the Religious Family of the Institute of the Good Shepherd founded by her, and of the Congregation of Eudists and of the Order of Our Lady of Charity, by Our Apostolic authority, through the instrumentality of the present document, decree that the Venerable Handmaid of God, Mary of St. Euphrasia, professed nun of the Order of Our Lady of Charity of the Refuge, foundress of the Institute of the Sisters of the Good Shepherd, be invoked in the future with the appellation, *Blessed*, and that her body and effects or relics may be exposed for public veneration, not however for solemn supplications, and that her images may be decorated with "rays." Furthermore, by Our same Apostolic authority, We concede that her Office and Mass be celebrated annually with the formulary of the Common of Virgins, with proper orations, approved by Us according to the rubrics of the Roman Missal and Breviary. But we concede that the recitation of the Breviary and the celebration of the Mass can be performed only in the Diocese of Luçon where the Handmaid of God was born, and in the diocese of Angers from where she went to the Lord, likewise that in the churches and in the chapels all over the world, which are used by the Institute of the Sisters of the Good Shepherd, by the Order of Our Lady of Charity of the Refuge, and finally by the Congregation of the Eudists, the recitation of the aforesaid Office can be performed by all the faithful who are bound to recite the canonical hours and as regards the Mass, that it can be said by all priests both diocesan or those belonging to a religious order, who happen to come to those churches or chapels in which the feast is kept. Finally, we grant the faculty of celebrating the solemnities of the beatification of the Venerable Servant of God, Mary of St. Euphrasia, in the above-mentioned churches or chapels on days to be designated by legitimate authority throughout the year, provided that all pertinent rules are observed, but only after the same solemnities have been enacted in the Sacred Patriarchal Basilica of the Vatican. In spite of any Constitutions and Apostolic Ordinances and decrees issued concerning non-veneration and all other legislations to the contrary, We desire that in all juridical discussions there be given to copies of this present letter, even though they are printed copies—provided they are signed by the hand of the Secretary of the Sacred Congregation—the same credence that is lent to the manifestation of Our will in this very letter.

Given at Rome, at St. Peter's under the Fisherman's ring, on the 30th day of April, 1933, the twelfth year of Our Pontificate.

E. Cardinal Pacelli

From the Secretariate of State

Addenda

THE POPES

During the existence of the Congregation of Our Lady of Charity of the Good Shepherd of Angers, the Chair of St. Peter at Rome has been occupied by seven Popes:

His Holiness Gregory XVI, deceased June 1, 1846.

His Holiness Pius IX, elected June 16, 1846, deceased February 7, 1878.

His Holiness Leo XIII, elected February 20, 1878, deceased July 20, 1903.

His Holiness Pius X, elected August 4, 1903, deceased August 20, 1914, canonized May 29, 1954.

His Holiness Benedict XV, elected September 3, 1914, deceased January 22, 1922.

His Holiness Pius XI, elected February 6, 1922, deceased February 10, 1939.

His Holiness Pius XII, elected March 2, 1939.

THE CARDINALS PROTECTOR

The Congregation has been under the jurisdiction of the following Cardinals Protector:

His Eminence Charles Cardinal Odescalchi, from May 30, 1835, until his entrance into the Society of Jesus in December, 1838. He died August 17, 1841.

His Eminence Joseph Cardinal Della Porta (1839–1841).

His Eminence Constantin Cardinal Patrizi (1842–1876).

His Eminence Raphael Monaco Cardinal La Valletta (1877–1896).

His Eminence Camille Cardinal Mazzella, S.J. (1896–1900).

His Eminence Joseph Calazans Cardinal Vives y Tuto, Spanish Capuchin (1900–1913).

His Eminence Louis Cardinal Billot, S.J. (1913–1927).

His Eminence Gaetano Cardinal Bisleti (1928–1937).

His Eminence Vincenzo Cardinal La Puma (1937–1939).

His Eminence Eugenio Cardinal Pacelli, later Pope Pius

XII. At his request His Holiness has continued in the role of Cardinal Protector (1939–   ).

SUPERIORS GENERAL

Six Superiors General have governed the Congregation:

St. Mary Euphrasia Pelletier, elected May 23, 1831, deceased April 24, 1868.

Mother Mary of St. Peter de Coudenhove, elected October 8, 1868, deceased May 26, 1892.

Mother Mary of St. Marine Verger, elected June 2, 1892, deceased May 30, 1905.

Mother Mary of St. Domitilla Larose, elected June 30, 1905, remained Superior until June 5, 1928, deceased January 21, 1940.

Mother Mary of St. John of the Cross Balzer, elected June 9, 1928, remained Superior until May 3, 1940, deceased November 21, 1942.

Mother Mary of St. Ursula Jung, Present Superior General, elected May 7, 1940.

Mother House of the Congregation of Our Lady of Charity of the Good Shepherd of Angers:

3 Rue Brault

Angers, Maine-et-Loire,

France

CONVENTS OF THE GOOD SHEPHERD IN THE UNITED STATES AND CANADA

PROVINCE OF ST. LOUIS

3801 Gravois Avenue
St. Louis 16, Mo.

2601 Bienville Avenue
New Orleans 19, La.

1126 Grace Street
Chicago 13, Ill.

20 North Avalon Street
Memphis 4, Tenn.

8830 West Blue Mound Road
Milwaukee 13, Wis.

7626 Natural Bridge Road
Normandy 21, Mo.

6724 Troost Avenue
Kansas City 5, Mo.

1410 Richmond Avenue
Houston 6, Tex.

1820 West Northern Avenue
Phoenix, Ariz.

501 Cambridge Street
San Francisco 24, Calif.

St. John Vianney's School
R.R. 2, Box 75
Bixby, Okla.

PROVINCE OF PHILADELPHIA

5301 Chew Avenue
Philadelphia 38, Pa.

Tekakwitha Hills School
Verree & Susquehanna Roads
Philadelphia 11, Pa.

3901 Pine Street
West Philadelphia, Pa.

St. Joseph's Protectory
Norristown, Pa.

Lourdesmont, Box 179
Clarks Summit, Pa.

Marymount-on-Schuylkill
Reading, Pa.

PROVINCE OF CINCINNATI

Our Lady of the Woods
Cincinnati 16, Ohio

518 South Eighth Street
Louisville 3, Ky.

Mount St. Mary
Price Hill
Cincinnati 5, Ohio

Broad and Sandusky Streets
Columbus 8, Ohio

2214 Bank Street
Louisville 12, Ky.

938 Highland Avenue
Fort Thomas, Ky.

Marycrest School
7800 Brookside Road
Cleveland 9, Ohio

111 West Raymond Street
Indianapolis 25, Ind.

20651 W. Warren Avenue
Detroit 23, Mich.

1315 Walker Avenue
Grand Rapids, 4, Mich.

PROVINCE OF PEEKSKILL

Mount St. Florence
Peekskill, N. Y.

Villa Loretto
Peekskill, N.Y.

841 Huntington Avenue
Boston 15, Mass.

250 Hopkinson Avenue
Brooklyn 33, N.Y.

126 Sussex Avenue
Morristown, N.J.

1225 Peoples Avenue
Troy, N.Y.

25 West Lawrence Street
Albany 5, N.Y.

584 Wilbraham Road
Springfield, Mass.

170 Sisson Avenue
Hartford 5, Conn.

189 Eaton Street
Providence 8, R.I.

Rest Hill
Wickatunk, N.J.

Euphrasian Residence
337 East 17th Street
New York 3, N.Y.

80 Pond Street
Jamaica Plain
Boston 30, Mass.

PROVINCE OF ST.PAUL

931 Blair Avenue
St. Paul 4, Minn.

Box 1706
Lousiana Avenue & Colorado
    Boulevard
Denver, Colo.

Box 915
Helena, Mont.

Sunnyside Avenue & N. 50th
Street
Seattle 3, Wash.

597 N. Dekum Street
Portland 3, Ore.

653 South 40th Street
Omaha 5, Neb.

2323 Court Street
Sioux City 19, Iowa

4819 Lidgerwood Street
Spokane 13, Wash.

PROVINCE OF BALTIMORE

Mount & Hollins Streets
Baltimore 23, Md.

301 Calverton Road
Baltimore 23, Md.

36th & Reservoir Road
Washington 7, D.C.

St. Euphrasia's School
Batesburg, S.C.

PROVINCE OF LOS ANGELES

1500 S. Arlington Avenue
Los Angeles 6, Calif.

Convents in the Philippines:
Manila
Batangas
Cebu
Baguio

Convents in China:
Hong Kong

The following two houses belong
to Guanajuato, Mexico:

Box 126
Mesilla Park, N.M.

Box 1150
Isleta, Tex.

PROVINCE OF MONTREAL

104 rue Sherbrooke Est.
Montreal 18, Quebec

411 rue Saint-André
Ottawa, Ontario

Asile Ste. Darie
1730 rue Fullum
Montreal 24, Quebec

Institute Ste. Marie-Euphrasie
331 rue Sherbrooke Est.
Montreal 18, Quebec

Maison Notre-Dame de Lorette
Laval-des-Rapides, Quebec

Maison Ste. Domitille
Laval-des-Rapides, Quebec

Sunny Brae
Près Moncton, Nouveau Brunswick

JAPAN

Yoki-Bokusha-shudoin
Hikari-ga-oka
Sendai-shi, Japan

Yoki-Bokusha-shudoin
Kamifukumoto 5500
Taniyama kyoku nai
Kagoshima-shi gai, Japan

PROVINCE OF HALIFAX

83 Quinpool Road
Halifax, Nova Scotia

14 West Lodge Avenue
Toronto, Ontario

562 W. 14th Avenue, Fairview
Vancouver, British Columbia

133 Waterloo Street
Saint-John, New Brunswick

442 Scotia Street
West Kildonan, Manitoba

3615 College Avenue
Windsor, Ontario

Minnow Lake
Sundbury, Ontario

St. Mary's Training School
Downsview, Toronto, Ontario